Faces of Korea

The Foreign Experience in the Land of the Morning Calm

Faces of Korea

The Foreign Experience
in the Land of the Morning Calm

Richard Harris

HOLLYM
Elizabeth, NJ·Seoul

Faces of Korea
The Foreign Experience in the Land of the Morning Calm

Copyright © 2004
by Richard Harris

All rights reserved.

No part of this book may be reproduced in any form
without the written permission of the author and the publisher.

First published in 2004
by Hollym International Corp.
18 Donald Place, Elizabeth, New Jersey 07208, USA
Phone (908)353-1655   Fax (908)353-0255
http://www.hollym.com

Published simultaneously in Korea
by Hollym Corporation; Publishers
13-13 Gwancheol-dong, Jongno-gu, Seoul 110-111, Korea
Phone (02)735-7551~4   Fax (02)730-5149, 8192
http://www.hollym.co.kr   e-mail: hollym@chollian.net

ISBN: 1-56591-214-4
Library of Congress Control Number: 2004108836

Printed in Korea

In memory of
Dr. Horace Underwood III (1917-2004)

CONTENTS

Author's Note   10
Acknowledgements   11
Preface   15
Introduction   18

PART I
WORKING IN KOREA

Brian* (30)_America_Corporate Lawyer_2½ Years   28
Joanne Uyede (54)_Canada_Vice President, CECN   34
Chined Paul Ogbonna (36)_Nigeria_Factory and Construction
    Worker_4 Years   40
Matthew Readman (27)_United Kingdom_TV and Radio Actor_6
    Years   51
Ronald Nielsen (61)_America_President, Seoul Korea Temple,
    The Church of Jesus Christ of Latter-day Saints_9 Years   59
Steve* (36)_America_Major, U.S. Army_10 Years   69
Sumalee* (20)_Thailand_Nanny and Waitress_6 Months   74
Martin Robinson (51)_United Kingdom_Lonely Planet Travel
    Writer_2 Years   79
Karis Thompson (23)_America_Fulbright Scholarship Intern_13
    Months   86
David* (27)_Australia_Human Resources Manager_5½ Months   94
Bruce Fulton (54)_America_Literary Translator and Professor of
    Korean Literature_5 Years   101

SECTION II
SOCIAL RELATIONS WITH KOREANS

Robert Holley/하일 (44)_Korea (America)_Principal, Lawyer and TV Entertainer_19 Years	118
Sarah* (31)_Australia_Actress, Singer, and Musician_10 Years	125
Eric* (29)_Philippines_Office Worker_3 Years	136
Antonio Patella (39)_Italy_Concert Pianist, Musical Director, and Restaurant Manager_5 Years	141
Yaira M. Resto (26)_Puerto Rico_E–4 Specialist, U.S. Army_1 Year	145
Nakashima Mayumi (40)_Japan_Waitress_7 Years	152
Samantha Brooks (37)_America_Freelance Artist_7 Years	158

SECTION III
PEOPLE OF KOREAN DESCENT

Mihee-Nathalie Lemoine (35)_Belgium_Multimedia Artist and Social Activist_10 Years	174
John (29)_America_Captain, U.S. Army_11 Years	185
Julie Kim (35)_Canada_Businesswoman_18 Months	191
John Hamrin (37)_Sweden_Volunteer and Teacher_16 Months	199
Maya West (20)_America_Translator and Student_14 Years	207
Monica Montero Lim (25)_Spain_Student_4 Months	214
Son Sang-kyun 손상균 (24)_Korea_University Student_4 ½ Years	222
Susan MacDonald (31)_America_TV Personality, Cross-Cultural Awareness Lecturer, and Interpreter_12 Years	228
Toney Dong Yul Shin (34)_America_English Teacher_8 Years	235

CONTENTS

SECTION IV
TEACHING IN KOREA

William* (32)_United Kingdom_*Hagwon* Teacher_4 Years	248
Fairlie Atkinson (26)_New Zealand_*Hagwon* Teacher and University Instructor_15 Months	255
Craig Service (32)_Canada_*Hagwon* Teacher and University Instructor_5 Years	263
Gumennaya Svetlana (26)_Russia_*Hagwon* Teacher_3 Years	271
Samantha Hanratty (29)_France_*Hagwon* Teacher_3 Months	280
Ted Gray (36)_America_University Instructor_8 Years	284
Nikki Berrington (26)_South Africa_*Hagwon* Teacher_6 Months	292
Fujiwara Yoshitsugu (34)_Japan_*Hagwon* Teacher and University Instructor_8 Years	301

SECTION V
LEARNING IN KOREA

Ron Schafrick (31)_Canada_Korean Language Student_5 Years	314
Fatma* (24)_Morocco_MBA Student_2 Months	321
Nicole Risse (26)_Germany_Korean Language and Korean Studies Student (B.A. & M.A.)_4½ Years	327
Yuki* (25)_Japan_Korean Language Student_6 Months	336
Jacques-Yves Le Docte (36)_Belgium_Korean Traditional Music Theory_1 Year	340

SECTION VI
AT HOME IN KOREA

Moon Hae-sung 문해성 (19)_Korea (North Korea)_Student_4 Years	354
Gary Rector 유게리 (59)_Korea (America)_Translator and Editor _35 ½ Years	370
Rowena de la Rosa Yoon (36)_Korea (Philippines)_President of ISKA, Public Relations Expert, Journalist, and Editor_8 Years	379
Dr. So Seung-gul 소승걸 (25)_Taiwan_Dentist_25 Years	389
Shapour Nasrollahi (34)_Korea (Iran)_Restaurant Owner_14 Years	397
Suzanna Samstag Oh (44)_America_Editor, Translator, and SamulNori Expert_23 Years	403
Dr. Horace Underwood III 원일한 (86; 1917–2004)_America_ Professor Emeritus and President of the Board of Directors of Yonsei University_71 Years	414

APPENDIX 429

ENDNOTES 444

Author's Note

THE VIEWS espoused in the following interviews represent the interviewees' respective private viewpoints, and this book shall in no way be construed as the author's endorsement of such statements. The author has not independently verified the facts contained in the interviews and makes no claim as to their veracity or accuracy, nor assumes any liability whatsoever for any unintentional damage they may cause to any party.

Acknowledgements

THANKS MUST first go out to all those willing participants who made this book possible. A total of 47 people from all walks of life were generous enough with their time to share their stories and, in many cases, generous enough with their hearts to open up about subjects that were both painful and traumatic to recount. The stories in this book not only tell of the ordinary day-to-day facts of getting by in Korea, but the realities of living, working, and functioning in the country on a very intimate level. This book is no less a testament to the diversity of the people who are living in Korea–or who once lived in Korea–than it is to the lives they have lived since arriving on these shores.

As the interviewer, this book was a valuable lesson in six degrees of separation. Although I knew a few of the people in this book before starting work on it-some vaguely, others well–it was mostly a case of plugging connections through interviewees who were kind enough to help out, and cold calling in the remaining cases. In the end, I was fortunate to speak with 47 very special people who have all had unique and diverse experiences in Korea.

Yet there is a behind-the-scenes team that deserves an equal amount of credit for the effort, the time, and the energy they put into this project. Every single interview needed to be transcribed, edited, and proofread. And, as in the case of four of the interviews, translated on top of all this, from Korean to English. This Herculean task required the services of many friends and acquaintances over the course of more than one year.

My brother, Matthew, always the rock with my writing projects, transcribed nearly half of the interviews by himself, a task for which I can never pay him enough. On top of this, he also edited and proofread the whole book, while providing a soundboard for me to weigh many ideas and approaches during every stage of this project.

My wife, Eun-ju (박은주), was also instrumental in bringing this book to life. She transcribed two of the Korean interviews, translated one of them and waded through the stormy seas that were an inevitable part of putting this project together.

There was also my "older brother" and chief confidante, Kim

Ki-young (김기영), who assisted by transcribing two of the Korean interviews and providing help in the English translations of each. Without his selfless dedication to this project, this book would not have been possible.

Although I only carried out four interviews in Korean, the length of time and effort needed to bring them to life in English was monumental. Maya West, Kim Hyun-kyung (김현경), Hong Joo-hee (홍주희) and Min Sung-won (민성원) were the architects behind this hugely labor-intensive job and deserve more accolades that can be doled out in a simple section like this. As each of these people provided their services out of nothing more than the goodness of the hearts, I in turn have to say, from the bottom of my own heart, thank you for de-complicating the most complicated process of this whole project.

Once there was actually a draft of this book to be looked over, however, there was an entirely different team that helped shape the book you see before you today. In Korea, Fairlie Atkinson and Craig Service were of great assistance in making each draft of the book look even better than the previous one, as were Dean Fealk and Krista Kim with their timely advice. Peter Atwood, thank you for employing your brilliant editing skills in record time. It won't go forgotten. Overseas, Maria Amore proved yet again that she could have an immense impact on one of my projects from thousand of miles away. Her astute attention to detail and unwavering eye for perfection made this a better book.

And, as seems to be the case with my books to date, the credit to the people who made this all possible from the publishing point of view come last, but certainly not least. Ham Ki-man (함기만), President of Hollym Korea, and my editor, friend and constant source of support, Julia Yi (이희정)–thank you. You were both enthusiastic about the book from its conception and made me believe after that fateful lunch long ago that this book would have a huge impact. Thank you once again, and as always, for believing in me. You are the ingenuity that fuels each of my projects in Korea.

Preface

I BEGAN WORK on this project for two main reasons. The first was to build bridges of understanding between the cultures and peoples that live in Korea. Although more than half a million foreigners from over 180 countries reside in this country, many of us have little knowledge of each other. More often than not we tend to spend time with people in similar professions; we like to speak our native language with others who share a common tongue; many of us socialize among those with the same socio-economic background.

And while this may be a reality of life for people around the world, for those men and women living in a foreign country like Korea, the reality is somewhat different, if only because we all share one major fact of life—we're all foreigners. It was because of this last fact that I sought to understand, and to bring to light to readers everywhere, the ties and the differences that exist between us all as foreigners in a country as homogeneous as Korea.

The second reason I wrote this book, however, was to educate Koreans about what it's really like for the foreign community to live and work and socialize in their country. As many of us can attest to, Koreans are often mystified at the lives we as foreigners carry out in their country. There simply has not been anything as honest and straightforward as this book published before.

The 47 interviews in this book are candid accounts of people from several different generations (19 years of age to 86 years of age), who have lived here for any length of time (2 months to 71 years), who have experienced hardship, difficulty, and resistance on any number of levels, and have, in every case, triumphed in at least one sense – they're still around to tell their story.

As the writer, or more accurately, the complier of this book, I have learned a great deal both about myself and about Korea by carrying out these interviews. Before doing the very first interview, I was under the ignorant auspices that I was unique, that my time in Korea was somehow remarkably special and separate from the great march of travelers and workers who have found themselves in this time-honored country over the years. I am not unique, though; I am merely one strand in a great line of people who now live in Korea and find some reason to stay here and make this country their home.

We all share a cause—some because we wish to, others because we feel it is self-imposed—and in that cause is something great, and something we can all learn from. By reading the interviews in this book, I believe we can all learn something, not only about this country and the people that reside in it, but about ourselves as human beings. More than that, though, you will feel connected and a part of an experience that, until now, you might have thought as singular. As much as you may feel that you are alone in this country and that no one else understands your story, that is not so. You are not alone in Korea; we are all a part of something much bigger.

Introduction

THE WORD "foreigner" has been become an increasingly slippery term in Korea in the last few years. Korea is a monolithic society that has historically claimed roots in one ethnicity, the *han* (한 - 韓) people. For most of its history, this has been a relatively easy term to define: you were either born of Korean parents or you were not; you either grew up in Korea or you did not. Today, however, the word "foreigner" is not so easily defined.

King Kojong (1880-1907), the second-last reigning monarch during the Chosun Dynasty (1392-1910), signed a proclamation deeming Korean emigration to the United States legal in 1889. It was then that the Hermit Kingdom, the self-proclaimed "Land of the Morning Calm," which for centuries until then had remained closed to the outside world, had its face changed forever. From that time forward, the way in which a "Korean" and the way in which a "foreigner" were defined would never be the same. With Korean emigration, and subsequently immigration into the country, the two terms came to have different implications forevermore.

There are currently about 48,000,000 Koreans living in the South, and a further 21,000,000 living in the North—nearly 70,000,000 Koreans living on the Korean peninsula in total. However, these are not the only inhabitants of a peninsula mired in a rocky past and, at present, a sorted political hostility. There are more than half a million foreigners living in South Korea today, and so the way in which a foreigner is defined depends upon the prism you look through.

On a semantic level, Webster's Dictionary defines the word "foreigner" as "a person belonging to or owing allegiance to a foreign country," while in Korean the word is defined as, "다른 나라의 사람. 외국의 국적을 가진 사람" (someone from another country; a person with a foreign nationality).[1] To de-construct this even further, the term "foreigner," *wae-gook-een* (외국인 - 外國人)[2], comes from the Chinese roots *wae* (외), "foreign," (or outside), gook (국), "country or kingdom," and *een* (인). The *wae* (외- 外) in *wae-gook-een* is derived from the Chinese character [外], meaning "divination of [a] turtle shell, cracks appear[ing] on the outside," while *gook* is derived from the Chinese character for "country or kingdom," [國], and *een*, from [人], meaning person.[3]

That being said, a foreigner in Korea today is not just "a person from another country," and a Korean can be something more than just someone "born of Korean parents in Korea." There are overseas men and women of Korean descent, *kyo-po* (교포), living in 151 countries around the world, some of whom currently live in Korea; there are half-Koreans, the children of parents who married interracially, that live, work, and study in Korea; there are adoptees who were born in Korea and of Korean parents, but who claim foreign citizenship; and there are people from countries on all continents that speak Korean, study Korean, and work in Korea. All of these people help to shape the fabric of what is Korea's modern face, a face that is becoming, contrary to popular belief, more multi-ethnic and multi-faceted.

Section I
Working in Korea

TRADE

Working in Korea

THERE WERE just over 500,000 foreigners from 182 countries residing in South Korea in 2002, on one visa or another, according to the Republic of Korea's Ministry of Justice.[1] The majority of these people were in Korea on one of the following visas:

Visa	Number of People
Diplomats (A-1)	1,237
Visa Waiver (B-1)	36,965
Tourist/Transit (B-2)	32,708
Short-term Business (C-2)	60,373
Short-term Visitors (C-3)	97,446
Students (D-2)	5,263
Industrial Trainees (D-3)	110,223
Religious Workers (D-6)	1,295
Treaty Investors (D-8)	6,594
Professors (E-1)	641
Foreign Language Teachers (E-2)	8,749
Arts and Entertainment (E-6)	6,938
Industrial Trainees Employment (E-8)	9,684
Visiting and Joining Families (F-1)	9,298
Overseas Koreans (F-1-2)	2,613
Spouses (F-1-3)	24,949
Residence (F-2)	16,035
Dependent Families (F-3)	4,045
Overseas Korean Residents (F-4)	11,655
Military (M-1)	35,613

The overwhelming majority of these foreigners (397,096 or 79%), came from other countries in Asia, those from China representing the largest number of foreigners in Korea (186,548). However, at least 10,000 people from each of the following Asian countries were also in Korea in 2002: the Philippines, Japan, Thailand, Indonesia, Vietnam, Bangladesh, Taiwan, Mongolia, and Uzbekistan.

There were 68,945 people from the United States in Korea, 35,511 of whom were military personnel and 33,434 civilians, while 6,519 Canadians were calling Korea home at the time. The largest contingent of South Americans were the Peruvians (658), while the majority of Europeans came from Russia (8,100), the U.K. (1,995), France (1,355), Germany (1,307), and the Ukraine (1,028). There were also 3,020 people from Australia and 1,580 from New Zealand. Finally, the African country with the largest number of its nationals in Korea was the Nigerians (1,563).

◘

However, not all of the people living and working in Korea were here legally. There was a staggering 301,747 illegal workers from foreign countries estimated to be working in Korea as of June 2003.[2] In some cases these unauthorized foreigners arrive in Korea as trainees, have their passports held by their Korean employers, and then leave to search for employment elsewhere. Some Korean employers, though, angered over the sudden departure of their employee, will then turn in the former employee's passport to the embassy of the country from which the trainee came.[3]

The mass arrival of foreign workers to Korea began in 1994 when the Korea Federation of Small and Medium Businesses

(KFSMB) began to invite and attract foreign workers to Korea and assign them to local manufacturers. Approximately 190,000 foreign workers, almost exclusively from Asian countries, have come to Korea under this program.[4] These people are obliged to work for at least one year at the original employer before being given an option for a two-year contract extension. As of spring 2003, the average monthly wage for foreign workers under this program stood at 967,000 won ($806), just 84 percent of the 1.15 million won ($958) that the average Korean made working at a small- or medium-sized business.[5]

People who work illegally in Korea face very different barriers in the workplace than those who are here with a legal visa. Problems in this field range from the length of stay to the work treatment (especially in factories, where migrant workers are protected by neither labor laws nor the government itself) to the secrecy required for the job. Many of these same people work in what has become known as Korea's "dirty, difficult, and dangerous" workforce, the infamous 3–Ds.

[]

While the number of investors in Korea is still small relative to other Asian cities like Tokyo, Hong Kong, and Singapore, the number is growing.[6] For the nearly 70,000 business people and investors residing in Korea as of May 2003, the value of their combined holdings on the Korean stock market, as measured by the Korea Composite Price Index (KOSPI), was approximately 34.5 percent of the KOSPI's total value of 261,399 trillion won ($210 billion U.S.).[7] Broken down by nationality, the total number of foreign investors stood as follows in 2003:

Country	Number of Investors
United States	5,573
United Kingdom	1,263
Japan	1,186
Canada	759
Malaysia	539
Luxembourg	428
Ireland	415
Others	4,398
TOTAL	14,561

With regard to foreign investment in stocks listed on the Korea Securities Dealers Automated Quotation (KOSDAQ), it totaled 41.404 trillion won in May 2003, accounting for approximately 9.9 percent of all investment on the tech-heavy market.[8] Foreign investment in stocks by country on the KOSDAQ was as follows:

Country	Purchase ('000 million won)
United States	2,394
Cayman Islands	1,319
United Kingdom	697
Malaysia	377
Singapore	325
Ireland	172
Virgin Islands	141
Japan	41
Others	1,098
TOTAL	6,564

Tourism is also growing. In 2001 the number of people that visited Korea stood at 5,147,000 people.[9] The regions people hailed from were as follows:

Area/Group	2000	2001
Asia	3,985,000	3,847,000
Oceania	54,000	60,000
Americas	535,000	507,000
Europe	452,000	429,000
Africa	18,000	18,000
Overseas Koreans	278,000	287,000
TOTAL	5,322,000	5,147,000

The eight men and three women whose stories are presented in this section represent a complete cross-section of employment in Korea, from the legal to the illegal, from high-paying jobs that draw the best and the brightest to occupations notorious for their mistreatment of foreign workers. They come from seven different nations on four continents and offer useful insight for people coming, or thinking of coming, to Korea to work, or for those simply curious about what it's like to work in a foreign country.

"Learn to love Korea. Learn to hate Korea. Feel that you are more Korean than you are anything else, and then become steeped in indignation at the fact that you will never be a Korean. When you ultimately leave, accept that you changed in a very positive way and that you've consumed and been consumed by a very special society—one unlike any other that's maintained traditions for hundreds of years—and know that you're a better person for it."

Brian*[10] (30)
America
Corporate Lawyer
2½ Years

An extremely voluble person, Brian has spent the last two years navigating his way around corporate boardrooms and legal offices. Unlike many foreign professionals, he has not only studied the Korean language, but has taken an active interest in all things Korean. This fact came through loud and clear in his interview, in which he showed keen insight into the culture.

I BECAME interested in Asia with the 1988 Seoul Olympics and most recently the World Cup. I became aware of Korea and I fell in love with the food long before I came over to Korea. I found the country fascinating because it is a seemingly modern society that is underpinned by some very interesting and often contradictory traditional elements. Korea is a tremendous economic success story: from ashes to industrialized society to top twelve economy of the world in fifty years—unprecedented. So it's very exciting to be here as a business person and it's very exciting to be here as a lawyer. I came to be near the action, and there's been a lot of action.

I sort of mentioned the idea to some friends that I kept in touch with in Korea from my first time here. I told them I was thinking about maybe coming back and then they just totally set the machinery in motion. They set up everything and introduced me to people. A connection of mine set me up with an interview with one department in our firm. It turned out they didn't need anyone, but they did pass along my application to another department and so I ended up interviewing there and they gave me the job.

With my job now, I probably get in a little later than you would in the States because this is not an early morning kind of society, probably because the working day tends to run later. If I'm working on a deal then there's so much negotiation, so much paperwork, so many issues, so many memos to write, so many people to talk with, that I spend a lot of my day answering questions from clients. I also spend a good amount of time talking to clients on the phone, meeting with other lawyers and having conferences and discussing legal issues before going back to the office to write opinion letters, answer questions from clients and orchestrate paperwork or documentation that needs to be done for a deal. As a result, I spend most of my time writing legal opinions about what steps companies should take in order to satisfy regulations and looking through contracts. All in all, I think that

I'm very well compensated for the work here, though. My salary here is slightly lower than in it was in the States, but I get housing provided, I get a slight tax benefit, and the cost of living here is substantially lower than it was in the U.S. Overall, I think I'm actually doing better here.

The corporate culture is different in Korea, however. In terms of my role there's also certain differences. What they like the foreign attorneys to do here primarily is serve as a client liaison. In the States, the people that generally deal with the clients are the more senior attorneys. Here, you effectively get a boost in terms of your seniority with respect to client interaction because they want you to build a rapport with the client; they want the clients to keep coming back, so you actually take a more integral role in terms of negotiating and in terms of dealing with the clients because the major firms in Korea are primarily focusing on foreign clients who have deeper pockets and generally are the bigger players. At the same time, foreign clients want to know how to do business in Korea. They're very concerned with the regulatory and cultural aspects and they need advice in Korea.

With respect to corporate culture, it's a lot different in that on the surface it's a lot more genteel. People are less combative than in the States, less confrontational. But by the same token, it can be just as competitive. The difference in Korea is that it happens much more subtly. People don't do it through verbal exchange. People aren't confrontational. Any kind of political cleavages in the firm could be situation specific, but people fight over territory and people want to be powerful and people find their allies. Hierarchy in Korea is so huge. Your age and how many years you've practiced is, I think, far more important than actual ability. In the States, I think ability can play a larger role. Now, because I get so much responsibility with respect to clients, it's hard for me to complain about something like age discrimination. But by the same token, for example, if there's a brief that's written and I think the legal analysis is wrong, it's hard for me to correct someone who's a lot more senior than me even if they're clearly wrong. In the States, however, if you stood behind your convictions and if you were clearly right and you could prove it, I think you would prevail. Here, I think the personal relationship remains supreme and the hierarchy would trump the actual merits of your case.

This all helps you develop very strong relationships with your Korean co-workers. But in many cases, at some point, you see that the mask slips, and you see there's a real limit to that relationship. You see that at the end of the day many Koreans approach you first and foremost as a foreigner and that limits the relationship. I'm speaking more on a social level, although of course that can impact a professional relationship. I believe that the limitation professionally is: they think that as a foreigner not of Korean decent you may not stay in Korea that long. Therefore there will be limits in terms of what they invest in you.

Socially, I think that the Koreans feel much more comfortable with one another. I definitely have social outings like lunches and dinners with Korean lawyers, but there are huge cleavages. I find that the Korean Americans tend to stick to themselves in terms of who they go out with and the Korean lawyers, for the most part, hang out with other Korean lawyers. That leaves the foreigners kind of straddling those two groups. There are, of course, a lot of exceptions, but overwhelmingly you see that.

In terms of the level of English in the office, the Korean Bar exam has an English component to it, so in theory everyone has a pretty good understanding of vocabulary, including some business and legal vocabulary and some reasonable grammar. Yet for the most part, the junior lawyers just entering the firm have fairly elementary spoken English. But then what happens is they use English daily—speaking to us, speaking to clients and writing in English—and I think that over the course of two, three, five years they tend to learn pretty good English. There's no question in my mind that the lack of fluency of English has definitely made some clients warier, however. Clients pay a lot of money for legal opinions and if it has a lot of grammatical errors it doesn't look polished. Also, with respect to client interaction, if there's a language gap I think that that's hard because you have to understand the client's needs. If you misunderstand them there's no way that you can get it right, and if you don't get it right the first time when you're billing by the hour, going back and doing something a second or third time means the client pays more money.

Fortunately, a lot of foreign lawyers in this country, primarily Korean Americans, bring a level of English competency to the office. Ultimately, the native English speaker gets into the act, but there's not enough of us to go around, so that can come to bear on efficiency. In other words, maybe the original document is written by a Korean but then a foreign attorney becomes kind of an English editor, which is fine, except you've paid for the document to be written in English by a non-English speaker which is more time consuming than writing in one's native language. And then you're paying for an English editor who is several hundred dollars an hour.

If I could offer advice to someone coming to Korea for their very first time, I would say learn the culture. Don't take things too personally and enjoy it. The Korean people are very warm. If you understand people's perspectives and their motivations it's very easy to navigate the waters. Don't get too caught up in your own ego because this is a country where people subordinate their ego for the collective good. Be willing to be a team player in a way that you're not used to. Try to understand Korean cultural dimensions, and you can thrive. Remember that you have certain advantages as a foreigner. Use those advantages and navigate in such a way that you can succeed. Be the aggressive one if you don't feel comfortable being aggressive. Use your strengths and minimize your weaknesses through cultural understanding. That way you can do very well while really enjoying yourself because this is a country that works hard and plays hard and it's a great place to be.

You have to come with an open mind. But by the same token you can't disregard all of your insights that make you unique and that give you a framework to understand the world. When you come to Korea and you have your odyssey, expect the unexpected, expect change. You're going to have your instincts turned on their ear and then you'll be flipped back over and realize that your instincts were right to begin with. As a professor of mine said in law school, "Sometimes you have to just let it wash over you." Let it change you. Feel balance through extremes. Learn to love Korea. Learn to hate Korea. Feel that you are more Korean than you are anything else, and then become steeped in indignation at the fact that you will never be a Korean. When you ultimately leave, accept that you changed in a very positive way and that you've consumed and been consumed by a very special society—one unlike any other that's maintained traditions for hundreds of years—and know that you're a better person for it.

"Discrimination is a funny thing. It can work to your advantage and disadvantage. I know full well that more often than not I gain an advantage in Korea because of the way I look. There's a good side and bad side, and I'll take the good side any day."

Joanne Uyede (54)
Canada
Vice President, CECN

As Vice President of the Canadian Education Center Network (CECN), Joanne is responsible for developing strategies to promote and market Canada as a study destination. She is also responsible for the overall management of the Center and for the CECN's Language Institute in Korea. Although she has never actually lived in Korea, she has stayed intimately connected with the country by doing business here for almost ten years.

I DON'T KNOW if I'm qualified to speak on Korea other than I think it is a beautiful country. When I come here, I usually spend my time in Seoul. I think my experience in Korea has been colored by frustration in my professional life. Part of what I find so frustrating is not knowing any Korean. I can't believe that after all this time I don't know how to say "hello" or "goodbye," but that's my shortcoming. I think it's interesting that in other markets, people have been far more helpful with language hints, much more open. Here, very often the Koreans that I've encountered in a non-professional setting have tried very hard to demonstrate that they can speak English, which is nice. That being said, I've never felt wholly comfortable in Korea, to be honest. I know that part of it is my own lack of familiarity with Korean culture. The more I try and learn, though, the more I get perplexed.

First of all, this is a very hierarchical society and the way that we operate as a network through decentralized management is a challenge because a lot of Koreans are used to daily supervision and I can't be here 365 days a year. Therefore, we put into place a series of mechanisms so that there is a budget that is going to be developed and has my approval. There is a strategic plan for each office. In Korea, I'm never wholly confident that I'm getting the full story, though. It's this hierarchical structure of society that impedes growth here. I expect my managers to take the ball and run with it, to take some initiative and think independently—a North American way of doing business. What it implies is an incredible amount of trust on the part of senior management, and my part, that we place in our managers overseas. Operating in what I see as a low trust market is a huge challenge, one I don't think we've managed completely yet.

I don't know whether this is completely cultural. Maybe business is just run differently here. I've looked at some of the businesses I've come into contact with while in operation here and there are layers of bureaucracy: people supervising other people supervising other people. We can't afford that. We operate on a team basis so our managers are expected to be carrying boxes and moving tables and doing everything that anybody else on the staff would do. I think that is a huge gap between Korea's management culture versus North America's. My sense is that there is a view that once you achieve a certain title in business here in Korea, there is an element of status that comes with having that title. When you're the most senior person you can relax and everyone else does all the work. However, that's not the way it's going to work in this company.

By the same token—without question—the fact that I don't understand the Korean language has affected my business relations here. For example, I would estimate that my employees understand forty percent of my English. But it's not just their lack of understanding; I'm also to blame for our communication challenges. They miss nuances in my language, and vice versa. In Asia, in particular, I'm very sensitive in the way that I deal with our staff. I think that may be a mistake in Korea, though I'm not sure. In Thailand, for example, people tend to be very gentle and avoid confrontation. The way I speak to our Thai staff is quite different from the way that I speak to our staff in Mexico. Singapore is quite different again. Singaporeans tend to be very focused and direct. So, this is as much my responsibility as anyone else's. It's also my challenge and so I feel that I have yet to get a handle on how to communicate effectively.

On another level, I think that discrimination is a fact of life in Korea. Of course I face discrimination—I look different: I'm tall, blonde and blue-eyed. I will broaden the definition of discrimination and define it as recognizing that someone's different. Yes, I'm different. I see people stare at me. So what? It doesn't bother me. Discrimination is a funny thing. It can work to your advantage and disadvantage. I know full well that more often than not I gain an advantage in Korea because of the way I look. There's a good side and bad side, and I'll take the good side any day. In this respect, though, I have to separate two things as a woman. One is the contacts I make outside of the CECN in Korea. For the most part I tend to meet with Korean men who give me respect, deservedly so or not. The second thing I have to separate is our own staff, which is all female. With them I sense a fair degree of manipulation, because I'm a woman.

As a result, I experiment with techniques because I've never felt comfortable here. Other managers in other markets will come to me and say, "You're the vice-president and you've been here a long time, you know what's going on and I need your advice. This is the issue that I have and I think this should happen but I need some advice." In Korea, I've not seen a lot of evidence of that. All too often I've found out after the fact that something has happened of which I had no knowledge. For example, understanding that we are funded in part by the government of Canada, if a significant federal minister comes to visit, either the office or the language institute should inform me, as it's very important that I know that. I should know ahead of time that this person is coming so that I can remind our managers to mention this or that to the given minister. In one such instance, I only found out after the fact that the minister had been through Korea. In a situation like this, I would send an e-mail that said, "How did the visit go? In future, it's important that we know ahead of time that we expect such visitors. As you know, we receive funding from the federal government, etc." However, e-mail has incredible limitations and so you have to be careful in how you word things otherwise something you write may come off as much harsher, or potentially sarcastic, or potentially as a serious reprimand. That's why I always try to be very clear, factual, concise and objective in any e-mailing we do, especially when you're dealing with someone whose first language is not English.

That being said, I believe the Korean market to be huge — absolutely huge. The numbers coming out of Korea, that being the number of students coming to study in Canada, are significant. There's the student recruitment part of it, and there's the language institute part of it. With marginal advertising we've managed to get a student base of 1400–1500, and we've only been open for a year and a half. We do have a quality product and I think that's attractive. I think there's a natural closeness, a natural relationship, between Canada and Korea.

In the end, though, I think the big challenge here is something that has been a big surprise to me. When I first came to Korea, I was operating according to Canadian business practices. Canadians operate in a high-trust environment; we shake hands and close the deal. That's it. The same is not true in Korea. The Canadian negotiating process can be understood, for example, as two circles of trust overlapping each other so that both circles share a common ground. This common ground is where Canadians begin to negotiate. To assume that the Korean business negotiations model is similar is a huge mistake. Many business deals in this part of the world go down the drain because the two parties involved can't locate that common ground to negotiate from. I hate to generalize, but in most Korean business negotiations the two circles of trust aren't expected to intersect, producing that common ground from where to begin the negotiation process. And so if I had any advice for other businesses in Korea I would urge them to hire people with cross-cultural experience. People who understand North American negotiation principles and North American business culture will help Korean companies deal with the challenge of working internationally. Like I said before, I hate to generalize about a country, but Canadians are very naive in that we treat people with a degree of respect and we expect it in return, and I think sometimes in Korea that behavior is viewed as weak. Loyalty and trust are hard to find in Korea, and that makes our office here very different from the other offices in Asia and Latin America.

"I found myself in Korea simply because some Nigerian agencies, working hand-in-hand together with Korean Embassy officials in human trafficking back home, deceived me. It's them that I blame. They were involved in human trafficking, and it saddens me to say that."

Chined Paul Ogbonna (36)
Nigeria
Factory and Construction Worker
4 Years

As if getting by in Korea as a migrant worker weren't hard enough, in July 2002, after an altercation at a club, Paul was arrested and held in prison for more than five months without being charged. Pushed away, beaten down and scorned, Paul is now fighting for justice the only way he knows how: through the courts.

MY AIM WAS to go to London, England because I'm a musician, but based on the problem that Nigerians have trouble obtaining visas, I thought it wise to come to Korea because getting a visa in Korea is easier. Actually, I never initially planned to come to Korea, but as someone who has traveled widely, I saw nothing wrong with it when I had the opportunity to come here. I knew a little about Korea before coming because we have Korean goods in Nigeria, and I also knew something about the 1988 Olympics.

When I arrived in Korea in April 1999 I came in on a C–2 visa. It was very hard when I arrived here because it's difficult to get to know Koreans quickly. One Nigerian guy told me early on that we couldn't even sit with Koreans on the subway or trains. He said if you sat down beside a Korean they would all get up and back away from the area. When I asked him why, he didn't really have an answer for me.

Actually, I had a big problem from the moment I arrived in Korea because my return ticket to Nigeria had been taken from me by a Nigerian guy who helped set up my trip to Korea through the Korean Embassy in Nigeria. This is why I think that the majority of illegal migrant workers in Korea are not illegal; like me they're the victim of a scam or someone who has lied to them.

Anyway, after arriving in Seoul, I went directly to Dongducheon[11] (동두천), near Camp Casey, and then made my way to Uijeongbu (의정부), northern Seoul. With the help of some Nigerian friends here in Korea, I got my first job at a textile factory, which was actually the very first time I had ever worked in any kind of factory. I was told I would be paid 700,000 won a month and have to work twelve hours a day. There were six of us altogether at the textile factory—me and five other Nigerians—where we dyed clothes. For those twelve hours every worker had his own specialization. The hours were especially tough, though, as we had to switch hours every week. One week we were working 8:00 a.m. to 8:00 p.m. and the next week we'd be working 8:00 p.m. to 8:00 a.m. My job was to take the clothes after they were washed and dyed in chemicals to another machine that looked like a big vat and pin them on so that they were dried almost instantly. From there, we then took them to a big dryer. That was what I did for six months.

All of us lived on the factory work site in an aluminum building next to the factory. The six of us Nigerians shared two rooms. Initially the Korean owner tried to force Korean food on us, but we told him we couldn't eat it because Korean food could not give us the stamina we needed to do that job, as it was a very hard job. The owner then got someone to construct a new kitchen for us so we could cook for ourselves with a gas cooker and we negotiated for rice and a few other things. We could eat Korean vegetables, as well as fruit, like melons, but we wanted to make our own food, like different kinds of soups and fish and meat.

As someone who just came to Korea, I knew the amount of money I was making was not fit for the job, but nobody told us they were deceiving us on our pay. What's more was that the owner of the factory told us that the first month's pay would only be half what we were promised. At first I couldn't find anyone to provide a clear enough answer as to why this had to happen. Only later did I find out that according to Korean law, or so the owner of the factory said, he had to keep the first half of the first month's pay in order to prevent workers from running off in the middle of the night or quitting without warning. He told us that when we finished our work, and gave proper notice—at least one week's notice—the remnant would be given to us with our final paycheck.

Soon after starting work we began working overtime. Originally, we were told we would be paid in cash right after that particular shift for the overtime work we had just completed. It was not part of our regular salary and it was not obligatory; it was optional any time they asked us to work more than the scheduled twelve hours. However, a few shifts in they suddenly made overtime obligatory. After this they then started breaching their agreement by not paying us our overtime as soon as the shift was over. Instead they told us they were going to pay us at the end of the month with our regular salary. I later discovered that the Koreans were making more money from us when we worked overtime, which is why they were trying to make us do it. Because of this fact, we decided that we weren't going to work overtime anymore, and only work the twelve hours we had agreed upon to work daily.

When I complained to the Koreans, they became aggressive. I knew we were in trouble. When it became clear that they were cheating us with the overtime work, I quit. We weren't the first ones to quit, though. We found out that before us Mongolians—even Koreans—had quit because of the conditions. One or two of my fellow workers followed suit and left after me. When I left, though, the owner refused to pay me the outstanding 350,000 won from my first paycheck. He didn't give me the remnant of my first month's pay because he said it was because of me that the other Nigerians left his factory.

During the time that everything had been falling apart at the textile factory, I had been fortunate to meet a few Nigerians who told me of other jobs around where I was working. In fact there was one Nigerian I met who had been in Korea for four years and told me of another job in a factory nearby. He said they were offering 800,000 won at this new factory and they gave you a bag of rice, something I did not receive from the first factory. After meeting the owner of the second factory, he promised to increase my pay if I worked there for a long time. At the time my friend was already making 850,000 won, so I knew it was true.

When I got to the other factory, I discovered our work had to do with chemicals and so I could only take it for one month. I told myself that my life was more important than that work or that money. I think what amazed me most at that time of my life is that I never thought I would be doing that kind of work. That's not why I came to Korea in the first place. Basically it was like being in the wrong place at the wrong time and I wasn't doing what I wanted to be doing. I was not pursuing my career in music or anything similar to it. It wasn't the fault of Korean society or anything like that; I don't blame anyone in Korea. I found myself in Korea simply because some Nigerian agencies, working hand-in-hand together with Korean Embassy officials in human trafficking back home, deceived me. It's them that I blame. They were involved in human trafficking, and it saddens me to say that.

Anyhow, it was November when I left that chemical factory and the weather was turning cold. I was totally alien to cold weather. Africans are not used to such cold and it became that I could not work under those conditions. Luckily with the money I had made up to then, I rented a place in Dongducheon to try and ride out the cold weather. The landlady was extremely kind and taught me a lot. She helped me out by cooking and getting me through the winter season, always making sure my room was warm, for example.

It wasn't until February that I got my next job, in Osan (오산), doing pipe work. The Korean man in charge there and his wife really liked me and we got along well. There was another Nigerian who had been working there for something like four years, so the rapport was established when I got there. When I worked overtime at that job, they paid me immediately, as soon as I was done the shift. It was a very tough job, but the hours were good. I only had to work from 9:00 a.m. to 5:30—everything after that was overtime. I worked really hard while I was there and ended up staying on for three months, making 800,000 won in salary, but with overtime I made 900,000 won a month.

After the pipe work in Osan I went back to Gimpo (김포) and started working part time. It was at that time that I learned it was more lucrative to work part time through a manpower agency than to work full time in a factory. We were paid 50,000 won every day and we weren't working with one person and one person only; we were moving around all the time. There were all nationalities working through that manpower agency: Nigerians, Russians, Mongols, men, women—people from all over the world. It was so lucrative working part time that by the end of the month we were paid one million won for twenty days work. If you worked really hard every day of the month, you could make upwards of 1.5 million or 1.6 million won. This was all in an effort to make sure at the end of the day that I could exchange my pay into a thousand U.S. dollars; everyone's goal was to have a thousand dollars by the end of the month. If you were lucky, though, you'd get hired from a construction company directly and be paid 70,000 won a day. Those who were luckiest would then be asked to work throughout the duration of the construction project. Everyone that was seeking work through the manpower agency was looking for this kind of opportunity.

It was around this time, while doing part time work through the manpower agency, that one of my Pakistani friends came up with the idea that we had to visit Jeju Island (제주도). Now, I really like nature and islands and I had been reading a bit about Jeju Island, so I told my friend I would go down there with him. It was September at the time and as soon as we arrived my friend had personal troubles and so he had to go back, leaving me all alone in Jeju. It was a very dicey situation for me. I was living in Seogwipo

(서귀포), and people recognized me all the time because I was the only black guy living around there. My situation was like Tom Hanks in *Castaway*. I tried to tackle the situation all by myself. Fortunately for me, the Koreans on Jeju Island are very nice people. They didn't care where I was from. They just wanted to be around me. Sometimes people would come up to me on the street and say, "Hey, let's go to a restaurant together."

By this point, I had met someone who was involved in part-time construction work and they had taken me on. They paid less than I was used to, only 40,000 won a day, but it was work nonetheless. It was nice being down there in Jeju, yet it was still 40,000 won a day. This went on for eight months until I finally decided to go to Seoul and get a visa so that I would be legal in Korea. When in Seoul, I went to a church and talked to someone there and he explained what the new visa entailed that was introduced for migrant workers under President Kim Dae-jung (김대중). The rules of the visa stipulated that you had to have an airplane ticket when you applied for the visa, proving that you would be leaving the country after the one-year term was over.

I went to one of the immigration offices soon after this and they issued me a visa. That was near the end of May and it was actually the first time I had been up to Seoul in about a year and a half. It felt good to see my black brothers, and with the World Cup of football starting in June, I decided to stay around Seoul for the month and relax. I had been working seven days a week in Jeju up until then—even when it rained—so I wanted to take some time off. I decided to go back to Jeju after the World Cup.

On July 7, however, as I was getting ready to go back to Jeju, everything changed. The whole thing began when an old Korean friend of mine and I went to a club in Dongducheon. A Filipino woman from the club sat down and served our drinks, but we never invited her so we refused to pay for the drinks when she said they were ten dollars each. I walked up to the bar and tried to make a complaint about what had just happened and just then two Korean men came in from the back door, walked up to me and told me that my friend and I had to leave. As the argument was going on, one of them smashed me on the head with something like a stick or a bat. I then tried to defend myself and was on the ground when the Filipino waitress hit me on the face with a glass bottle. Some foreigners then jumped in to try and break up the fight. My friend then called the police. When the police came, they asked me who smashed me on the face with the bottle. I told them who did it and then we all went to the police station to work things out, but they didn't bring the Filipino girl in, the person who did this to my face. While at the police station, the Korean owner of the club took one of the police officers outside, gave him money—we saw him give the money—and when the officer came back in he closed the file. All of a sudden, the case changed. They let my Korean friend go and then told me that I had to go to the Uijeongbu police station. By the time we left, I had already been there for about five hours.

We arrived at the Uijeongbu police station around 7:00 a.m., and for the next seven hours I was offered no food or water, nor was I offered any treatment even though I was bleeding from my face. The police refused to take any pictures of me for evidence to be used later in court, although I asked them many times to do so. They were asking me where I lived and whether I wanted the Nigerian ambassador notified about this case. I told them yes. They checked out my visa and phoned immigration to make sure my visa was in working order, which it was. After that, they called my

Korean friend and asked him some questions. I think my friend did all that he could, but he couldn't help.

At this point they handcuffed me by clipping one of my hands to the roof. I was still bleeding and asking to go to a hospital, but they didn't listen. They said they were going out for some food. When they came back they unclipped the handcuffs from the roof, handcuffed my two hands together, and told me that we were going to the hospital. I asked the officer if I needed to be handcuffed to go to the hospital when I was the victim of this crime, but they didn't take me to the hospital in the end. They took me to the Uijeongbu immigration department instead. On the ride over to Immigration I kept asking them to take a picture of my face, but all the officers in the car were doing was laughing at me, telling me to go back to my country.

When we got to Uijeongbu Immigration at about four in the afternoon, they changed handcuffs and took me to a room where a Korean man talked to me for about an hour. After this they took me to Mokdong (목동) Immigration, where I ended up spending the night. The next day I finally got in touch with my embassy. They asked me what I had done wrong and I told them exactly what had happened. I spent two full days at Mokdong, yet nobody was questioning me during that whole time. I was left alone! I was asking for treatment for my wound all throughout this, but they never did anything about it. Without laying any charges against me, they then moved me to Hwaseong (화성), the foreign prison outside of Suwon (수원). I managed to get in touch with my embassy again, but it seemed like they could do nothing for me.

In the end, I was in that prison for four months and ten days. For those nearly four and half months, I was treated inhumanely on several occasions. For example, one night the officers in the prison came at the prisoners with a big video camera, laughing at all of us while they tried to film us. The next day they came at us with the same camera and we complained. Later that same night, when I went to the washroom, some men came at me and tried to film me in the toilet. Back in my cell twenty minutes later, about 10–12 men told me to come out of my cell, which I did. The first thing I saw was a pair of handcuffs and an electric prodder. They wanted to put the handcuffs on me but I refused, so several men jumped on me and started ripping off my clothes, after which they began hitting me. They then used the electric prodder on me, and I could feel it run through my veins before I fainted. Chained, and mostly naked after this, one of the men then took the video camera and started filming me again.

I eventually got in touch with some activist groups and one of them suggested that I go on a hunger strike to protest the maltreatment I was receiving in prison. I took the advice and went on a hunger strike for three weeks. They were begging me to end the hunger strike, but before they could release me, they told me I had to pay a fine of two million won! I told them my release had to be unconditional, though. It was incredible because this whole time I had been in prison there was never one single charge brought against me. They never—not once—read to me the charges they were holding me on.

Anyway, towards the end of my hunger strike, they took me to a hospital, partly because of what the hunger strike had done to me, and partly, I believe, because of what the malnutrition at the prison had done to my body coupled with the psychological problems of being locked up. Still a prisoner in the hospital, I was there for three weeks and the whole time they kept telling me that I had to pay this two million won fine. I again refused and so they went to court to get an answer from a judge. On December 12, I was finally released, the day after MBC (Munhwa Broadcasting Corporation) filmed me in my hospital room. From that club in Dongducheon to being released out of the hospital was five months. It was just one big mistake after another.

Since then, I've been trying to bring these injustices to light. I was in severe depression when I got out of the hospital and could not work for some time; you just can't move on when you're living with manic depression. Anyhow, I've handed my case over to a human rights group. I want the people responsible to pay me for the inhumane treatment I received while in prison, so I'm going to sue for punitive damages. If I win this case in court and receive a fair settlement, I would be appeased. They have to compensate me because justice has not prevailed yet. I want the law to prevail.

"Why do people want to put me in a lot of their programs and why did people want to put me in a lot of their programs? Part of it was my skills, but more was because of my energy, my open-mindedness, my willingness to be flexible with the Korean system and to be an easy person to work with."

Matthew Readman (27)
United Kingdom
TV and Radio Actor
6 Years

Matthew has more experience on Korean television and radio than the vast majority of foreigners who work part time in this medium through a second visa. A natural performer, Matthew has had the unique opportunity to work at a television station in Seoul full time, doing a wide array of programs.

MY SISTER had been here for one year, teaching English in Jeonju, North Jeolla Province (전주, 전라북도), and I came over to visit for a month and a half in the summer of '96. I had a very, very interesting time, and because I wasn't working I learned a lot very quickly, as I was socializing all the time. I remember that it was hammering down with rain, the middle of the rainy season, when I was here visiting my sister. It was sweltering and it felt like *Blade Runner*. There were big video screens with women advertising ramyun and it really seemed like something out of *Blade Runner*. But what I was most amazed with was that it was low in terms of elevation. I had expected it to be like Hong Kong and it wasn't. Also, I had never been anywhere where everybody looked ethnically similar. That was the biggest thing. Wham! I'm a white person amongst many, many people who are not Caucasian.

When I went back to England, I worked three months and thought, "No, this is something I want to do now. I'm going to go back and I'm going to teach in Korea for one year." That was my original plan. When I arrived back in Korea, though, I wasn't at the school I was meant to be teaching at—my contract had already been sold because I spoke British English. I had to go through those difficulties of people saying, "You're English is wrong because it's not American English." I felt disoriented and not empowered because I couldn't read and I didn't know where to go on my own to order food that I could eat. I was in Jeonju, where not many people spoke English, so I couldn't get any advice. But aren't those the times when you learn the most and you feel the strongest? One day I was lost and I couldn't find my *hagwon*[12] (학원)—private academy. A man on a motorcycle came up and drove me around the city until he found the *hagwon*. So, to tell you the truth, I embraced it.

After three and half years in Jeonju, I came to Seoul. First of all, if you live in the countryside, things don't change from the day you're there. Even if you speak Korean you're still considered different, a foreigner, that you don't know how to use chopsticks, you don't know how to eat kimchi. And even though I had been in Jeonju three years I wanted to be a little more accepted, and it wasn't happening there. Therefore my tensions would build up about the friction between the two cultures, because no one was adapting to me, even though I tried so hard to adapt to Korea. I came to Seoul partly because of that, but more specifically because I was interested in television and radio and if I was going to do that in Korea there was only one place to do that: Seoul.

At the time, everybody knew I was a frustrated artist in Jeonju. I was always trying different theatre projects and using drama in the classroom, but I wanted some way of really performing. Somebody in the *hagwon* came up to me one time and said, "There was a tiny article in the newspaper: actors wanted for EBS (Educational Broadcasting System)." I called up and they said, "Well, you live in Jeonju, it could be a bit far, but come anyway." I went and I did an audition at EBS. I had nothing to lose. I felt no pressure at all, particularly as I had the advantage of having so many opportunities of doing theatre. I did the audition, they called me back and it went from there, really. I was commuting every Friday night at nine o'clock until 2:00 a.m. to get to Seoul, working all weekend and then going back Sunday night. Obviously people appreciate that kind of thing because it shows you're committed to your work.

When I first started on television I was doing a program called "Listening Special," which was a quiz show for university students, and was on TV for an hour on Sunday mornings. There would be skits that we made at EBS, with questions testing listening. After six months of doing that, decision time arrived: go home to England or do something much more permanent with a television company.

EBS fought and fought with visa problems and management problems and finally I secured a full-time position with them. Nobody knew what that would entail, though, because no other native speaker of English, no other foreigner, had had a full-time position at EBS before. I guess they just thought they would find me the work and I would be in the office nine to five to help out with all the language problems, and indeed that's what happened.

From that point on I started working on skits for teaching programs, short scenes as an actor, script writing and lots of what we would say "advising and researching work." My boss at the time was very, very committed to helping me and also my skills, and she would give me a lot of personal projects. Slowly over a year it grew so that everybody knew me there. I became involved in many different programs. It wasn't until a year later, though—when I started children's programs—that it affected anyone outside of EBS. Suddenly, for some reason unknown to me, I became very popular with young learners. That's when the audience reacted to me, and the people started writing in. My popularity grew tremendously and I had a lot of demands to be on many different programs. All of a sudden people at EBS were relying on me, aware that my popularity had grown, so I had something which was marketable. Also, I had been there a year and a half and I spoke more Korean, so I was involved in so much more research and giving ideas for programs. Once I started speaking Korean it was very different. It was more difficult because they would forget that I was a foreigner and that Korean wasn't my first language. They'd expect me to understand everything and sometimes it wasn't going to happen like that. When I misunderstood stuff, when I would misunderstand a direction or something, I would be reprimanded and shouted at the same way as if Korean was my first language. The more I spoke Korean, though, the stronger my relationships were and the more they would be impressed that I had learned the language.

At the beginning of this stage of my career I was mostly a

presenter of the program, very much a teacher image. Everyone said I was very over-the-top, and I attribute that to the fact that I'm a theatre actor. When I started doing children's programs I did a lot of singing, a lot of dancing and a lot of acting as other characters. Many people feel, "I'm not getting dressed up as a banana. Why would I do that on national television?" But I like to think I do everything, and if you take it seriously—not yourself seriously, but your work seriously and the meaning of what you're doing seriously, what you're providing for the children of Korea, not just English, but cultural exchange—then you don't look stupid. You look committed and you look like you're having fun. Everything I do I have fun with.

So, for six months to a year, everything was, "Thank you, Matthew. You're so kind. You always help us. You help us to understand. I don't know what we'd do without you." Later on, as I became more popular and my Korean got better, I was giving more ideas and challenging images there. As a result, life became more difficult at EBS; the negotiation between the two cultures became much more difficult. If I did something they felt was wrong, I had to bow down and apologize. I'm not used to doing that. If I challenged the system or challenged the content of the programs, potentially there would be huge offence taken, and straight away they would say, "Oh, Matthew's arrogant. He's too big for his shoes. He thinks he's more important than other people." I had to adapt. I'm a very emotional person at work, within my work. Koreans embrace that, and that's why I developed a lot of very close friendships at EBS. There were people I could talk to and confide in. But that's a very fine line because if you're dealing with emotions in personal relationships, people can get offended and that's when the problem would arise. One of my biggest achievements was being able to work at that company as the only foreigner. To be sure, it did get to me sometimes. It got to me hard. But I always somehow found a way through within a couple of weeks.

At the height of all this, when I was doing six or seven programs at one time, I would work from seven thirty in the morning and on average get home at nine or ten. I would work all day and be completely exhausted, but in a satisfying way. That's the way it goes with work in television and radio; it comes, it goes. You take your rest when it comes, you work hard when you have to work hard. I was completely and utterly submerged within a Korean company during my three years at EBS full time.

High points? I'm sapped, almost in tears, very stressed, chain-smoking, drinking coffee at midnight, saying, "I can't go on." Somebody will then come up to me, sit with me for half an hour, and totally listen to all my complaints, my moans—which could sound critical to a Korean company—and try and make everything okay and support me and go and talk to other people and say, "We should help you. You're a foreigner within a Korean company." Low points? I worked one day with a heavy, heavy cold and flu. I started work at seven thirty and finished live radio at nine o'clock. From nine thirty till eleven o'clock I filmed in a small studio, very intensely, all in Korean, trying to remember the Korean properly, with people kind of giggling at my mistakes. I then went and rehearsed for three hours for a brand new show, giving lots of ideas, working hard with children and motivating them all day long. At the end of the day I was exhausted, and even though I was sick the director said, "Okay, we meet Tuesday morning."

"I'm sorry I can't do it Tuesday morning. I'm filming again," I replied.

"What? What do you mean?"

"Well, I'm really sorry."

"Okay, then you don't have to do it."

"Sorry?"

"Well, we'll take away your money."

"Okay, you can't kind of be flexible with me, so you just cut my time and you cut my money?"

The producer got very angry and started shouting, so I left the studio. On Monday morning when I arrived at work, she stripped me down, shouted at me and accused me of swearing and using foul language in front of children, which was not the case. She had gone to the management and had me cut from the program, and told people what an arrogant person I was. I didn't say anything except, "No, I don't think that's true. No, I'm sorry that's not true." Finally, I conformed to Korean culture. I went on bended knee and apologized. I said, "I was unprofessional. I brought stress into the studio. I should not have reacted like that." Since then I'm her golden boy. I can't do anything wrong. She wants me in all the programs she does. Every time she sees me she wants to talk to me. She's back to being very polite to me, very kind. There's an example where you just have to swallow your pride and conform to something which you do not believe in very strongly as an independent-minded person. That is an experience I will not forget.

For people who are thinking of getting into television and radio work in Korea, however, I would say do it. Absolutely. You don't have to be a star; you might just really enjoy doing the work. But you've also got to be aware that you're working within a Korean system. Why do people want to put me in a lot of their programs and why did people want to put me in a lot of their programs? Part of it was my skills, but more was because of my energy, my open-mindedness, my willingness to be flexible with the Korean system and to be an easy person to work with. If you're aware of that and you can be flexible and you can be fun to work with, there are so many opportunities.

"The drive for academic, and thus economic success, has shut out the room that used to be there for spirituality. Economic conditions and overall standard of living in Korea have greatly improved, but with a price. The innocent, natural, spiritual nature of the average Korean has been greatly reduced."

Ronald Nielsen (61)
America
President, Seoul Korea Temple
The Church of Jesus Christ of Latter-day Saints
9 Years

A spiritual and devout man, Ronald Nielsen has been in intimate contact with Korea and Koreans since he first visited the country as a missionary in 1962. His three separate experiences in the country over almost forty years have afforded him a special insight into the country and its people, especially with Koreans' affinity towards Christianity.

I FIRST CAME to Korea in February of 1962 when I received a call from the LDS (Latter-day Saints) Church. The call was for a two-and-a-half-year mission, and at that time I didn't even know where Korea was! I quickly found out the mission consisted of Okinawa, Japan and Korea. Still, Korea didn't register in my brain, I thought "Oh man, that's interesting. I am going to Japan!" I went to the library and checked out about twenty different books on Japanese history, language, and culture, and then I had a friend's mother make me some tapes that had to do with the Japanese language. I would just listen to them and mimic them. Those were the days before the MTC, the Mission Training Center. Back then there were about five to six thousand missionaries worldwide—now we're over 60,000—most of whom were young men and women of about 19 or 20 years of age.

Anyway, to get back to the story, I spent about one week in Salt Lake listening to our Church leaders speak about missionary work and how to be a good missionary, and then three of us were off on a plane to Tokyo, Japan. We were interviewed by the Tokyo mission president and I remember one question in particular: I was asked "Elder Nielson, are you willing to give your life to the Church?" And I responded "Uh ... I guess so?" "Good!" said the president, "We've assigned you to the Korea district!" That was the first time that Korea had entered my head and I was so flabbergasted. I couldn't even tell the president that I'd been studying Japanese for three months and that I had fallen in love with Japan and everything Japanese. So, for the next two weeks as we were waiting for our visas to clear, I even prayed that I wouldn't have to go to Korea. Obviously that didn't work, and thank goodness because the Lord knows where he wants you and the experiences I've had over here have certainly surpassed my expectations.

I was 19 years old when I started out on my thirty-month mission. These days, all missions are two years, but back then the foreign speaking missions were an extra six months long. Also, my mission was extended an extra four months on top of that to help with the translation of the Book of Mormon, so I was here for almost three years.

Actually, many people are not familiar with Mormons, but the word "Mormon" actually comes from a prophet in the Book of Mormon. Mormon was his name and he did the editing and abridging of that book. The Book of Mormon is a companion scripture to the Bible. It talks about a group of Israelites that came to the American continent at about 600 B.C. Sometimes we're accused of not being Christian, but we're the Church of Jesus Christ of Latter-day Saints! We believe Jesus Christ to be the son of our Father and the mediator between us and God. That's why I find it odd when some of the more mainstream denominations accuse us of being less Christian or simply not Christian at all. We do differ from the Protestants, for example, in that we're a restored church, not a protesting church against the Catholics, and we're not Catholic in the sense that Catholics trace their authority back to Peter and the bishops. Essentially, we believe that there was an apostasy that took place in the second century and that there was a watering-down of the true doctrine, hence the need for a restoration. Joseph Smith, the modern-day prophet in the early 1800s, was called upon by the Lord to restore the Church of Jesus Christ, hence the Church of Jesus Christ of Latter-day Saints.

Anyway, getting back to when I arrived in Korea in 1962, I first labored in Seoul. I served also in Daegu (대구) and Busan (부산). The LDS Church was still very young in Korea at that time. Missionaries arrived here after the Korean War (1950–53). A number of Koreans were converted by members of the Church who were here with the U.S. military. Then, under the auspices of Dr. Kim Ho-jik (김호직), who was converted to the gospel back in 1952 when he was doing his doctoral work in agronomy and food science at Cornell University, LDS missionaries were able to get visas to come to Korea. Eventually, he became the minister of education in the cabinet of the Syngman Rhee (이승만) administration. With his help, the first missionaries arrived in Korea in 1956. Six years later, when I got here in 1962, there were still only 18 of us.

In 1962, Korea was an entirely different country from what it is today. It was literally a third-world country. We lived in homes that had no plumbing. To use the outhouse in the winter time was so cold you'd quickly want to do your business and then get back inside. In the summer time it was so hot, and the ammonia was so strong, you couldn't keep your eyes open, as tears would stream down your cheeks. You could hardly breathe while the maggots below were cheering for more. Thank goodness we were permitted to employ, because of the economy, local people to help with the cooking. In most cases, the cooks couldn't cook any American food. When I was in Daegu it was rice, squid, bean sprouts, and kimchi three times a day.

My first impression of Koreans was that they were a very humble people who were eager to help foreigners. They were always curious, wanting to know more, and anxious to learn English. The modern economic approach to life I think has taken a great toll on the spirituality of the average Korean, however. For example, in missionary work we used to be able to talk with almost anybody. They'd never turn you down at the door, always inviting us in as special guests. We could go out and knock on doors anywhere and get in and talk. They may not have agreed with what we had to say, but they were never rude. Back then we were teaching and having discussions all day long, in contrast to the missionaries today who can hardly get in the door. Today, Korean students have hardly any time to discuss anything with missionaries because they're enrolled in *hagwon* (학원)—private academy—classes before and after school. The drive for academic, and thus economic success, has shut out the room that used to be there for spirituality. Economic conditions and overall standard of living in Korea have greatly improved, but with a price. The innocent, natural, spiritual nature of the average Korean has been greatly reduced.

So, after my initial call in Korea, I went back to college to complete my degree in engineering. You have to understand that "the call" in the LDS Church is for a specific amount of time. For us young men who were aiming for a college education, we were taking a two-year break. These missionaries are here to provide a service for members of the Church and the people of the community. After their two-year service, they return back to whatever academic or other goals they have in life. Midway through my junior year, however, I wasn't satisfied with my direction and so I switched to Asian Studies. I graduated with a dual major in History and Asian Studies, and then went on to do a master's degree in Oriental Studies at the University of Arizona. For my doctorate, I switched from East Asian to Near Eastern Studies because that's what I was teaching. For the last 32 years I've taught at the college level for the LDS Institute of Religion.

It was while I was teaching there that the Church called me to come to Korea once again in 1992. I was called back to supervise the activities of the younger missionaries. From 1992 to 1995 I supervised some 500 missionaries here. Upon arriving back in Korea, after almost thirty years away, the country was entirely different economically, which in turn impacted the work of a missionary. In the past, if we had any time to go around knocking on doors, we loved that. Most missionaries today hate it because that's about all they have to do. They don't have anywhere near the amount of teaching appointments that we used to. For example, back in the sixties we probably had as many "teaching discussions" in a day as contemporary missionaries do in a month. It's hard to get people to sit down and talk with you, compared to the old days. Today the missionaries work in many other activities, such as working with other members, getting involved in service work, etc. They're required to do four hours of community service, such as working with orphans or simply picking up trash off the street. The Church has also refined the art of missionary work to the point where lesson plans have been designed and training created to enhance missionary skills.

Our Church has been very successful in Korea and part of that has to do with the nature of Christianity as a whole. Christianity has had a large impact on Korea, with about 25–30 percent of Korea being Christian. In the past century, Koreans have associated Christianity with modernization, democracy, and the successful economy of the West. More importantly for the Koreans, Christianity was linked with the rising anti-Japanese feeling of the first half of the twentieth century. Under the Japanese occupation, the foreign Christians residing in Korea were looked upon as aiding the Koreans against their Japanese imperial masters. The modernization of Christian countries undoubtedly had an alluring effect. Also, there's an affinity between Korean culture and Christianity. The term for God, *ha-na-neem* (하나님), for example, lends itself to a monotheistic deity, compatible with Christianity. The LDS Church places emphasis on the family, and teaches that marriages can be eternal and not just "until death do we part." We believe the family is an eternal unit. We also believe departed ancestors can accept the Gospel in the spirit world. This teaching on family and our ancestors is very appealing to the Koreans, since they have a deep respect and connection to their ancestors.

When someone decides that they want to become a member of our church, what happens is that usually the missionaries will engage you in six basic discussions: God's Plan of Happiness, the Gospel of Jesus Christ, the Restoration of the Gospel, Eternal Progression, Living a Christ-like life, and Membership in God's Kingdom. We don't view the commandments of God as—limitations, but we view them as guidelines for happiness in this life. Take one for example: "Thou shall not commit adultery." Even if you don't believe in God's judgment or in the afterlife, this commandment makes good sense in this life. Whenever this law is broken, there is much misery, not just with the immediate parties involved but other members of the family are often involved in this pain. If people follow the Lord's commandments, they'll lead a happier life.

After a person agrees to lead a Christ-like life, they're baptized, which is a symbol of a cleansing into their new life. That's just the beginning, though. Our Church is made up of volunteers—the bishop, the officers, and all the teachers that make a ward or a branch function as volunteers. The bishop may have a job that he works at for forty hours a week, but then he spends another forty hours overseeing the activity of his ward and delegating to others. Everybody with the Church pitches in and that's how people are of a service to fellow Church members and the community at large.

On top of that, there's also an Old Testament principle that a member of the Church tithes ten percent of his or her earnings. We donate both our money and time. Of all the charities out there, and I've seen a lot of them, the Church is the best charity for me because I know that every penny of my donation is going exactly where it is needed. There is no administration cost. The bishop and all the other volunteers of the Church do not receive any salary. That's how it functions in America and anywhere in the world where Mormons operate.

With Korea, there are of course specific challenges for our Church. One example of this is the drinking and smoking culture in this country. In the vertical society that is Korea, if you work in any company, you're expected to drink with the boss. Failure to do so could cause problems, such as alienation or loss of promotion. To convert a person that lives in this reality poses a problem. Funny enough, though, when I was here as a missionary, we would baptize about two men to every woman. The vast majority of our converts were young men and women such as ourselves because it was hard for a younger man to persuade an older man in Korea. Now, because we've utilized the member-missionary system, you have families and members within the branches who have family members and friends who aren't members of the Church. The truth is that we gain access to most of our converts through our members, however. When I was a missionary in the 1960s, this superstructure didn't exist. We've had to build it from the ground up. So, it isn't uncommon for an older man or woman to bring in their children and grandchildren for baptism. It's also much better this way, I believe.

Conversely, one of the advantages that the Korea mission has to work with is that probably Korea, more than any other place in the world, has developed a local leadership in the Church a lot faster. Again, I think that has to do with the fact that whole families are being baptized in place of just one or two members. Our role should be that we're here to set the example and provide the framework within which to operate, and then encourage the local population to take care of it themselves, remaining here on a supervisory level.

Anyhow, I'm presently on my third mission, which began in November of 2000, and will last for three years. I'm now the president of the Seoul Temple here in Seodaemun-gu (서대문구). How it works here is that there's the local ward that's run by a bishop. This bishop answers to a stake president who may be responsible for as many as eight or ten wards. The stake president then answers to the area authority, which is in Tokyo. The area president supervises the various stakes and missions. For example, here in Korea there are 17 stakes and four missions. I have no ecclesiastical authority over any of the stake presidents in Korea; I answer directly to Salt Lake.

The most positive experience I would take from my nine years over more than four decades in Korea would definitely be the chance to work with the Korean people themselves. There's a very special spirit and discipline in Korea. The special relationships here, particularly once you're in one of those groups, as we are in the Church, are simply amazing; it's amazing to witness the things that people here will do for each other. I've had the fortune to listen to some people's stories from the Korean War and all of them were a humbling and life-affirming experience for me. On the other end, very little has rubbed me the wrong way here. That may have to do with the fact that I'm somewhat insolated from the negatives in Korea, and therefore see mainly the good that this country has to offer. I've seen Korea go through the process of changing from a third-world country to the modern nation that it is now. They have done in forty to fifty years what America and the West took 200 to 300 years to do.

Something else that I've learned over my years here has to do with language. Language has to be lived in order to be understood, and in that sense I still have a lot to learn! As a young missionary I learned quickly just how careful I had to be in Korean. You may think that a word has only one meaning, when in fact it may have a plethora of meanings, given the situation in which it's used. Take for example *sheel-chun* (실천), which means "to practice." Now, there's also *oon-dong* (운동), which is another form of "practice," as well as *yun-seup* (연습), which is yet another type of "practice." Although Korean can be very confusing for foreigners, it facilitates some words and ideas about Christianity a lot better than Chinese does. For example, when saying the word "deity" in Chinese, you have to choose between the words tien, which means "heaven," and shangti, which means "the guru on high." The Korean word for "God," *ha-na-neem,* is more in harmony with Christian monotheism.

Looking back, my time in Korea has had a wonderful effect on me. It's been a great blessing, really. The time spent here wasn't much of a sacrifice. Nowadays, the electricity might go out once a year in our house in Seoul but back in the sixties it would happen every day! I used to tell myself how much I wanted to get out of those uncomfortable situations, but I look back now and laugh at the situation. A crisis plus time equals humor. People that are able to laugh at themselves are grateful for the experience, no matter how hard it was at the time. Over my time here I've also learned that the average South Korean is a very spiritual person, and as long as they're able to balance the growing materialism of modernization while maintaining their traditional value system, I think they'll be okay.

"Living among Korean officers and their families was a great experience for my family and me. It was one that we will always cherish."

Steve* (36)
America
Major, U.S. Army
10 Years

A graduate of the prestigious United States Military Academy at West Point, Steve should be an inspiration to all those people of Korean descent who are trying to find the right balance between retaining their important Korean cultural and linguistic traits and their upbringing in a different country. Loving husband, devoted father, and U.S. Army officer, Steve has certainly experienced a great deal—and benefited from this experience—in his years living between the United States and Korea.

I SPENT SIX years in Korea after my birth in 1967. I have two elder sisters. My first language was Korean, but I learned a little bit of English just before we left for the States, to Virginia Beach, in 1973. I have no memories of the transition being difficult. At that age I was going out, having fun, playing with my friends. I picked up English the fastest in my family, just because I was the youngest, and the younger you are the quicker you pick up languages. The neighborhood we lived in was great. The people were very friendly, very helpful, and we had children my age all around us. My first memory in the United States and of the people there was just fabulous. To this day I'm still grateful to the people in our neighborhood.

While I was growing up in the States, I did return to Korea on several occasions. The first time was back in '83. We were part of a government-sponsored program that still runs to this day where they bring *kyo-po* (교포)—overseas ethnic Korean—from all over the world to Korea to learn all about their country and culture. It was a first-rate program. I think it lasted two weeks and I got to meet other Korean *kyo-po* from other parts of the world. I have vivid memories of the ones from Canada because they spoke French, and it was so odd to see someone who looked Korean and spoke French. We got to see all the different sites of South Korea and everywhere we went it was VIP treatment. Yet it wasn't a thing where I became more culturally aware that I was more Korean. I didn't see myself any differently, actually. The thing that I was opened up to was that there were Koreans who went to different countries and had different backgrounds.

In my second year at West Point, I went to Korea once again for what's called a CTLT, (Cadet Troop Leading Training) where you actually go to a U.S. military unit and act like a platoon leader for about a month. I went to Camp Humphreys, near Pyongtaek (평택), South Korea and had a great experience. That was the first time I was away from home as an adult. However, I didn't learn a lot about Korea, just because I spent most of my time on base and I didn't speak the language that well.

My next two visits were also for short military exercises. The next extended time I came back to Korea was 1995, and that was to do my company command in the 2nd Infantry Division at Camp

Casey, after graduating from West Point. I didn't want to be anywhere else because, quite frankly, I considered the 2nd Infantry Division the most important unit in the army at the time, and so I came with the mentality that everything I was going to do was going to be work-oriented. I knew that after the company command I was going to start my preliminary officer training program, where I would go and learn Korean, and then go to graduate school. I didn't get off base a lot during that time because, one, I didn't have any interest to go out and explore, and two, I didn't have the time, so I didn't learn much about Korea during that year here. My vocabulary in Korean was that of a kid then. I was illiterate and so could only write my name. I had no idea of the difference between the familiar tone and the honorific one. Initially when I spoke Korean, I turned a lot of Korean people off because I was speaking in the base level and not as if it was the first time I was speaking with them. It was only at the Defense Language Institute that I learned to read and write and that was in 1996, a year later.

The next time I was back in Korea, 1999, it was a total shift. The reason I came back was to finish out my training as a regional specialist, what the Army calls the Foreign Area Officer Program. I had done my language training, and I had done my graduate studies, so I was going to finish up by going to a Korean university to further learn Korean, travel all over the country and the region, and also attend the South Korean Army Staff College in Daejeon (대전). My tour from 1999 to 2001 was to totally learn about Korea, its culture, its military, and its society. We had to live off the installation so we could learn how Koreans lived, learn how they paid utilities, how they got along with their neighbors—things like that. It was as much of an immersion as you could get.

I chose Korea to do my Foreign Area Officer Program for two reasons. Professionally I thought I could give the most back to the military because of my interest in the region and because of my background, and secondly, it was a journey for self-improvement, self-discovery, if you will, because I started realizing that being Korean American I had a lot to learn about the language and about the culture. It was also very important to my wife, Grace, who was born in Korea, but did most of her growing up in the States.

My travels within the country were really eye-opening then. I had no idea of the diversity and the beauty of the landscape. What I really learned, though, was how the Korean military and Korean army officers were trained, what their thinking processes were like, and how they differed greatly from the American way of thinking. Living among Korean officers and their families was a great experience for my family and me. It was one that we will always cherish. They are truly dedicated and hardworking, and their families endure many sacrifices. The differences between us, I think, are largely cultural. The Korean Army, for example, focuses heavily on the education. In the Army, we try to focus on learning, and once you learn the concepts in a school you go out and try to apply them. My observation of the Korean Staff College was that they would focus more on grades, because for them, if they didn't finish in the top of a certain percentage, they weren't going to get promoted to lieutenant colonel. This forced the officers to focus on cramming for tests. I discussed my observations with instructors and classmates, and they told me that the system was a reflection of Korea's education system, but that they have been looking into possibly disconnecting grades from promotions.

In terms of my future, I'm making a conscious decision to come back to Korea. Yet that's not necessarily for cultural reasons. It's a career decision. As a regional specialist, the majority of jobs for me are here in Korea. Obviously the great thing about that, on the periphery, is that my son and daughter will be able to grow up a couple of years here in Korea, though I feel we will never live here. A couple of years at a time is fine, but my wife and I will raise our children in American schools with English as a primary language. I have no desire to live in Korea for the rest of my life, because the U.S. is home to us. When I think of all the places that I've traveled, I always think within the concepts of liberty and freedom and I think in terms of the standard of life. There's nowhere else I can do the things I want except in the United States. The thing that makes us unique about being American—and this is going to sound really egocentric as a country—is that we are the greatest country in the world. I believe the things we stand for and the things we're trying to do around the world overall are good. You can't always do everything right, you can't always do the best thing, but I think overall as a country, we have the power to do good, and so I'm proud of that.

"I think if you want to work and live here for a long time you have to have a lot of patience."

Sumalee* (20)
Thailand
Nanny and Waitress
6 Months

For good reason, Sumalee did not want have her real name printed in this book. One of hundreds of thousands who are working illegally in Korea, Sumalee is doing her best to make ends meet by working crazy hours almost every day of the week.

I CAME TO Korea in December 2002 to work. I know that this country is a rich country, so I thought I could get good pay. In fact, I tried to go to Taiwan but it's hard to get a visa there for Thais. In Korea I don't need a visa, so it's the main reason I came here, though I can only stay for three months at a time. I came with my Canadian boyfriend because he wanted to work and make money, too.

When I arrived in Seoul, I had no idea how to find work. My boyfriend, on the other hand, was an English teacher so he could use the Internet to find work. When he got a job he asked everyone he knew if there was any work I could do, but it was difficult finding anything for me. After about a month here, though, I heard from some Filipinos that there was a market in Itaewon (이태원)

where you could post work-wanted signs. My boyfriend helped write a sign for me that said I was seeking work as a babysitter or housekeeper, but all this only took place after being here for a month.

In the beginning I stayed home and cried a lot. I wasn't working for almost two months. I became really upset and sad when I realized I had no money. My boyfriend had to give me money to buy food and that was really hard. I've been working since I was young and giving my mother money, and so when I didn't have any money to do what I wanted it made me crazy. If I wanted to buy something to eat, I was too scared to ask—too shy—and this made me feel irresponsible, and made me think negatively. I wanted to work at the time, but the thing was, if I went back to Thailand, what was I going to do? My brother had a loan that I was helping to pay back, so what was I going to do? I could get a job in Thailand, but it wouldn't even be enough to support myself and my boyfriend, let alone my family, and so I had no choice. I tried to take it easy, thinking, "Everything will work itself out," but all I could really do early on was cook for me and my boyfriend—always Thai food! Most of the stuff I cooked with I brought from Thailand myself.

Anyway, after those first two months of loneliness and sadness, I got my first part-time job babysitting, but it was only one day a week. It would eventually take six months to find work that kept me busy everyday. These days I usually work eight hours a day and it's 60,000 won per day. If I work like this, six days a week for eight hours each, plus two nights in the bar, I can make a lot of money. I have to say that I love the work I do. I even love babies now! Usually they're five or six months old. There's one girl—she's seven months old—I've been looking after since she was three months old, so now I'm like here mama. She's so cute! But the thing is, some of these families leave all of a sudden and then I have no work, which is part of the reason I'm also waitressing in a bar. It's good for me because all the customers are foreigners, so I can talk to them in English. I work there two nights a week. It's fun, but it's a little hard and it gives me a headache and makes me sick because I don't smoke, and the bar is really smoky.

To tell the truth, when I first started working illegally I was very scared. I was never scared when I was in someone's house and babysitting because all my employers were very nice to me and they loved me, so I had no problem with them. Also, the police don't come to people's homes. Yet when I'm working in the bar I'm frightened because I'm always thinking the police are going to come to the bar. Early on I was so nervous when I saw the police come to check people in the bar. I would start to shake and say to myself, "Oh my God!" But I soon realized that the police were not coming to check the regular people in the bar; they came to check for American soldiers and were military police. Yet because I didn't know who they were or what they were doing in the beginning, thinking they were coming to check for illegal workers, I got really scared.

These days things are okay with work, though. I'm satisfied with the amount of money I'm making, and I'm sending home some money to help pay off my family's debt. Doing all this, however, leaves me with no spending money for myself. I make enough to pay back, but that's it. Also, sending money home can be complicated, as I usually give it to a friend when they're going to Thailand. I have some Thai friends here in Korea, and when they go back to Thailand, they get the money to my mother. When I'm done paying back that loan my brother took out, I'll try and save more money for myself.

With life in Korea things are not as good, unfortunately. I like Korea less now than when I first arrived. Some Thai people have a problem being here because they think Koreans are not friendly or they're rude, but I have no problem with Koreans. They like me and they're really nice to me. I've been fortunate because I've never experienced any kind of racism from Koreans—never. But I do like it less here because if you've been to Thailand you will have seen that everything is cheap and you can do anything you want. Here in Korea, you can't do everything you want and things are expensive. Sometimes I want to do something around town, but I have to stay home because it's too expensive for me to do it. That's why I just think there's nothing to do here in Korea.

Thankfully, though, English has been enough for me to survive in Korea because I haven't learned very much Korean. To be honest, I don't need to know how to read Korean because I go from home to work and that's it, and I can read the English on all the subways and buses. Whenever I have a problem I ask a Korean and they always help me, even if they cannot speak English. They always help me, and so I've had no bad experiences with the people here. Yet the truth is that it's very hard for many Thai people coming to Korea. I've heard that some Thais are sent directly back to Thailand at Incheon (인천) International Airport. I don't know, I guess they're afraid they're coming to work illegally.

As far as advice goes, I think it would be good to have a Korean husband or a foreign husband here. For someone coming to work as a babysitter, or something like that, I would tell them to put signs up and try and meet people. There are Thai restaurants in Itaewon with Thai people that might help you. The people at the Thai Embassy are helpful but they cannot do much to help you when you're looking for a job. I'm from Thailand and Korea is also in Asia, a country not so far from my country, so it's easy for me to go back and forth. I think if you want to work and live here for a long time you have to have a lot of patience. Most foreigners that I've talked with are not so happy living here. Most of them have been to Thailand—and loved it—so they're working here for the money. So, if you want to make money you should come to Korea, and then do what you want afterwards.

"If you just stay in Seoul you miss so much, not just the history of the other areas, but the regional foods, the beaches, the islands, the fantastic seafood restaurants. It's a pity that some of the foreigners don't realize that they can also have some great experiences outside of Seoul."

Martin Robinson (51)
United Kingdom
Lonely Planet Travel Writer
2 Years

You're unlikely to meet many people that have done as much traveling around Korea as Martin Robinson. Seemingly introverted and reserved on the outside, he becomes very talkative when it comes to his globe-trekking adventures, which include trips to five continents and fifty countries.

I WAS HERE in Korea in 1997 because the Korean president had an initiative on globalization, and part of that initiative was employing lots of native English speakers to work in Korean middle and high schools. I had worked already in Tokyo, Japan for four years and was thinking about going somewhere different, either Taiwan or Korea. Korea won out. How this happened was I went back to England after working in Japan and saw an ad in the newspaper completely by accident. I was in the local library reading some sort of newspaper and there was an ad saying:

"Teach English in Korea with EPIK" (English Program in Korea). I rang them up and I got someone at the embassy and he gave me a very strange interview, which I passed, and then I landed up in Korea, in Jeonju, North Jeolla Province (전주, 전라북도).

I was with the EPIK program there for two years, and in a good school. The Korean English teachers were very kind to me, as Koreans are famous for their hospitality to foreigners. It was interesting being in a school situation rather than being in a *hagwon* (학원)—private academy. I was the only foreigner out of 1,000 people, I think, so it was very Korean.

It was while I was living in Jeonju that I wrote a hiking guide to North Jeolla Province, the name of the province that Jeonju is located in. This was by no means my first travel writing, though. I had written travel articles for one of the English dailies in Japan for years. I also wrote freelance for magazines for some time before that. Anyway, it was while I was living in Jeonju that I put out the travel guide. At the time there was no information in English on the area—just trying to work out the buses was a great nightmare! Actually, North Jeolla Province has a lot of good hiking places, lots of national parks, provincial parks, that are worth seeing, so I sort of amused myself on weekends by traveling out to all these different parks, writing about them and keeping a record of it all. I even drew my own maps! Although it took a year to put together, I ended up publishing that hiking guide by myself. After I self-published, one of the local English bookshops was selling the hiking guide and it was also in the tourist information bureau in Jeonju.

Some time after this, the previous writer for *Lonely Plant Korea* came across my hiking guide and sent it to the Lonely Planet offices. Someone there liked it and they asked me to submit a test piece. I live in Auckland, New Zealand now, so I picked Thames. Thames is a very small, old mining town not far from Auckland, so I thought it was a good place to write up. I wrote the place up, sent it off to Lonely Planet and they just about liked it. After that, I was offered the fantastic job of roaming around the outback in Australia in a 4x4 and writing that up for the Australia Outback book. They then needed someone to write up Seoul, and they thought I was the person to do it. So, I came out and did Seoul—that was in 2002—and then they needed someone this year to do Korea, and they liked the Seoul one, so they gave me the Korea job.

Doing the Lonely Planet guide for Korea has been a challenge in many ways. First, you're working twelve hours a day for long periods of time when you're researching, so it's stressful because you have to try and cover everything. You have to do as good a job as you can and you can't go back if you miss something, even if it's a telephone number of a hotel because it's fairly hard to go back and pick it up again. There are so many things that you have to cover and they all need phone numbers and how to get there and how to get away, etc. To get everything right is really a concentrated effort. You can easily burn out. That's the biggest problem, I think, trying to avoid burning out and getting fed up and getting driven mad by traveling and writing it all down. I think all travelers find that after a month of hard traveling they need a rest, but if you're a Lonely Planet writer you can't rest. You have to keep going.

For me, it's been a long time in Korea doing research, covering Seoul, as well as Gyeonggi Province (경기도), Gangwon Province (강원도), Chungcheon Province (충청도), and North Jeolla Province (전라북도). One thing I've found very unique about Korea is its history. I guess the history of every country is unique, and that's what makes countries different to some extent. However, I think it's interesting the way the history of Korea relates to how people behave and what you can see here nowadays. Another area that is special is the food. I think Korean food is unique and different from anywhere else. Every time I come here I find out more and more things about food, so it seems a never-ending task to try and write about and recommend to people the incredibly various types of food that you can get here. If you just stay in Seoul you miss so much, not just the history of the other areas, but the regional foods, the beaches, the islands, the fantastic seafood restaurants. It's a pity that some of the foreigners don't realize that they can also have some great experiences outside of Seoul.

I've been really lucky to see some other great places in Korea. You know, some people are just born unlucky. They go to India and they get sick for a month and so all they see is the inside of a hospital. They can't walk the whole time, and then they just get out of the hospital and a monsoon arrives. It's too hot to move and then they have a bad experience with a moped driver who rips them off fifty dollars, so they have a thoroughly miserable time. That's life; it's unfair. I'm just one of the lucky ones.

For me, I like finding new places, and in Korea I liked finding places that weren't in the previous book. For example, I'm just amazed by all the different things there are in Korea that people don't know about, like Daecheon Beach (대천 해수욕장). People say it's commercialized, but beaches everywhere are commercialized! The beaches of Korea are great. And the lakes! This is something else that should be more famous. National Geographic should do something about these lakes and the really beautiful boat trip you can do from Danyang (단양) to Cheongju (청주). That's a really great boat ride, but so few people have heard of it. I think there are lots of undiscovered things in Korea, and this is what makes it interesting.

On the other hand, the worst part in Korea is probably the hardest thing to write about: the Korean *yaw-gwan* (여관)—traditional inn. Generally you go into a *yaw-gwan* and the owner is asleep. It then takes a bit of time to wake them up and they're probably not very happy to see you, even if you're a customer. When you explain to them that you're not actually a customer, and that you just want to look around and put them in your guidebook, they're even less happy than before. Also, they all tend to be the same. With Korean hotels, *yaw-gwan*, and even the *yaw-in-sook* (여인숙)—small inn–it's actually hard to find differences between the same price levels. 20,000 won *yaw-gwan*, for example, are all pretty much the same; 300,000 won hotels are pretty much the same; 10,000 won *yun-sook* are pretty much the same. My editor keeps telling me that I've got to somehow differentiate them and say something about them, like "One is friendlier than the other," or "One is cleaner than the other." I find it difficult to put that in, so that's one part of Korea that's pretty hard on the travel writer. With Korean *yaw-gwan* everything's similar, right down to the toothpaste, the toothbrushes, the half-empty shampoo bottles, the free drink in the refrigerator, and the sleeping *a-jum-ma* (아줌마) middle-aged woman—in the entry hall of that dingy corridor.

For us Lonely Planet writers, there's no typical day. Every day is different. I suppose that's one good thing. Guidebooks cover everything. That's the thing people have to realize. A lot of people are pretty good about writing about food they enjoy or discos or clubs, but in a Lonely Planet travel guide you've also got to write about national parks, hiking, bungee jumping, *bun-dae-gi* (번데기) —silkworms—animals and everything else. If you're only interested in certain things then travel writing is not for you. You can do travel writing articles, but not travel guides, because they have to cover everything.

Essentially I think being a Lonely Planet writer is like being an actor. You have intense work periods and then you have rest periods; it just depends on which books are needed and which books you're chosen to do. Although you're paid pretty well when you're actually working, it's quite difficult for people to do as a full time job. Some people manage it, but others supplement it with English teaching or home gardening or something like that. I think there are around 150 writers at Lonely Planet, some will be full-time and others will be less than full time—just like the actors.

With the work itself, choosing the countries and cities, it's not entirely up to the writer because writers have editors and editors are the boss—that's the reality. Of course writers, particularly Lonely Planet writers, are generally given quite a lot of freedom so that each book is quite individualistic in some ways. I tend to favor live music, so you'll probably find more live music in my Lonely Planet guide than you might find in other Lonely Planet books. I must say, though, that the best part about writing these guides is that I can travel around for free. Lonely Planet pays for everything. In fact, that's a difference between us and other magazines. Some travel writers for other magazines might get free trips offered by hotels, but in fact Lonely Planet writers never get anything free from anyone. That's their policy, so we never take any free hotel tours or eat free meals in a restaurant. We're paid expenses that cover just about everything.

After leaving Korea, the write-up is then twelve weeks, which is quite generous, actually. The editing then takes at least six months and then another two months, maybe, to get printed and so on.

    I should mention that while writing this new Lonely Planet guide to Korea, one of the major problems has been Koreans' level of English. I guess you're supposed to say that it's getting better, but I'm not sure that it is. I don't know why it's not getting better. There are so many English teachers here that it should be getting better, but it's still a major problem. So, like in other countries around the world where English is not widely spoken, travelers have to resort to sign language and here, *han-geul* (한글)—written Korean. That's always a challenge of travel. It's helpful if they speak English, but if they don't you just have to accept that and try your best to communicate in other ways.

" ... come knowing you are a guest in someone else's country, as a homestay guest, and that it's up to you to adjust to Korea and not vice-versa."

Karis Thompson (23)
America
Fulbright Scholarship Intern
13 Months

As an adoptee of Korean descent, Karis came to Korea in Korea for a much different reason than most every other foreigner. Despite being led to believe that she would never find her birth family, her long journey proved successful almost from the start. Today she is in constant contact with her birth family and enjoying a job that allows her the time to reconnect with the people and culture of Korea.

MY FATHER was the eldest son in his family and needed to conceive a son to carry on the family lineage, and so had taken a second wife to have a son. I was born from his first wife to a Korean family that had four daughters already. I also had an older half-brother who was two months older than me. My mother's older sister, who had been like a mother to her, counseled my mother to place me for adoption instead of raising five daughters and needing a dowry for each one when we eventually got married. My mother and aunt also thought I would have a better life in the United States, so I was adopted three and a half months after I was born. My mother and aunt were the only two people who knew I went to America. The rest of the family had been led to believe that I had died shortly after I was born. Five years ago, however, my mother and aunt told the rest of the family that I was indeed alive and in America. The family said they were very upset and considered looking for me, but didn't know how to do so or even if that would be the best route.

I came to Korea thinking I would never find my family because the story I had heard when I was young, and the story my parents had been given, was that I had been abandoned at the police station and there were no records of my family or parents or location of birth. People in Korea also told me I would never find my birth mother, and that birth mothers don't usually want to be found, because they were once single and unwed but maybe have remarried and started a different family since the birth. But I still wanted to leave my information at the orphanage just in case she was looking for me or curious. Mainly, though, I wanted to thank her and tell her that I was okay and had lived well in America.

The decision to come to Korea to work was a long time coming. I had considered teaching abroad for some time; my first choice since before college had always been Korea. My adopted parents had offered many times when I was growing up to bring me back to Korea, but I wasn't interested at the time. I became more interested in Korea in high school and in college when I interacted with some Korean American communities at churches, and also through academic projects.

When I arrived in Korea, I went to the orphanage where they brought out my records and informed me I had living parents. They gave me their names and ages and told me I had four older sisters. They also had an address and phone number for them, and so a few days after that, I met them at the orphanage, my mother and aunt and two of my sisters and their financés. We then went to their home after the orphanage meeting and met the rest of the family before going out for dinner and coffee. Since then I've seen them many times and we've developed a real family relationship.

Initially, the reason I chose to come to Korea through the Fulbright program was because it looked like the ideal program. It seemed like a very intense cultural immersion experience, but with the guarantee and security of an American organization there to support and train us. Also, the Fulbright program offered cultural training and had no language requirement.

The program itself serves a need for English language instruction throughout the world, but we're also sort of an egalitarian organization. Most people who have access to native English speakers in Korea are wealthier or have certain privileges in life, so they can afford the *hagwon* (학원)—private academy—with the native English speakers or even travel abroad. But we're with every student, like the student whose parents could never afford to send them to Canada or Australia or even to a *hagwon* in the city. We teach everyone. This year, in fact, over 190 schools applied for the sixty odd teachers who came through the Fulbright program.

When I arrived in 2002, I came with 47 new people. On top of this number there were five people who extended their contract from the previous year. I never counted, but I think one third of the group was of Korean descent, with a handful of others being half Korean or of Asian descent. Last year, there were also two other adoptees. At the time of our arrival it was the middle of July, right after the soccer World Cup. It was very hot at that time of year and

I was very homesick. I had only had minimal contact with Asian communities growing up in the Midwest, and so to walk out the back gate of Kangwon National University (강원대학교) and be in this sea of people that looked like me, yet with whom I felt very little connection, was extremely overwhelming. It was then that I was struck with the thought that for one year I would only have contact with Korean people who only speak Korean and have such a different cultural framework than I do. At the time, I believed there was very little hope of conversation, very little hope of connection, and it made me fall even deeper into the homesickness, which ended up lasting for only a few days.

It helped incredibly to be sharing the experience with fifty other recent college graduates in a university setting, though. Mainly it was just "America camp" in Korea for the first six weeks. We explored the country and learned Korean and took taekwondo lessons and had language partners and younger "brothers" and "sisters," but it was all very safe and American-oriented for those first weeks, which helped the acclimation into the full immersion experience. Korea was a lovely place for the first six weeks.

Then, after those first six weeks, we all went to Yonsei University (연세대학교). All the Fulbright scholars lined up, our principles and co-teachers lined up, and we were paired off with the people who would determine our life in Korea, at least partially. The co-teachers all spoke English, and my principal also spoke English fluently, which was very nice. Shortly after this, we all went off to our respective placements, and for me that meant Jeju Island (제주도), where I lived and taught for a year.

In Jeju, I was teaching at the best girls' middle school on the island. I have a background in English and education and we talked a lot about classroom management and teaching strategies, yet very little was applicable to this situation because Korean students are very different from American students. Classroom management doesn't really exist because Korea's very infraction- and punishment-oriented. If students misbehave they are punished accordingly. I tried almost every strategy: different point systems, positive reinforcement and negative reinforcement, and some classes were angelic and other classes were not so angelic. It was a challenging year. In the classroom it was difficult, as a lot of them didn't have much incentive to learn English. Others, though, had a great desire and interest in English, so it was a huge range of students. Sometimes they just didn't want to study at all and so some days in the classroom were pretty brutal because it was very hard to communicate with them. This is when I would try to use as much Korean as possible and slow down with English, using many gestures to aid me in what I was doing. Sometimes I would be almost dancing in front of the room but they just didn't seem to care to learn.

There were about 1,000 students in the school, about 35 to 40 girls a class, and I felt I got to know a fair number of them outside of class by doing things like playing basketball. Other times students would stop by my desk at lunch and we'd just talk or not talk, as our language abilities dictated. It was wonderful to cultivate such relationships with students, and it was very good that I had middle-school girls because it never felt awkward or hierarchal. We felt like older sisters-younger sisters.

For that year I was in Jeju, the school was paying me directly. The Fulbright scholarship pays for the six-week orientation course, two conferences, and our plane ticket to and from Seoul. They cover all our outside benefits too, like insurance, but it was the school that paid me a monthly salary and provided me with my homestay family. I was paid 1.3 million won and my homestay family received 400,000 won every month for putting me up. Everyone in the English Teaching Assistant Program (ETA) had to stay with a homestay family. During the first year, all the placements are outside of Seoul and with a host family.

With my own homestay family, the mother was an English teacher at my school, so she was sort of the translator for everyone in the family. She and I were colleagues, but more than that, I think we both enjoyed having another woman in the house. Sometimes we would go to a movie together. She was a very typical Jeju woman: strong and independent. She told her husband what to do, told her students what to do, told her sons what to do —and everyone listened! With the other family members, I tried speaking Korean—with the father and the two sons, one of whom was a second-year middle-school student and the other a fourth-year elementary school student. But the middle-school student asked me not to speak Korean because it was easier to understand me if I spoke in English. That curtailed the Korean language learning in the household. They tried early on to teach me a few words, but it was too confusing. They came up with six different ways to say "go," for example! They were a really great family, though. Once they grew accustomed to my American-lifestyle way of doing things in the evenings and on weekends, they just became comfortable with that and less worried about my safety, so I could take classes and meet friends at night and it was not a problem. At the same time, though, living with any family involves a lot of compromise. It's intense to be a guest in someone's home and to realize that they're hosting someone for a year. That takes a huge toll on the family, so I would try to be as flexible and as helpful as possible.

Towards the end of the year I really wanted to go home to the States. My American family had come to visit me in March and it was kind of a dreary month for weather on the island, so I kept thinking, "I need to go home." I hadn't really considered staying another year in Korea until someone suggested that doing the intern position at the Fulbright Committee in Seoul would fit my interests and abilities. I started thinking about my goals for the next year and I really felt like I hadn't had enough time with my Korean birth family, since I was in Jeju and they lived in Seoul. I hadn't learned the language and I knew I would definitely be coming back to Korea often for the rest of my life, so I thought, "I can't not talk to my Korean family." That's when I decided one more year would allow me to learn Korean, see my family and just deepen the foundation for a lifelong relationship with them.

In Korea, the intern position at the Fulbright Scholars Program was created as the program grew, from nine people in the beginning to now 65 people, as a way for the grantees to stay connected to Fulbright without everyone calling the director or assistant director at all hours of the day and night. I'm sort of the liaison between the people who are out teaching and the office in Seoul; sort of the buffer, the strainer. I have some of my own projects that I'm starting to get to, but a lot of it is just responding to their needs, ranging from "I don't really like my cell phone. Can I get a new one?" to "my host family is not really feeding me and I'm hungry." Fulbright is still paying me, and I'm paid the same as all the English teaching assistants under the program. Like the teaching assistants, as well, I also get a free apartment.

I have to say that I feel the Fulbright program to be a success. I believe the American Fulbright Organization considers the ETA one of its finest programs, in terms of impact on the country and the relationships formed. The Korean government loves it too because most of us come and are not really motivated by money; we want to learn about Korea, spend time in Asia, experience a different culture, and teach English well. So, to have that kind of presence in Korean classrooms has been positive for us, and also for the Korean schools and the students who make their first contact with a foreigner, as well as the teaching faculty.

However, the ETA program is not the only option for those interested in working in Korea. There are also research grants. Last year I believe there were 20–30 research grantees of different levels: senior, junior, and graduate school. They come and are able to work and live in Korea, and by year's end they will hopefully have something to contribute to Korean and/or American society. They don't live with Korean families like the ETA program teachers do, though. They get a housing stipend for the place they're living in and enough to cover their expenses.

If I were to offer advice to people coming to Korea under this program, I would say come knowing that you are a guest in someone else's country, as a homestay guest, and that it's up to you to adjust to Korea and not vice-versa. There will be times when you're very frustrated, but it's just a completely different culture here, and to be a foreigner in the culture here is very jarring. Ultimately it's up to you to make concessions. Be flexible and be open and expect to change a lot yourself, more than you will change Korean culture and society.

"It's a particularly pro-employee labor law that we operate under here, which can be restrictive and, at times, counter-productive."

David* (27)
Australia
Human Resources Manager
5½ Months

Having worked in two diametrically opposed job environments in Australia and Korea, David's experience in the Korean workplace has benefited him with invaluable advice to pass on to future business people, as well as to those simply interested in learning what it's like to work in Korea.

I'D BE LYING if I said it was Korea that I had aspirations for, or that it was even Asia that I was looking specifically for experience in. I definitely knew that it would be good as a development opportunity to not only work outside of Australia, but to work in a completely different culture. The more I thought about it, though, the more excited I was about coming to Korea, being so different as it is.

Initially, not being able to get around and feeling like I was a child were the most difficult challenges. I couldn't speak the language at all, and so had to think hard about every move I made. For example, if I was going to the Ministry of Labor, I'd ask myself,

"How am I going to get in a taxi and give the driver directions? How do I even find the Ministry of Labor? I can't exactly pull out the Yellow Pages or the White Pages!" That feeling like I needed people to get around all the time was hard.

The language was also a challenge. We're an American company, so the standard of English should be fairly high compared to most Korean companies, but the overall level of English in my company is mediocre. There's plenty of people that have good English—great English—but there's just as many that have none. Even though our official language in the office for documents is English, there's still just a mass of staff that still can't speak English. About 99 percent of our staff is Korean, and I would say maybe twenty percent of those people are fluent. You could say as a generalization that the younger generation coming through have a higher level of English than those that have come forward a generation before. The managers, the middle and senior managers, are probably on a fifty percent basis. You can be surprised sometimes, though. You can have someone working in a laboratory in Ulsan (울산) who has worked in South America and has studied in the U.S. and speaks English fluently, yet they're in a job that typically wouldn't put an emphasis on speaking English.

The big shock of working here in Korea, however, was using the Korean title system, where there's a hierarchy, and the bulk of the emphasis is on your seniority. How you're treated is based largely on your age and, to a lesser extent, your experience, rather than a merit-based system. As a relatively young manager or supervisor, I'm asked how old I am so many times just because my age is considered an anomaly in a supervisory position. This has a big impact on business because one of the things that a big organization tries to capitalize on is common business practices, and sharing those common business practices across the board. The way that we would promote people through the organization back home, for example, is based on merit; things that are based on age play a far more secondary role. In Korea, the fact that it's important to ask someone their age so frequently makes one very conscious of it. Personally I didn't take it as rude and I wasn't offended by it because after the first time it happened, and through a little bit of reading and talking to other people, I understood that it was quite normal. Truth be told, though, it's hard not to be somewhat offended or a little bit shocked and irritated by it when it happens so often. But to let that show would certainly have not got me any votes.

There's always an element of pressure to try and break down the Korean system, to try and roll out the common system and conform with the U.S., or a global model. I think that's one of the pitfalls that I could have easily fallen into—and I'm sure I did to an extent. Even though it's a cliché, everyone says before you leave for Korea, "One bit of advice I can give you is don't try and go in and run it like an American company," or, "Don't go and try and run it like it's an Australian company." It's very easy to say, but then you've got the same pressures that everyone else has around the world to conform and to be seen as being aligned with global models, striving towards the same key priorities. Having to swallow a bit of that, I realized that if I was going to go in and say, "Well, this works back home or this works in the States," that's the worst thing I could have done. It might be difficult, but if I do show some sensitivity to the Korean title system, if I do treat those that the Korean social structure system doesn't demand respect for and give them that respect, I can form allegiances. I can have help from the people who are the real decision makers within the organization.

As a whole, I do think that this is a detriment to business in some ways. If you were to look at something like the perception of power distance, it seems to be that the average supervisor–employee relationship in Korea is far less equal than that in the U.S. or in the U.K. or in Australia, for instance, where if you've got an idea, you speak freely. If you need to get your idea across there is certainly no fear of reprisal or fear of being disrespectful in that public forum, let alone just incompetence to your supervisor. Yet I don't think that happens a hundred percent of the time in Korea. I think it flows through into organization structure, too. You'll see a much flatter organization in most Western countries, which is, from a headcount and costs of labor perspective, much more efficient. Here it's not uncommon to see a manager supervising a supervisor, and then that supervisor supervising a group of people underneath them. In this system the only direct rapport for the manager is with one person where that person might be overseeing a team of twenty. As a result, sometimes they're more of a figurehead from an HR perspective.

In most other organizations, HR would be seen as a facilitator. We would provide the tools or managers to help manage their people, but we step away from that direct management role, unlike in a Western country. Here we found ourselves being an intermediary, actually siphoning things back and forth between supervisor and employee when we thought, "Surely if you felt comfortable talking to your supervisor this would save time. It would certainly free up our resources."

I think it's precisely because some Western businessmen and women come to Korea and try and change the culture by turning it on its head that there can be a stigma against us from a Korean point of view. In other cases maybe Koreans are just a little bit paranoid about whatever you're going to do because they just assume the worst, that you're going to try and disrespect the current way of business—see it as outdated and Eastern—and implement a Western model as a way for the company to move forward. Regardless of the changes you're suggesting, even if they have merit and are changes that every country and organization have to go through, it could be passed off like that's not the way we do things here in Korea. Maybe if it was coming from a Korean national it wouldn't have been seen that way. It wasn't common, but there were times when you thought the little resistance could have stemmed from that fact.

Another area of business that is unique to Korea, from the U.S. or Australia, is the differences in labor laws and the different expectations on HR whenever we want to make a change. It's a particularly pro-employee labor law that we operate under here, which can be restrictive and, at times, counter-productive. We've had substantial difficulties when, for good business reasons, we've either had to reorganize, downsize, separate low performance employees, or change compensation and benefits, which maybe was to the detriment of the overall level, based on sustainability of business. The whole concept of developing a "comfort money package" to help ill-performing employees separate voluntarily from the organization was, I thought, just a good indication of how restrictive the laws are here that you're going to be operating under, when you're paying someone—who may have stolen from you, mind you—to voluntarily resign! Another example of these labor restrictions is when you want to change a policy, a company perk or a benefit. In cases such as these you need to attain a greater than fifty percent consent from the employee base. I found this all the more ironic because our company, which does not have a union presence, had to follow through with this, too.

Something else that people often ask me is whether the North Korean threat affects business here adversely. I think it does a little bit. I don't talk about the North Korean threat as much to my friends here as I do every time I get a call from family or friends back home. But it's got to have some effect otherwise you wouldn't see stock prices go up and down based on investor and consumer confidence. It doesn't affect us day to day, apart from maybe having an evacuation plan in place for the two expatriates in our company to know where the first port of exit is. Actually, I don't see it affecting our business at all, really. I read our evacuation plans and sometimes wonder about their ability to work effectively in a time of crisis, anyway. If there was, God forbid, an invasion from the North or some sort of catastrophe, then you can be sure that everyone's evacuation plan is going to have a few similarities. You wouldn't be able to get to an airport because everyone would be going to the same ports of exit, anyway. As far as having some sort of plan in place, the embassies are as good a place to start as any.

For business people coming to Korea in the future, I think it's important to keep in mind that making a good impression is worth so much at the end of the track. The little social etiquette that you think, "Okay, I can pick that up as I go along"—don't wait to pick it up as you go along. If you can, talk to others who are already working here, read a little bit on social issues rules 101, like who to pour a drink for in a business meeting, how to hold your hand when you're receiving a business card, how to address a person by a title. If you can show some sensitivity and research up front, and a little bit of Korean, being able to give a traditional greeting is going to work wonders down the track because so many people who come here don't. And then after that, because you don't have as many networks as you would back in your home country—where you may be less inclined to be a member of AmCham (American Chamber of Commerce) or the equivalent—utilize those so you can talk to others that are in similar roles in other organizations.

One more thing: learn a song that you can sing, even if you've got as hideous a voice as mine, because as a foreigner you will be expected to sing in a *no-rae-bang* (노래방)—singing room. There is no question. Expect to be taken out, in the early stages particularly, and shown the sights and sounds of normal business life, and what goes on after the business day, such as drinking soju. You're bound to end up in a *no-rae-bang*, or worse, in front of a packed auditorium full of employees, and there'll be a mike and there'll be no question who's singing first because if you're the only foreigner there, or you're one of the few, everyone wants to hear you sing first. So pick a song, a common song, that you think possibly you could carry on and be ready to sing. Don't turn it down.

"I will forever be indebted to the kindnesses I have received in Korea over the years. What I do as a literary translator is kind of a small token of my wish that I can somehow bring some visibility to a literature and the literary tradition of a country that's been overlooked by the rest of the world."

Bruce Fulton (54)
America
Literary Translator and Professor of Korean Literature
5 Years

A giant in the translation community that is only now starting to make waves outside Korea, Professor Fulton was a bastion of knowledge and insight into a literary world that many are unaware of. Although he's the first to admit that there are limitations to Korean literature from an English point of view, he's very optimistic that the future holds great things in store for a country with a long and distinguished literary tradition.

KOREANS WOULD call it fate, whereas I would say serendipity. The way it happened was that I was living in the state of Maine in July 1977 and I had graduated from college seven years earlier. I was beginning to feel like I was getting kind of set in my ways and decided I needed to do something very different, and so I applied to the U.S. Peace Corps, the institution that was set up by John F. Kennedy in the early 1960s. In the summer of '77 I got a call from Peace Corps headquarters in Washington D.C., telling me that my application had been accepted. They inquired as to whether I wanted to go to Afghanistan. I wasn't sure if I wanted to make that kind of commitment so I asked them to give me a few days to think about it. I called them back and they told me that Afghanistan was full-up. "How would you like to go to Korea?" they then asked me. I knew that if I was going to do this that it couldn't wait any longer, and so I took advantage of the opportunity and I went. I knew absolutely nothing about Korea, so I went to my college library and checked out every single book I could find about Korea—a grand total of five! One of these books was a language primer that dated from about World War II; I was pretty much flying blind.

In February of 1978, our group, in which there were maybe 43 or 44 of us, gathered for a three-day staging in San Francisco where we were administered our vaccines and did some last minute paperwork. After a briefing of what we were to expect upon our arrival, we were taken to a Korean restaurant in Oakland, and I remember developing an immediate attachment to Korean food, thinking, "If this is the way I'll be eating every day for the next two years, I'll be very happy."

We landed at Gimpo (김포) Airport and one of the first things we noticed were the gun placements alongside the runway and the realization that the Korean peninsula was, although technically in a cease-fire, at war. We spent the weekend in Seoul and then it was off to Cheongju, North Chungcheong Province (청주, 충청북도) where the Peace Corps training center was. Originally, the very first Peace Corps groups were trained in Hawaii, but the staff soon realized that it was really very difficult for people with no previous exposure to the Korean language and culture to learn it outside of Korea, and so they moved the training base camp to Korea. We spent ten weeks there studying Korean four hours a day, six days a week, and also studying English language teaching methodologies, as virtually none of us had any exposure to teaching the English language, either. We kind of got thrown right into it.

The real culture shock came when we were billeted with a Korean family. In addition to the language barrier, we encountered the norms of Korean family life: comparative lack of privacy and people living within relatively close contact with each other. It was a very busy life. I remember walking the streets at night and noting how dark they were. Another thing that comes to mind is the lack of public toilet facilities. I remember one of the best survival skills that we learned, especially in Korean cities in the late seventies, was being able to ferret out public toilets—if you had some kind of intestinal disorder it would have posed a serious problem.

Anyway, in the Peace Corps the volunteers usually ended up fulfilling some need that the host country had, and in the case of Korea we were either English teachers or we worked in rural health centers, specifically with leprosy and smallpox. Everyone in my group was involved with education. We were all going to be working at a provincial training institute or teaching English at a teacher's college at a university. In our first year, in order to kind of prepare us for this, we got a little exposure to the Korean education system, which gained us experience and legitimacy in the eyes of our Korean counterparts. Most of us taught English at a middle school in our first year, and then moved on to other assignments our second year.

The conditions were far from ideal, let me tell you. I was teaching at a middle school in a remote area of Jeolla Province (전라도), where our class size was near to seventy students. In some situations, we had classes twice that size! Realistically, I don't think we taught those kids much English, although there were a few kids who wound up going to university in Seoul, and we hoped that some of them could become involved in English language education in the future.

After my term with the Peace Corps was over, I left Korea and went to Nepal with my wife, whom I had met in Korea, before flying back to the States. Back home, I decided to go to graduate school in Korean Studies. At the time, the University of Washington in Seattle had one of the few Korean Studies programs available in the U.S. After the two-year program at the University of Washington, my wife and I went back to Korea in the summer of 1983 and I entered the Korean language program at Yonsei University (연세대학교), which was also the first time my wife and I really had an opportunity to translate a novel by the man I ended up doing my PhD dissertation on, Hwang Sun-won (황순원). That's also essentially where our translation career started, because from then on our work has progressed steadily. After that, 13 years later, in 1996, I began my residency at Seoul National University (SNU 서울대학교) for my PhD.

Actually, I should backtrack a little as this story goes back to 1979, when my Peace Corps assignment was at Seoul National University. It was at SNU that I met a man named Chang Wang-rok (장왕록), who was a professor in the English department and a specialist in American literature. At the time, he was translating a novel by Hwang Sun-won and he asked for my help in proofreading his translation, which I did. By then my wife and I had been married a couple of months and had been introduced to a man who published a series of translations of Korean literature in Korea. Among these translations was the novel that this colleague of mine at SNU was translating. This publisher saw my spouse and I and surmised that a native English speaker, coupled with a native Korean speaker, would make an ideal translating team. He asked us if we'd like to translate one of the books in his series and we accepted. The book we ended up translating was a collection of the publisher's own stories, the publisher also being an author. So that was actually our first translation. We completed our second book-length translation upon returning home from Korea in 1983, a novel whose title we ended up translating into English as *The Moving Castle*.

    I hate to say it, but I don't think the state of translation from Korean to English has advanced all that much since my wife, Ju-Chan (주찬), and I first started doing translations over twenty years ago. We here in Korea got off to a late start compared with China and Japan, where frequent comparisons are drawn from. Potential non-native Korean-speaking translators of Korean literature in Korea have been pretty much limited to people who've had first hand experience here, namely Peace Corps volunteers, military personnel, and missionaries. Understandably, only a very small percentage of these people have a strong enough interest in literature to parlay that into a career in literary translation. The result is that, by necessity, the bulk of literary translation in Korea is "outbound" by nature, that is to say native Korean speakers translating their native language into a foreign language, as opposed to translators like myself who are "inbound" translators; I'm translating into my native language. There have been some capable translations by outbound translators in Korea but on the whole they are quite uneven. There are very few of us who have kind of stayed the course, continuing to translate full time, and there doesn't seem to be much training of the next generation to come, or as Koreans would say, *cho-bo-sang-tae* (초보상태), which means we're still taking our first steps.

Fortunately the government has been very supportive. The Korean Culture and Arts Foundation has been very generous to us over the years. Their translation program has since been subsumed by the Korea Literature Translation Institute, which was founded a couple of years ago. Translators of other countries' literature are amazed—and envious—at the amount of support that we get from Korea. We're very fortunate in that respect. Without their support it would have been very difficult for us to have produced the translations we have. On a personal note, I will forever be indebted to the kindnesses I have received in Korea over the years. What I do as a literary translator is kind of a small token of my wish that I can somehow bring some visibility to a literature and the literary tradition of a country that's been overlooked by the rest of the world.

Some people might think that a husband and wife translation team sounds strange, especially to those that are used to individuals doing translations, but for us it works really well. When we decide on a story or a bunch of stories, my wife will read over the original text in Korean and annotate it. What I ask her to do is annotate expressions, or maybe dialects I may not be familiar with. Also, in situations where there's subtext, the necessity to read between the lines becomes imperative, and so I'll ask my wife to flag those as well. I'll then look over the annotated copy of the original and make a first draft. Later, we'll get together again, side by side, and I'll read to her what I have on the computer and she'll read the original. That way we try to make sure we've solved all the lexical problems. Once we've done that, in the case of a short story, which is the usual situation, I'll put it aside for a while and I'll move on to the next story. After some time I'll go back to it and read it silently to make sure it flows, consulting the original if need be, and pestering my poor wife for her help and expertise. In the final stages, I'll read the translations out loud to myself to ensure it's right. If we're at a reading, and I read the whole document without any part of it sounding awkward, then I know we've done the job to the best of our ability.

The length of time this takes depends on a number of factors: the author and their writing style, for instance. For a writer like Oh Chong-hui, for example, who is a bit difficult—even for Korean readers—a thirty-page story may take six months or more. But we can work on several different stories simultaneously; we might be on the first draft of one while putting the final touches on another. Some stories we've gotten into take shape in a month or so, but that's kind of pushing it. You really need time to let it sit and then come back to it with a fresh perspective. So, if there was an average time, I'd say maybe three months or more, yet there are some stories where we don't feel we're able to let it go for the better part of a year.

For people who might not be very familiar with Korean fiction, I guess one way to start is to explain that there's a long tradition of fiction in Korea, dating back to at least the 1400s, but the fictional genre that modern Koreans excel in is a foreign import: the short story. The argument that's put forth by Kevin O'Rourke, a professor in the English department at Kyung Hee University (경희대학교), is that Koreans found the short story congenial in the same way that people in other lands and in other times who were kind of suffering from miserable political and social situations found the short story congenial, like his native Ireland in the early 1900s, czarist Russia and France after its defeat in the Franco–Prussian War in the late 1800s. Indeed, modern Korea has produced a number of very fine short story writers, of which Hwang Sun-won is a distinguished representative. Novels, on the other hand, tend to be closer to the pre-modern Korean prose literary tradition, and are regarded more or less as hack work, and not as serious as the short story.

I should also mention that the Korean literary establishment is extremely conservative; 95 percent of it is overwhelmingly male. And by that establishment I mean the men who teach Korean literature at universities, the editors of the various literary journals, and those who work at the various publishing companies, where often these roles are interchangeable. There is a thriving market for novels and popular fiction in Korea, but it's always been short fiction that's achieved the highest critical acceptance. On the other hand, some of the most popular works of modern Korean fiction are similar to the most popular works of the pre-modern era, and they're these massive tomes of multi-generational family sagas of Korean society and culture. There's this long tradition with regards to writing these long multi-volume novels. Finally, there's also a tradition of newspaper serialization, which goes back to the early twentieth century, when the first Korean newspapers hired people for the singular purpose of serializing novels. This is very much a part of Korean literary culture, and again that may be evidence for viewing the historical works, not as some tour de force, but rather as a culmination of something that they read day-by-day in the newspaper.

If I had to sum up the most engaging Korean authors, and the ones Western readers would gain the most from, I'd have to begin by mentioning the authors that my good wife and I concentrate on. The first one, of course, would be Hwang Sun-won, whose 100-plus short stories are the pinnacle of achievement of the modern Korean short story. I think I would then move on to Cho Se-hui (조세희), someone who has written very little, but has written a linked-story novel which is comprised of 12 distinct stories linked by character and theme. That's probably the best selling novel of modern Korea, well over 200 printings. In English it's called *The Dwarf*, and is a very clever series of stories written in the mid to late 1970s that was pretty much a veiled exposé of the evils of industrialization under the Park Chung-hee (박정희) regime. Yi Mun-yul (이문열) is also an important author—there's no doubt about that. My wife and I have never translated anything by him, but he is very close to the pre-modern Korean literary figure in terms of his "didacticism." In Korean literary history, didacticism is not a dirty word. It was something that an educated man was expected to be. Yi Mun-yul is a traditionalist, and he works very hard to keep that in the consciousness of younger Koreans.

There are two more authors I would add to that list. One is Oh Chong-hui (오정희), who was recommended to us by Hwang Sun-won back in the 1980s when we'd finished translating *The Moving Castle*. She is one of two women largely responsible for the success that Korean women writers have enjoyed for the past ten years now. The second is a writer by the name of Choe Yun (최윤), who is not only a creative writer but also a translator. I think that anyone who reads these four authors will get a good idea of the richness of modern Korean fiction.

SECTION II
SOCIAL RELATIONS WITH KOREANS

LOVE

Social Relations with Koreans

Social relations between Koreans and foreigners have a short history in Korea. At least officially they do. Confucianism was institutionalized under the Chosun Dynasty (조선시대 1392–1910) and this had a severe effect on marriage. Like almost everything else that fell under the direction of Confucian doctrine, there was a set list of what was acceptable and what was not. In the ideal Confucian family system, for example, only paternal-line relatives were seen as relatives; social rights—and therefore class—were only passed on from fathers to sons; authority over the family rested solely with the father; marriages were only deemed acceptable between two people of different blood clans; and only first-born males held rights to lineal succession.[1]

This codified set of customs for Korean marriages and families remained virtually untouched until the Korean War (1950–53). It was only after the nation's bloody civil war, and more than 500,000 foreigners—predominantly American—came to live and socialize with Koreans, that marriage began to change in any meaningful way. When Korean women began bearing the children of United Nations' soldiers new kinds of relationships formed that eventually blossomed into the union of marriage. This process only accelerated when missionaries began arriving in significant numbers in the 1950s and 1960s.

However, in a society as conservative as Korea, change was met with much resistance. Until quite recently, in fact, most courtships between foreigners and Koreans were conducted in secret and away from the public eye. So great was the stigma attached to dating—let alone marrying—a foreigner, that Koreans risked being expelled from their families and, in extreme cases, written out of the semi-sacred system of family lineage papers, called *ho-ju-jae* (호주제)[2] in Korean.

Until the 1990s, the majority of international marriages were between a foreign man and a Korean women, and so, the unfair and often prejudicial treatment that the woman received from Korean family members (and Korean society at large) would become that much more acute. Yet in the last decade a remarkable transformation has taken place in Korean society, a transformation that has changed the traditional family unit in Korea forever. Whereas men were much more reluctant to marry foreigners in the decades after the Korean War, this group now represents the majority of foreign marriages in Korea. In 2002, almost 75 percent of all marriages between Koreans and foreigners were Korean men tying the knot with someone of another nationality. And although the majority of Koreans getting married to foreigners—both males and females—do so with Asians, women are still clearly the leaders in breaking down ancient taboos and beliefs, as they marry men from all corners of the globe and of all faiths.

There were a total of 15,913 international marriages in Korea in 2002, up 679 couples from the year prior, which represented a total of 5.2 percent of all marriages in the country. Statistically speaking, international marriages in Korea in 2002 were broken down as follows:[3]

Korean Men and Foreign Women			Korean Women and Foreign Men		
Total	11,017	100%	Total	4,896	100%
China (female)	7,041	63.9	Japan (male)	2,377	48.5
Japan (female)	959	8.7	U.S.A. (male)	1,210	24.7
Philippines (female)	850	7.7	China (male)	272	5.6
Vietnam (female)	476	4.3	Canada (male)	174	3.6
Thailand (female)	330	3.0	Pakistan (male)	126	2.6

In an effort to provide friendship among foreign women married to Korean men, and to form a network among its members, the International Spouses of Koreans Association, was founded in March 2000 with forty members from 15 countries. Today, the group claims a membership of more than one hundred women from more than 25 countries and is further proof that people of different nationalities and citizenship are helping to form the new fabric of the modern Korean family.[4]

[

Another group of Koreans that has been stigmatized over the years, and at times, even demonized, is the gay community. Although there is very little mention of any form of homosexual behavior in dynastic Korea, we do know that as early as the eighth century there was reference to homosexuality in the Korean royal family. King Hyekong (혜공), the 36th king of the Shilla Dynasty (신라시대 57 BC to AD 918) was ordained king in 765 at the age of eight, but killed fifteen years later by subordinates who could not accept his abnormal "femininity."[5]

One of the earliest, and easily most controversial, instances of early lesbianism in Korea dates back to the fifteenth century, when King Sejong (세종 1397–1450) convened a meeting to discuss rumors that one of his daughters-in-law was sleeping with another woman. According to the Annals of the Chosun Dynasty, the daughter-in-law was expelled from the royal family, but under different pretexts.[6]

In some ways, many Koreans view gays today as they did in the Middle Ages, though this is changing ever so slowly for the small group of Koreans brave enough to make their voice heard publicly. Without doubt, people of different nationalities have helped the gay community advance its cause in Korea. The clearest evidence of this is probably the fact that the biggest ("big" being relative to Korea, mind you) gay entertainment street in Korea is in the foreign-dominated area of Itaewon (이태원), Seoul.

Fortunately, the last decade has seen huge strides in the government's, as well as society's, view of gays in Korea. In the early 1990s, gay and lesbian support groups were formed in the United States for Korean Americans, a lesbian support group was formed in Korea in 1991, the first gay campus organization was formed at Yonsei University (연세대학교) in 1995, and the first lesbian commitment ceremony in Korea was held in 1995.[7]

Not long ago, in late November 2001, when the Ministry of Information and Communications formally enacted an Internet content rating system that classified gay and lesbian websites as "harmful media" and mandated their blockage (under the guise of protecting the youth), the lesbian, gay, and bisexual community in Korea fought hard to repeal it. In August 2002, a court concluded that freedom of speech and expression were not applicable to homosexuality, allowing for outrageous penalties, including two-year imprisonments, to be enforced. Fortunately, half a year later, in April 2003, the Korean National Human Rights Protection Committee officially advised Korea's Youth Protection Committee to remove anti-gay language from the 1997 Youth Protection Act, which had underpinned the 2001 Ministry of Information and Communications decision. This is where the law stands today.[8]

❍

The three men and four women in this section offer a very personal insight into the different social relations that foreigners have with Koreans. Some are heterosexual males and females who have married and, at times, divorced their companions. Others are gay men and women who have faced challenges while living and working in Korea that few can relate to. Without doubt, every one of the interviewees in this section proved to be extremely candid about his or her life, providing great understanding about rarely discussed issues.

"We're basically a normal family, and my kids love life as much as I do."

Robert Holley/하일 (44)
Korea (America)
Principal, Lawyer and
TV Entertainer
19 Years

One of the best-known "foreigners" in the country, Ha Il (하일) as he's known to Koreans, has been living in Korea for almost two decades. Missionary, lawyer, TV entertainer, and principal, Robert Holley is an anomaly in many ways. Aside from being fluent in Korean, he is one of the few Americans of non-Korean descent to hold Korean citizenship. Today, while shuttling back and forth between Gwangju (광주) and Seoul for work, he and his wife are busy running the school where their three boys receive their education.

I WAS 19 WHEN I came to Korea in 1978 as a Mormon missionary. I was sent to what's called the Busan (부산) Mission for the church and the first area that I lived in was Daegu (대구). I spent about ten months in Daegu and the rest of the two-year period I was in Gyeongsang Province (경상도), but I did spend two months in Yeosu, South Jeolla Province (여수, 전라남도).

I can still remember my first impression of the country. I

arrived in Korea and the next day we went to this church, and I looked out this window there and thought, "Oh, this place is crowded. Look at all these houses just bunched together!" I remember these people had a fire burning on the roof of this three- or four-story building next to the church, and I was looking there, thinking, "What kind of people would put a fire on top of a building like that?" I thought, "I'm going to be here for two years. I don't know how I'm going to make it!" I can remember those first feelings because they were really strong, and it was just like a big sense of homesickness. Korea was the first country I had ever been to outside the United States. Within a week or two of this first experience of homesickness, though, I really came to like Korea and Korean people.

Korea was quite a bit different then than it is now. For us to get a hamburger, for example, we had to go down to the local bakery and get a soybean burger with cabbage instead of lettuce. That was the only thing that we could get in terms of foreign food. We had no indoor plumbing any place that I stayed at. In order to take a shower we had to go to the local *mok-yok-tang* (목욕탕)—public bathhouse— to do it, but it was still quite fun. I came to love Korea at that time.

After my two years as a missionary I left Korea. My goal in life was always to be a lawyer and while I was here I thought, "Why don't I become an international lawyer and go back to the States and maybe minor in the Korean language, go on to law school and maybe come back here as a lawyer?" So I set that big goal and went back to the States, and before I graduated from Brigham Young University (BYU) I went on a semester-abroad-thing and came to Korea. I spent a semester sitting at Yonsei University (연세대학교) with Korean students in political science. I really had a fun time. I went back and finished minoring in Korean and majoring in political science and graduated from BYU, after which I then went to law school in West Virginia.

I then came to Korea to clerk for my third year of law school. When I was back in the States I had somehow kept up my connections with Korea. After I had been here for my missionary work, I got a job at a big plant when I was at law school in West Virginia, where there were a lot of Koreans. During my second year I roomed with three Koreans in one house—big mistake. Every Friday night all the Koreans would come over to this huge house we had and they'd sit on the first floor and complain about Americans and tell each other how much they knew about Americans.

Two or three months before I graduated, though, I was hired by a firm in Seoul—Kim, Chang and Lee—and started working for them shortly thereafter. I spent four years with them, working in Seoul, living in Seoul. It was at that time that I met my wife. Actually, when I was a missionary, one of the places I was stationed was Jinhae (진해), and she happened to live next door to us. She and her sister both attended the Mormon Church in Jinhae, so we knew them from there. I had always thought, "Hmm, she's really cute," and the nice thing about her was she was always laughing about this and that. She had a nice smile too, and always laughed. I got to know her then, but I never thought I'd marry her at that time. Actually, I can still remember the first time I came to Korea when my grandmother told me, "When you go to Korea, enjoy your time there and make a lot of nice, white friends."

Anyway, when I was living in Jinhae I wasn't dating my wife, and in fact, I had got her address and given her name to several Koreans I knew who were looking to be introduced to a cute Korean! When I came back to Korea after graduating law school, I was walking down the street one day and saw her. She had just graduated from college and was working as a salesperson at Kia Motors. We got to know each other again and by that time I was getting older and wanting to get married. I had dated one or two people in the States, one girl who even came to Korea to teach English and spend time with me, but things didn't work out, and it was at that time that I met my wife.

After seeing each other again, we became friends. I had other friends who said, "Try dating a Korean girl." I had actually dated a Filipino girl for a time and my parents were all for it, but when I decided to marry my wife I went back and broke the news to my parents and they were just adamantly opposed to it. My father took me way out into the desert of Utah and said, "Why do you want to marry this Korean girl? Think about this. Your kids are going to have a hard time and they'll be teased and what not. It just won't be good." My mother tried the same thing when I was there and it didn't work out very well—my parents couldn't convince me and I couldn't convince them.

When I got back to Korea my mother continued to send me little letters that said the family was split. Four of my siblings were on my side and four were on their side. I wrote back to my parents and said, "Look, I've decided that I'm going to marry her. Now, you can either support me in this or you can oppose me in this. If you oppose it, then if things didn't work out in marriage, and we did end up getting a divorce, then you would certainly be a contributing factor to that." It was at that time all the opposition stopped.

In the end my mother and my father came to Korea for the marriage. My mother even wore a *han-bok*! (한복)—Korean traditional dress. After the wedding my wife and I went to the States, and I was so worried because I told her that my parents couldn't stand kimchi. One night we went to this Korean restaurant and she just gobbled down some kimchi. I told her she'd eaten too much of it and that she was going to smell like kimchi when we got home. My wife just broke down and cried and that was one of my most regretful moments of married life.

Last year, however, when we were back in the States—we had been married 15 years at this point—we were having dinner with my parents and my dad said, "You know, Hyun-suk (현숙), a long time ago, before you got married, I was really, really adamantly opposed to your marriage." And my wife said, "I know that." My father then said, "Well, I know you know that. But in all my years of life that was the biggest mistake I ever made."

My wife's parents, on the other hand, knew me when I was living beside them as a missionary. During that time as a missionary, when things were hot outside, me and a Korean companion of mine would go up to the roof where our toilet was, which was right against my wife's building and their toilet, and spend the night there. My wife's mother would always be out there working. She had plants that she took care of and late at night she'd be out there when we were sleeping and she'd talk to us. She remembered those times with me, and so was all for our marriage, even though her husband, my father-in-law, was not. I can still remember asking for his permission to marry Hyun-suk, and him just sitting there and clearing his throat a few times. He then lit up a cigarette and walked outside. That was it. My wife and mother-in-law said that was enough, though. He apparently was opposed to it, but told my wife, "Whatever you want, I'll go along with." We ended up getting married at a Mormon temple here in Seoul.

Our first child was born in 1988, the second in 1991, and the third in 1994. We have three sons. We've brought the kids up in both languages. We don't just speak English to the kids; I even yell and swear at them in Korean! The oldest one speaks both languages almost perfectly. The second one I was really worried about growing up because the language between him and his brother was Korean. Now he's probably ninety percent fluent in English, but he'll make grammatical errors when he's not thinking about it. His Korean is probably around 20–30 percent. I don't know whether he's joking, but he pretends not to understand Korean sometimes. The third one speaks Korean much better than he does English, but they all go to a foreign school, so they're speaking English all the time.

I'm a strong proponent of teaching your kids the same morals you believe in, so we're very strict with our kids. They're not allowed to go to PC *bang* (Internet cafés) or game rooms (arcades), for example. My kids are very introverted and they're not very talkative. They're kind of shy, so they don't really go out all that much. In terms of language, I think if you have a bilingual couple it's very important that you use both languages with the kids and raise them to know both languages. Like I said, my youngest son speaks Korean better than he does English, but he cannot read Korean because he goes to a foreign school. We're trying to teach him to use some Korean programs and I think it's very important that parents do that. I know that some other people think differently. I have many friends who are married to Koreans and even though they both speak Korean and English, they'll only speak English to the kids and because of that the kids only speak English.

My kids are now at an international school, but they were originally homeschooled. The reason my wife and I decided to homeschool our kids was that we wanted to be deeply involved in their education. My wife and I were both spending a lot of our time teaching our kids in English through several different school programs that we used from the States. By doing that, we were able to impart on them our own values and beliefs while we were teaching them the basic subjects. My oldest son is now a straight-A student and I think that he is that way, basically, because of the period when we were homeschooling him. Because of that period, that time we spent with him, we really gained a greater appreciation for education and Mormon values.

After several years of homeschooling, the kids went to an international school that I helped set up with a friend in Busan. This had a really positive effect on the kids. Because of that, they were in a regular school with a lot of kids who were half Korean and half American, and other kids who spent three or four or five years in the States, as well as other foreigners.

To my knowledge, my kids have never experienced any kind of prejudice or racism, not even in Utah or in the Mormon Church. Everyone told me horror stories about having kids that are half Korean and half American, but my kids have had no problems whatsoever. They're regular kids with regular friends. Kids are abused if they're fat or skinny or ugly—kids will be teased—and my kids are never teased, although they tease each other a lot. We're basically a normal family, and my kids love life as much as I do.

We've spent six months at a time in the States with my kids on two or three occasions, and my kids had no problem fitting in there as well, just like they've had no problem fitting in here. The only problem that I see arising is that I have Korean citizenship and my kids, when they turn 18, have to choose between one or the other, American or Korean citizenship. I take the position that my kids are free to choose. I'm not going to force it on them.

"I couldn't forego my pride and return home to my family. I wanted to make it work over here. I wanted to have someone in my life over here who cared about me and would be on my side, because I felt like I was fighting a losing battle in Korea all by myself."

Sarah* (31)
Australia
Actress, Singer, and Musician
10 Years

If not for her patience and perseverance, Sarah would still be locked in a relationship she says almost crushed her on more than one occasion. Trapped in an abusive marriage for eight years, Sarah's experience in Korea has left scars, but made her stronger and more self-aware.

I'M A MUSICIAN by trade. When I left high school, I was offered a spot at a very prestigious music school in Australia. My father was against a career in music so I went to study economics instead and worked at the futures exchange in Sydney. I was very unhappy, though; I was dying inside. Then a girlfriend rang me up and told me she needed a singer for this Las Vegas cabaret-type-of-show that would be going overseas to Asia. I hadn't auditioned for anything like that in a long time but I thought, "What do I have to lose?" so I went and auditioned. The woman said to me, "Can you go to Korea next week?" And that's how I arrived in Korea.

An agent picked me up over here and when the show finished he wanted me to stay on, doing hotel gigs. While I was with the show we traveled all around the country, performing at large hotels in Jeju Island (제주도), Busan (부산), and Seoul. I ended up staying in Seoul and doing solo gigs for a while. Those people you see in the lobby of hotels in an evening gown, singing "My Way"—that was me.

My parents weren't happy with my being in Seoul, and so I felt like I had to be successful and make some money over here, otherwise I'd go back home with my tail between my legs. My agent was a complete ass and very cunning, though. He would only give me a certain amount of my earnings, and usually only when I was without any money at all. This would result in me saving nothing and therefore it would ensure my having to continue working for him. He was manipulative on top of everything else.

When I first came over to Korea, my sister had cancer. I talked to her on the phone one time, after not being here for very long, and asked if she wanted me home. She assured me that she was all right and not to worry because she was on the mend. Two days after that phone call she died. I didn't know this, however, because I had no phone at my apartment and this was before the days of cell phones in Korea. My family had to call my manager's office and my manager surmised that if he told me about my sister's death, I'd leave Korea for Australia, so he didn't tell me. I found out 13 days after she was dead and buried in the ground. And I only found out because I called my mother. That completely screwed me up. I didn't want to tell my family about my situation because they had enough on their plate, with my sister's death, so I sucked it up and tried to make a living with that asshole. Those were my days of drinking and partying all the time. It was unavoidable as an entertainer. It didn't take long before I got really sick from all the alcohol and drug abuse. My hair fell out. My nails fell off. I lost 13 kilos (29 lbs). When I finally went to the hospital, the doctor took one look at me and said, "I'm not even going to ask you what you've been doing. I know you're doing something to yourself. It's your choice: you can change your life or you'll be dead within the year." I figured I'd better clean my act up before my family had to deal with another crushing loss. I got on the wagon and tried to make some money, which was difficult while still under the thumb of that manager.

I had been dry for ten months when I met my husband in a bar, which was about 18 months after arriving in Korea. We had a ten-year age difference—I was 22, he was 32—and my Korean sucked, which made things difficult for us because he didn't have much English. Within two years of meeting him I had learned to speak Korean, though, because I wanted to be able to speak with his parents.

My husband is a musician and was making an album at the time and wanted me to do some work on his album, which I did. He actually helped me get out of my contract, which was really helpful. But he had a huge drinking problem and basically I started drinking again right after I met him. About a month after we'd met he had gotten me out of my contract and I proceeded to move in with him. There wasn't a lot of dating. I was still working every day and he would come and see me after I finished work. We'd drink until five in the morning and that was the extent of the courtship.

I should have seen the warning signs back then. The alarm bells should have been ringing. It was a difficult and confusing time. I couldn't forego my pride and return home to my family. I wanted to make it work over here. I wanted to have someone in my life over here who cared about me and would be on my side, because I felt like I was fighting a losing battle in Korea all by myself. When women are young, the "White Night" syndrome is such a comfortable and romantic belief. The idea of a man coming into your life with all the answers to your problems is still a very attractive fantasy for a young woman. I was so sad, vulnerable, and disillusioned, and my husband made me feel safe and appeared to have all the answers. He proposed to me about four months after moving in together. We were married three months after that.

I had some doubts at the time, but I guess because I was young and naive I thought that if it didn't work out I would simply extricate myself from the marriage; people do that all the time. But when you take your vow and you listen to his, the seriousness of the situation takes over. I've always been a person who sticks to her word and if I say I'll do something, I follow it through. I felt that I had moved into his life and that I should fulfill my responsibility. I felt indebted to him for getting me out of my contract. Also, I had this kind of Catholic–guilt syndrome which, coupled with being very young, had a lot to do with my decision to get married, I think.

On our actual wedding day, we just got married at City Hall. We always said we would have the big wedding later. It's not like back home, though, where you actually have somebody marry you. Here in Korea, you simply fill out papers. They didn't have carbon copies, so we had to fill out something like twenty documents. The person looked over them, stamped them and then handed them back to us. No proclamation of "You are now husband and wife." Nothing. On the way out, I asked my husband what we had to do next and he said, "That's it. We're married!" Very romantic. So, we went off to eat *kal-bee* (갈비)—Korean ribs—and drink soju. Every girl's dream wedding!

When my parents-in-law first learned of our relationship, they didn't take it so well. However, his family is wonderful and extremely nice people. His mother's quite old and his father had already passed away by that point, which, if he'd been alive, would have made it even more difficult, because he would have most surely been against it. Initially his family would say to him, "Are you out of your mind? This will be too difficult. She's from another culture and she won't understand anything." I used to come home and there used to be hour-long messages on the answering machine for my husband, from his mother, saying, "You have to think about this. This is not a good idea, my son." Eventually, it was at *Chusok* (추석)—Korean Thanksgiving—when I brought a load of food with me and cooked for his family that I made a huge impression, I think. It helped them to see how genuine I was and how devoted to my husband I was. I learned their customs and found out what was important to them, and always respected those things. I never spoke *ban-mal* (반말)— informal language—to his mother or smoked in front of her, and I think she realized that. She was also very happy that I was Catholic because she had converted to Catholicism when her husband was dying.

With my own parents, they thought I was too young to get married and they were right. My father was worried about the age difference, but they weren't at all concerned with his nationality. My parents wouldn't give a shit who I married, just as long as he was good to me. They actually met my husband a few times. A year after we got married we went back to Australia for my brother's wedding and they met him for the first time. I think my father loved how respectful he was. Asians are very respectful to their elders, and my father is very old–school and high up in the chain of command in his police force. He likes that quality in people, and he liked that about my husband. They knew we had problems, my mother especially, as our marriage was the same as theirs in certain respects. And they were right.

We actually had problems right from day one. I kept a journal at the time and when I left my husband a year ago, I read it over. What's scariest to me is the fact that I wrote those words down on paper. They came out of my head and were written by my hand, but I didn't see them or heed them. For example, his drinking was out of control and he would get violent sometimes, especially when he was drunk. His attitude to life was dangerous because he wallowed in self-pity. He felt the world owed him something and was pissed-off he wasn't getting it, so he'd go out, get drunk, be miserable, and then come home and bother me. I was totally sleep deprived for the first year of our marriage. He'd come home, wasted, and demand I sit with him while he drank. If I didn't, he'd get violent, so I felt I had to. I would hope he'd pass out so I could get some sleep and make it to work. I think it was because I was young that I didn't know how to get out of it. I didn't even know what angle, if any existed, I could approach the problem, so I developed a belief in my ability to solve his problem because of the success that I'd had with my own alcohol and drug abuse. Unfortunately those types of problems are rarely fixed by others. It got better, though, in the sense that it stopped being an every day thing and evolved into a two or three times a week thing.

His major problem was that he never worked. I was the one who would get up and leave the house to work in the morning. I still believed in his ability as a musician at that point. It was never the fact that he didn't have talent; it was his lack of motivation to get anything done that was his setback. I played a part in it as well, to a certain extent. My going to work and paying our bills further cemented his lack of desire to create. He had no reason to get off his ass and do anything, and that's the way it went for eight years. I can count on my hand the amount of days he worked during our marriage.

I focused on my career because he wasn't bringing any money in. I had to do that. I had to work very hard for as long as I could and as often as I could, and it paid off because my career took off. By that point in our marriage, I had finished the hotel work and was getting studio work on a more regular basis. I was working with a Korean singer for a while and ended up dabbling in everything: television, radio—you name it.

However, my resentment towards my husband started to boil over after three or four years of his behavior and our life—I never slept! I had three hours in bed and then I was up to try and make it to work again. I had no time to myself when I got home; it was all about him. He was like a vacuum sucking out all my energy. He'd want to be fed, and so we'd have a fight over dinner. If I went out with my friends, he'd call every half hour. He sucked so much life out of me that I had nothing left to give. By the end, I'd become the stereotypical male of a relationship: I was working 12 fucking hours a day and paying for the house!

This was towards the last couple of years, when I was 26 or 27, I guess. I just felt like I had so many responsibilities. I bought a house, but there was a mortgage and when the IMF (International Monetary Fund) crisis hit Korea we didn't have fixed interest rates so one interest payment alone was 1.5 million a month! I didn't know how I was going to make it work. His response to financial difficulty was to ring up a family member and ask for money! My husband's type of behavior was so irresponsible. We never saw eye-to-eye on that. His belief was that his parents owed him that security.

I would always say that our problems were just typical marriage problems, but that wasn't true; we had cultural problems too, such as the way he viewed women. He never liked women. I tried, on several occasions, to address the issue and he never saw his lack of respect for females. And women with careers were fair targets. If I tried to broach the problem he'd complain that I was a feminist. He would always tell me that, even if I could learn to love all of his faults, our relationship would always be flawed because I could never be led. He believed that every relationship needed a leader and the leader should be the man. Men all over the world are proud creatures, and so much more so in this country. Even if they're a bum on the street without clothes and are begging for a buck, if you call them a "bum" they will fight you to preserve their pride. My husband's pride was completely unfounded; there were no grounds for it. He would say to me that everyone had to respect him. He would beat his younger brothers into submission. I would try to explain to him the Western concept of respect as being something that is earned and not given upon demand or request, but he never understood that.

In the end, I stayed for as long as I did because I felt pity for him. He was very good at manipulating my kindness. My bleeding heart has been one of my bigger downfalls, but I'm a little older and wiser now, thank God. I felt sorry for him and every time I did try to leave there were tears and promises. I wanted to believe him. When you stay with someone for that long you don't want to think of it as for nothing.

One day, though, I was taking a shower before work and the words of a good friend of mine, who's also married to a Korean, came back to me: take it day-to-day, he told me. The epiphany came to me in the shower that day and I thought, "Oh my God! I'm going to be barely making it through my days with this man until I'm eighty!" I panicked. I couldn't breathe. "I can't live like this," I thought to myself, "just because I feel sorry for someone!" I knew I'd rather kill myself than have that be my life, so I started asking myself some really important questions about myself and my marriage: do I want babies? Can I have children with this person? I couldn't answer the first question, but I knew the answer to the second one was absolutely-fucking-not! No way did I want this individual to be the father of my children. There were not a lot of things that I liked about him, so how could I bring a child into a value system like that? I knew that was impossible. I met some really good friends after that and they were very supportive and I got strong—I got a backbone.

When I finally made the decision to leave him it was so easy. I don't know what happened, exactly. It was just this grace period that the universe had given me. I went home and I told him I was leaving him. He didn't think I was serious, of course. I proceeded to tell him that I'd found a house and I was moving in there the following week. He panicked, and then the tears and the threats ensued. I never caved, though. Not once. I wasn't even a bitch, just strong. "I wish you the best. If you kill yourself I think that would be a real shitty thing to do, you knowing the person I am, and that it wouldn't be easy for me to live with that guilt, but I won't be responsible for that. You're responsible for your life," I told him.

After I said that it was just like this textbook psychology jargon coming out of my mouth. But I never had a guilty moment. It wasn't easy; it was really hard, but it was right. Those first couple of months were especially difficult because all I'd done for eight years was concentrate on making it through the day. I never once picked through the things that had happened to me in that relationship and the toll they had taken. To have to go back and remember the things that had happened to me was more work than I've ever done in my life. I can't believe that I had allowed myself to be treated that way for so long. I was so disappointed that I had such little respect for myself.

I used to be bitter towards him—and I still am—but I have to learn to let that go. I've seen it destroy people's lives. Life is too short. I was more angry and bitter at myself than I was at him. I'm sad that I allowed him to treat me that way. Now I just want nothing to do with him. I want to get on with my life. I'm happy these days and I feel excited about all the things that I could never do before. I'm enjoying being single and having my own space. I love going home at the end of the day and doing whatever-the-hell it is I feel like doing. There're no negative forces there to suck away my energy. I've got a great group of friends and I really like being on my own. And though I don't miss him, sometimes I'll get the old pangs of thinking that the situation is easier for me than it is for him. It's then that I remember that I've worked for everything I have. If there's a reason that things aren't going well for him it's because he sat on his ass and did nothing. The pity-pangs don't take long to dissipate once I remember the truth.

If I were to offer any advice to intercultural couples, first of all I'd have to point out that a Western man marrying a Korean woman is an entirely different situation than the opposite. For a Western woman marrying a Korean man, it depends on what your ideals are. If you're a traditional type of woman who's happy to stay at home and raise a family, just make sure he has a good job and a sustainable income. Communication is an important thing, as is compromise; it's all give and take, right? Personally, I gave everything and got nothing in return. I learned the Korean language; I learned Korean history; I learned to cook Korean. I imagined that if he came to Australia he'd be willing to do the same thing but he didn't. He wasn't willing to change anything about himself for me. You need to explore your husband-to-be's personality and behavior. Meet his family and friends and get him to interact with yours. Take him home and get him to go out with your friends. I still believe that a way to gauge how far a relationship will work is to watch your partner with your friends.

Maybe the opposite dynamic is at work when Western men pick a Korean woman to marry because there's the hope that she'll be subservient and cook and clean, just like their mothers. And maybe it's the opposite dynamic happening when a Korean man chooses a foreign wife: they want the subservience, obviously, but then they realize that their woman has a career and brings home the bacon so they don't have to go to work and they can just sit on their asses—they get their mother, too!

I do, however, think it's possible for intercultural or interracial relationships to work. A huge amount of effort and compromise must take place, though. And then there's his family to worry about. It's a hard transition for any Western woman who comes from an educated background and has a strong sense of who she is to come here and be placed inside this box, a box that is governed by rules that you'd never adhere to under normal circumstances. For me, Korea's made me a stronger person. I take nothing but strength, knowledge, and gratitude when I leave.

"The thought of my boyfriend getting married truly scares me. If he doesn't want to marry he should learn to defy his culture. You don't have to follow your parents' wishes all the time. Your parents aren't always correct."

Eric* (29)
Philippines
Office Worker
3 Years

Eric is not your average Filipino in Korea. Highly-educated and fluent in English, he's also a gay man living in a society that makes it very difficult to be open about sexuality. This has not stopped him from developing intimate relationships with Korean men, however. In fact, his experience has led him to gain many insights into a part of the culture that is greatly misunderstood and rarely talked about.

I WAS WORKING in Manila at the time, when I got a phone call on my birthday four years ago from my uncle. He told me he was sending me a plane ticket to Seoul to visit him. I ended up staying in Seoul for one month, and when I returned to the Philippines, I knew I'd come to Korea again. When I stepped onto Korean soil, everything was so new to me. For example, I could go somewhere in Europe or America and feel very familiar, but when I landed in Korea, everything was new and fresh. I looked to Korea for a challenge. I wanted to learn new things and I wanted to learn about Korea's culture, its food, its language, its people—everything piqued my interest.

When I was here the first time around, my uncle and aunt were always out of the house. One time I told my uncle that I wanted to go out because I was so bored. He told me to go to the bank, take out some money, then take the bus to Itaewon (이태원), and get off at the McDonald's. So, I got on the bus in Sinchon (신촌), saw the McDonald's not long after, and got off the bus. I felt so stupid and helpless. After that, my uncle told me that if I wanted to live here I would have to learn Korean, so he bought me some books and I studied on my own.

When I came to Korea the second time, I arrived on a tourist visa and was soon after offered a job doing computer design. That was three years ago. Working here in Korea was very different, I must say. The Philippines is the most Americanized country in Asia, so the two experiences have been totally different. If you work in a Korean office, the first things you have to learn are patience and understanding; you're not encouraged to express your opinions when working in a Korean office. My experience would have been different if I were a white man, yet because I'm Asian I'm treated equally. I have fair skin but I've been told that Koreans discriminate against dark skinned Asians. The experience was a bit paradoxical, actually. If you were to read a book about Korea, the book would tell you that Korea is a country of manners, for example. However, based on my experience, Koreans aren't that friendly, initially. You need to have a lot of interaction with them before you can become friends with them. It took me a long time to develop a feeling of closeness with anyone in my office.

Now, I'm Filipino, and the one thing that brings all us Filipinos together is the church. That's actually why many Koreans are interested in my community; we're the only foreigners in Korea that gather every Sunday in one place and that's a captive market for them: telephone cards, home appliances—you name it. This all takes place in Hyehwa-dong (혜화동). Some Filipinos come all the way from Suwon (수원) and Uijeongbu (의정부), in fact, because the church in Hyehwa is bigger and the interior is nicer. There are also churches in Ansan (안산) and Suwon, though.

That being said, though, I don't have many Filipino friends in Korea. One reason why it's hard for me to make friends with some Filipinos here is that they speak their own dialect, which is different from the dialect spoken in Manila, where I'm from. This makes us Filipinos from Manila feel uncomfortable. Some of these people have never been to Manila, so what are we going to talk about? We don't have a lot in common. I want to meet people from whom I can learn something new, but with them I'd be too busy teaching them everything I know! I don't want to waste my time with that.

That's partly why I have so many Korean friends, many of whom are gay. Korean gay men are pathetic, though. They don't have any freedom and are always trying to hide. They have to marry a woman because of their culture—they have no other choice. They're locked in this box and their family expects them to be married with children. They don't have any options, but I blame that on the society and not on them. I hate the pressure that's put on men to get married. My boyfriend is the eldest in his family so everyone expects him to get married. I can't imagine myself without him in Korea. We've been together for seven months now, and it's the longest relationship I've had. I used to have boyfriends for two months here, three months there. I'm surprised we've lasted this long, actually. The thought of my boyfriend getting married truly scares me. If he doesn't want to marry he should learn to defy his culture. You don't have to follow your parents' wishes all the time. Your parents aren't always correct. In fact, all the Korean boyfriends I've had here in the past have had girlfriends at one time or another. I think it's peer pressure that leads to this. The schooling here is not usually co-educational and most of the young teenage boys are forced to have a girlfriend because they're not confident enough to tell their parents and their friends the truth.

All in all, however, I think Korean boys are very cute and sweet, even though many of them can be spoiled brats and very rude. Sometimes they forget their manners. They're sweet in the beginning of a friendship, but then they tend to try and control you. They want you to act according to their expectations. "Don't say this", "Say that", "I want you to meet these people", "You can't meet those people." These are the kinds of things they say all the time. I've met many Koreans, some of whom I consider my friends, but I still feel as if they're all hiding little secrets within themselves. For instance, my relationship with my boyfriend right now is okay, but whenever I ask him "Why is this like that?" or "Why is that like this?" or "Why is your mother acting like this?" he gets very angry with me, and tells me that it's none of my business. But I think it's my business because we're friends. There are more obstacles to friendship here in Korea. I'm actually older than my boyfriend but he still tries to control me. "You can't hang out with that crowd", "Don't drink too much", "Don't smoke or else," he often tells me, so I come back and say, "Hey, I'm not your wife, you know!"

On another level, Korean men have a strong bond between

them. They long for male companionship because most Korean fathers are never home and they don't make time for their children. Korean men grow up as "momma boys." For example, with heterosexual males from the West, I could never convince them to have sex with me, if only because they're from the West. In Korea, however, I know there is a strong possibility that I may be able to persuade a friend to be intimate with me, even if he "thinks" he's heterosexual. It doesn't even have to be sex, though. It can just be experimentation.

To me, cross-cultural dating makes perfect sense. It shows that relationships between two people know no boundaries—color, language, culture, or otherwise. One needs to have a lot of patience and understanding, more than what ordinary couples from the same background require, for instance. There should also be respect for each person's culture, and one must not change the other for his convenience. In other respects, though, cross-cultural relationships are difficult. Yet the fun, excitement, and the mutual feelings that we share as a couple far outweigh all the terms of endearment one can express. It has no boundaries or rules. And, as they say, love is not seen nor heard: it is felt. As my boyfriend and I near our first year of togetherness, I simply cannot imagine being with anyone else.

"After five years I think it's right to learn Korean because I have to respect this country. They offered me an opportunity to work, to make money, so of course I work. They gave me an opportunity to stay here and they like me."

Antonio Patella (39)
Italy
Concert Pianist, Musical Director, and Restaurant Manager
5 Years

There are few people as well-known in the Itaewon (이태원) community as Antonio Patella. Manager of the very popular La Tavola restaurant, Antonio is known to many in Seoul as a wonderful man to socialize with, and a great person to see when you want some of the best pizza Korea has to offer!

I ARRIVED in Korea in May 1997. I was working with the Seoul Ballet Theatre (SBT) at the time, and stayed with them as the music director for three years. Actually, before I ever arrived in Korea we had some exchanges between me and the SBT, because my brother is part of the company—he's a dancer—so I invited them to Italy two times and they had performances. When I finished my studies in Italy at the Academy of Arts in Bologna, the SBT offered me the opportunity to be their music director and I accepted, so I came to Korea.

When I first came to Korea, it was also my first time to Asia so my first impression was, "Wow, what is this?", because in Italy we have one fixed idea about Korea. We think about Korea as a Vietnam or a Cambodia, not a developed country. When I arrived in Seoul I said, "Oh, my God. This is Seoul?" Of course we see Seoul in every magazine in Europe now, like Tokyo, New York, Paris, Rome—it's very beautiful. Seoul is not Korea, though. Seoul is something different; it just happens to be in Korea. I was very impressed with the huge buildings and just very surprised overall.

It might sound strange to some people when I say that when I arrived in Korea five years ago I didn't speak one word of English —no English at all and no Korean—but it's the truth. I spoke Italian and French very well at the time and so thought those two languages would be okay. But I quickly realized it wasn't okay. I had to study. However, I had no time to study because I was so busy with work, so I learned day by day, step by step, meeting people and trying to understand what they said and afterward, right away, English came. The problem with the languages from the very beginning was Korean. It's not like English. English is easier to learn. With Korean, you need to sit down at the table and study hard. If not, forget about learning Korean. It took me three months just to learn the characters, the *han-geul* (한글) characters! In Europe, and in English, we have just five vowels: A, E, I, O, U. Here, though, it's like ya, yo, yaw, yoo, ee, and on and on. Korean is really very difficult, "한국말 진짜 어려워요." Koreans say that to me all the time.

Anyway, after three years of working at the Seoul Ballet Theatre, I became the manager of La Tavola, a restaurant in Itaewon. Incidentally, it was actually while I was with the SBT that I met my wife three years ago. Being a pianist, the Italian Cultural Center would ask me to play at every event they hosted. It was at one such event where I met my wife, who was in the audience at the time. We dated for two months and during this time when we were dating we cooked for each other a lot. She sometimes cooked *jjee-gae* (찌개)—Korean broth—for me and I loved it. I also cooked for her sometimes, usually something like pasta. I don't have that much time to stay at home to sleep because I really work a lot, but when we have free time together she cooks for me sometimes, I cook for her sometimes. I don't know everything about Korean food, but I love a lot of it.

It was after two months of dating that I proposed to my wife. It was then two years after that when we finally got married. I was a little bit scared actually because it's not my country, but she was so kind, so nice. The thing is, the mother of my wife, she's so wonderful. She gives me a lot of support. Of course she helps us, like giving us a sofa and some other things. I have to say, I'm just very happy about that.

We technically got married at the embassy at first, got married on paper that is, just to make sure of everything. But for me that kind of marriage is not important. I come from the south of Italy where we're very religious and have to keep the rules. My mother goes to church two or three times a week, so for me church is very important. I should point out that when my wife and I first met, she didn't have a religion. However, she became a Catholic soon after our meeting, which was wonderful, because as a result the two of us were able to have a real marriage. And thank God, because the bishop of Korea married us here in Hannam-dong (한남동), at the International Catholic Church. Bishop Morandini of the Vatican Church married us, so it was really fantastic! Afterward, everyone came to my restaurant and all the staff were really wonderful to us.

It was only after our wedding ceremony last year that I went to Italy with my wife for the first time, though. My parents accepted her as a daughter right away; there was no problem with her being Korean. Fortunately my wife likes to learn Italian and I like to learn Korean. After five years I think it's right to learn Korean because I have to respect this country. They offered me an opportunity to work, to make money, so of course I work. They gave me an opportunity to stay here and they like me.

"Actually, it's not really different being gay in the military in Korea from anywhere else. If you've been in the military for a year or two, then it's not going to be a lot different in Korea."

Yaira M. Resto (26)
Puerto Rico
E–4 Specialist, U.S. Army
1 Year

For the nearly five years she was in the U.S. Army, including the year she was in Korea, Yaira faced a daunting number of challenges covering up her sexuality. Though she had a girlfriend back home whom she cared for deeply during her tour in Korea, she was never once allowed to talk about her in public for fear of being discharged from the army.

ORIGINALLY I wanted to move to the continental U.S. after I was born and raised in Puerto Rico. I didn't just want to move and look for a job by myself, though, which is what led me to the military. In the military, they take care of you in some ways and so that was my safety net. Also, I wanted to travel to other places; I was looking for a little adventure.

I came in as an E–4 Specialist (Enlisted, Level 4) right from the beginning because I had a college education prior to the military. Depending on how much education you have, that determines your starting rank, but E–4 is the highest you can start at. I did my basic training in Fort Jackson, South Carolina for three months, then moved to Fort Meade, Maryland for three more months of job training. It was at basic training when I met a lot of gays. I met even more gay people while training in Maryland. We would all talk about it and became friends with each other. In basic training, everybody separates in little groups. It took me about six months to talk about it, and this only happened after a friend came up to me one time and talked to me about it, even though she didn't know I was gay, too. We were together through all of basic training and job training in Maryland. It was after talking to that girl that I realized we weren't the only ones.

Anyway, after those three months in Maryland I was then stationed at Fort Eustis, Virginia for three years. It was in Virginia that I finally met some people from around the area. As fate would have it, the same day that my girlfriend and I decided to get together, I picked up my mail saying I had been assigned to the Republic of Korea. My date to ship out was six months from then, so my girlfriend and I were together for just six months before I had to leave.

Once I got to Korea, the military gave me a couple of briefings, a few phrases in Korean, and they taught me a little bit about the food, the culture and the weather, how to behave in the shopping areas of Korea, but nothing much in depth. Our training was mostly concerned with military matters.

My own cultural experience began when I started learning stuff from different Internet websites that I looked up once I got here. I then went out and actually started experiencing Korea from there. I knew a couple of people whom I had worked with in Virginia that I had e-mailed, letting them know I was going to be here. This friend of mine who was a captain called me up when I got to the hotel in Seoul and took me out for my first Korean dinner in Itaewon (이태원), which was *kal-bee* (갈비)—Korean ribs. The food was great; I was really impressed.

After that experience, I started going out with my camera and visiting the museums. I'm not much of a talker, so I would just go off by myself, pretty much as a tourist, and take pictures. I don't think I tried to communicate with any Koreans until I was here for several months. In the beginning, I went off base just on weekends. That was mostly because the first few months I didn't have my property shipped over here, so I didn't have a television, I didn't have anything in my room—it was just me—so I had to get out. During the weekdays I would go around the base and get to know post, and on weekends I would go out to Itaewon. Once I got to know Itaewon well, I then got on the subway and tried going other places as well.

Living in the military, especially out here in Korea, most people don't have their family with them, so it's all social interacting among the soldiers all the time. And once you're socializing, everyone starts talking about their family and their boyfriends and their girlfriends and sons and daughters. You don't get asked directly if you're gay, but there's a pressure to avoid certain questions, and start making up stuff. For example, I've said that I have a boyfriend to a couple of people, even though I don't. I've pretty much put my girlfriend's information in there. Most of the time I don't say I have a boyfriend, but if I'm talking one-on-one with a person and we're getting into a conversation about family and relationships, and I really, really want to talk about it, I say I have a boyfriend.

When I first came to Korea, I started to put pictures of family around my room. The pictures of my partner I put up very discreetly, pushed to the back, so as not to bring up a lot of questions and avoid anything with that at all costs. One time I was out with a group of women, and a couple of guys that I work with saw me walking around with them. Apparently the guys who had seen me had been in Korea for quite a while and knew one of the girls, so when I got back on-post, one of them said to me, "Oh, Resto. I saw you out there in Itaewon. You were hanging out with the German lady." And I said, "The German lady? Who's that?" I assumed he was referring to one of my friends who was walking in front of the group, holding hands with her girlfriend. And so this guy said, "Yeah, you were hanging out with the German lady. What are you doing with her?" so I said, "I'm not doing anything with her. We're just friends." But these guys were giving out the looks.

I think that maybe started a rumor somehow, and a little bit after that I got a roommate and she totally avoided contact with me at all costs. She didn't say anything about it, but we were roommates for about four months and she talked to me maybe two or three times in the whole four or five months we were roommates. She never even looked me in the eyes. She would always talk to me facing the other way or something like that, and only when she really, really had to. I suspected it was the rumor that led to this behavior on the part of my roommate because one day I was coming out of the shower in the bathroom—roommates all have to share a bathroom—and she was coming out of her bedroom in her bathrobe. She covered herself, started to run into the bathroom, and then slammed the door, like I was going to see something. I just stood there wondering what ever happened to her. It was then that I noticed that every time I went into my room and locked the door she would come out and go in the bathroom. It was actually quite funny to think that somebody might be intimidated by me; it's like being afraid of a mouse. I never worked up the courage to address that with her, or to tell her anything about it, but if I would have, I just wanted to tell her there was nothing to be worried about whatsoever.

That's part of the reason I don't feel comfortable in the military. Right now I have a steady relationship with a woman who's back home in the States. She has a son, a five-year-old boy whom I consider my son too after being together for a year and half. Now, because of our relationship, there have been a lot of instances where I've had to lie in front of her boy or try to change things for him, and I really don't feel right doing that.

For the year that I've been in Korea, the women from Seoul Sisters have really helped me deal with issues like that. Seoul Sisters is a group of women here in Korea that enjoys the company of other women. We get together about twice a month, and even though I've heard there are a couple of straight members, most of us are gay women. I think they have around 200 members on the list, but that includes people who were here in Korea and are still receiving e-mails from the group. Right now, I think we have about twenty people who are active members and go to the meetings regularly. Of the 20–25 women who are out at a Seoul Sisters meeting, most of them are English teachers. There's one housewife, one student, and one military servicewomen, but everyone else is a teacher. We have quite a few Australians, a lot of Canadians, a lot of Americans, and a couple of British women.

I'm a big a computer enthusiast, and so I was able to find them listed on a website about gay places in Asia. I then sent a message to the president of the group and she wrote me back and I decided to go to one of the meetings. However, it took me about three months to go to the first meeting. Before the first meeting, I was a little bit nervous because I thought it was going to be either a really politically active group, something too active for my tastes—I was just looking for friends—or maybe it was going to be a meat market, some kind of a dating service, and I wasn't looking for that either. But when I stepped in there we just started talking and everyone was really friendly. I ended up making so many friends who I know I'm going to keep in touch with once I leave.

Nonetheless, I'm going to leave the military soon, and my girlfriend back home is a lot of the reason why I'm doing this. I've always had a problem with my weight. I had to lose a lot of weight to be able join the military in the first place, but that requires a lot of focus and lot of personal motivation, and after a while it became too much effort. Once I got into a relationship and didn't want to be here, I became totally depressed, and so it became almost impossible to keep up with the physical fitness schedule or what I was supposed to do to stay in shape. Plus, my girlfriend is having a hard time being a single mother and paying the bills and everything. I've been sending money back home for a while, but there's not a lot I can do from here. Right now, if a male service member has a problem back home with his wife, like she had an accident or something, the military would authorize him to go on leave and go to his family and take care of any kind of difficulty they might have back home. Once I realized that anything could happen to me or my girlfriend and we would have no way of traveling on demand to give each other support, and that our little boy who is just starting school would have to be taught to lie and hide our family ties because of my job and the intolerance of my peers, it was all over me. I didn't want to belong to such an organization anymore.

In the beginning, I joined the military mostly because I wanted job experience; a college degree is not very good unless you have a few years experience. My degree is related to graphics, so now I have a college degree and four years experience and I got what I wanted. I've been able to take advantage of that opportunity so far. In that way, I'm really happy with my time in the military. Actually, it's not really different being gay in the military in Korea from anywhere else. If you've been in the military for a year or two, then it's not going to be a lot different in Korea. For gay women coming to Korea in the future, or here right now, I would definitely suggest getting in touch with the Seoul Sisters. They have been such a breath of fresh air out here, just having somewhere I can go and talk to people who I don't have to lie to.

"My husband helped alleviate any fears about getting married when he told me that I didn't need to bring anything but myself to the marriage ... when he told me that he would treat me like a princess..."

Nakashima Mayumi (40)
Japan
Waitress
7 Years

Nakashima Mayumi is not unlike many Japanese women who have married a Korean man, in that she has learned the language, the culture, and many of the traditions of her new home. Deeply respectful and brimming with kindness, she prorides a great window on how two cultures, historically at great odds with one another, can mesh beautifully.

IN THE SUMMER of 1992, my husband was transferred to the company I was working for at the time, which was in Nagoya, Japan. He had been in Japan for about a year and a half before we actually met. When we first started dating, we spoke Japanese. Actually, it's funny because before he met me, my husband had always said that he would never marry a foreigner, let alone a Japanese woman, even though his father spoke Japanese really well and used to keep saying that he wanted his future daughter-in-law to be from Japan. These days, we speak mostly Korean, but we do speak with each other in Japanese from time to time.

We were together for one year before we got married. At first, my husband asked me if I could help him with his Japanese, which was how we got to know each other better, gradually falling for each other as time went by. He seemed like my older brother when I first met him. I didn't get intimidated or anything by that, but rather, I felt comfortable with him, even though he's eight years older than me. I can't say it was exactly love at first sight, though. Actually, in some ways I think my husband acts like a woman. He's really into clothes, accessories, and those kinds of things. Even more so than I am! At first I didn't really like that about him. The fact that I got married—and to a Korean man at that—is still somewhat of a mystery to me, because when I was growing up I saw through my own parents how much a woman, or a wife to be more exact, sacrifices for her family when she gets married. For a long time that made me think that getting married was not the right thing to do.

My husband helped alleviate any fears about getting married when he told me that I didn't need to bring anything but myself to the marriage, however. Fifty years ago, there were people like my husband all over Japan. That's not true any longer, so I was sort of amazed when I was dating my husband years ago because it really isn't easy to meet a person with such pure and innocent thoughts nowadays. Also, when he told me that he would treat me like a princess if we got married, that gave me the confidence I needed to get married. He truly believed that I would never experience any hardships with him, which showed me that he had a lot of inner strength and confidence in himself. I can't tell you how happy it made me when my husband told me that he would take care of me and protect me until the end of the world. Japanese people, particularly Japanese men, don't ever say things like that.

With my parents, even though most Japanese people like Korea, they thought my husband appeared too narrow-minded when they first met him. He kept his head bowed while he was with them. I'm not sure why, but maybe it was because of the Japanese greeting customs. He talked to them in Korean and I had to act as the interpreter.

Anyhow, my husband and I got married in Japan after being together for a year. We had a traditional Japanese wedding in Nagoya, inviting only close friends and relatives to the wedding. In Japan, it usually takes a long time for the bride and groom to get ready for the wedding ceremony itself, especially the women who have to go to a beauty salon and get their hair done before putting on very special wedding clothes. After this, the woman has to go to the wedding hall and pray to the Japanese gods and then she and the groom greet the guests and sing. A typical Japanese wedding ceremony usually goes something like that.

After the wedding, we spent six months in Japan before coming to Korea in 1993. However, I'd been to Korea a couple of times for fun before our wedding. I always thought the night view was really fascinating, partly because there were so many crosses here. Initially, when we first got to Korea, my husband and I were renting a house—we weren't living with my husband's parents—and sometimes the landlady would come to my place out of the blue to share some of her food with me. It embarrassed me a little at the time, but now I understand that Korean people just want to treat anyone they care about like they're part of the family. I can't speak for every single Korean person, but I think Koreans tend to be very polite and respectful, which, surprisingly enough, actually made me feel a little uncomfortable sometimes. Koreans are also very positive and assertive. You can interpret that aspect in both a good way and a negative way, though. For example, it seems to me that Koreans will sometimes just go and criticize someone in a very direct way. There's a saying that goes like this: a Japanese man who has had a little to drink is the same as a sober Korean man. I think there's a lot of value in that statement. At the same time, however, I've now learned after years of marriage that Koreans are very good at making a living under difficult circumstances, which is a very good point.

Anyway, it was after arriving in Korea that I first met my husband's parents. They were living in the countryside at the time. I'm not sure why, but for some reason they didn't really understand what I was saying to them. For me, I also had a hard time understanding what they said because their dialect was so strong. Since I didn't know much Korean, I basically just said hello to them. My mother-in-law asked me if I cooked well or not. We had nothing but Korean food then so it was hard on me. From time to time I would get an upset stomach after eating some spicy food. These days, however, I like Korean food. I've even learned to make kimchi a little bit after all this time. In the beginning, though, it was more the weather that caused problems for me. I wasn't used to the weather here in Korea and so I went through some difficult times because of it.

For the first few years we were in Seoul, I just stayed at home and took care of things around the house while my husband continued working at his company. I went through a very difficult time then because everything on TV and on the radio was in Korean. That was part of the reason that I began studying Korean. I studied for a few months at the language institute of Ehwa

Womans University (이화여자대학교). It was at that time that I discovered Koreans seemed to think women should just stay home and take care of all the housework. I actually knew a Japanese woman who was trying to get a job, but everyone around her kept telling her to just stay at home. She ended up relenting and doing what they said, staying at home and being a housewife.

When I had no friends and acquaintances before going to study Korean, I just stayed around my home like a fool. Of course it didn't help that my husband told me to stay at home as well. Yet while I was attending Korean language classes, I got to know some Japanese students pretty well. Back then, I didn't feel lonely at all and had a lot of fun. However, after I finished my studies, I felt all alone once again; there were only Koreans around me. It was then that I had a lot of chances to talk to Korean women, especially those who were married, and I learned how to cook Korean food.

Then, in 1997, my husband and I went back to Japan because of his work. We were living in Saitama, and I was working part-time. I felt really comfortable and relaxed being back in Japan. When I was living in Korea, it was like living in a battlefield. I never really felt relaxed and at ease. People drive like bullets in Korea and Korean society itself seemed a bit too complicated for me. By the same token, though, I must say that there's never a boring moment in Korea. There are so many great places to go shopping and have fun here, and the prices are so great! Also, there are so many things in Korea that are different from Japan. For instance, Koreans always say that they are going to be successful in life, while Japanese people normally don't say things like that. I like it when Koreans say they're going to be successful in life and in work no matter what, because whenever I hear something like that I feel like something good will soon happen in the future.

Anyhow, in 2000 we returned to Korea once again because of my husband's work. We're both at the mercy of his job. However, these days married life is really good for us. People often say that life becomes boring after a couple of years of marriage, but that isn't the case with us. We enjoy a great home life. Maybe it's because we don't have any children yet, but my husband is really attentive to my needs—he even cleans around the house and does a little cooking! Though my husband and I don't have any plans for a baby yet, we're not ruling the idea out. The thing is, my husband doesn't really want to raise a baby in Korea because he thinks it would be really hard for us to do that. For me, I also realize that it would be tough for us to have a baby in Korea and to bring it up and educate it here. We're actually planning to go back to Japan in ten years. My husband likes Japan more than Korea, and I think his personality is better suited to Japan, anyway. He likes Japanese culture and Japanese food a lot, too.

"... we both decided that if everything ever fell apart we would both grow garlic somewhere on some island."

Samantha Brooks (37)
America
Freelance Artist
7 Years

Samantha is a survivor. At 6'1"—and blonde—she knows what it's like to stick out in Korea like few others. She's put up with the stares, the gawks, the fawning, and the occasional insult. Now married to a Korean man she says she fell in love with at first sight, her marriage has been one of resilience and perseverance. Initially she was ostracized from her husband's family based on nothing more than her skin color and nationality. It was only a tragedy years later that provided the silver lining to this story.

MY MOM DIED my senior year of college, and I used my student loan money to buy her headstone and pay the mortgages on the house until I graduated. Then my student loans started coming due. My sister had a baby, so I had to support the family and keep up the household with money I didn't have once the student loan money was used up. That's when I started working like a mad woman—all kinds of different jobs in different vocations until I graduated. I thought my degree would pull me through, and it should have, were it not for the Rodney King riots breaking out. I then did what any desperate, broke woman would do; I got back together with my ex-fiancé. Life wasn't any better under a middle-aged, controlling suit like him, though, so I sought assistance from my alma mater—USC—and went to the employment agency. "I need to get out of here. Where can I go and work for a while?" I asked. They gave me a list of agencies and I picked one that sent people to Asia. I told them I wanted to get into corporate training, paid them $175, and then they sent me to Korea.

Everything was a farce from the very start, though. I thought I would be working in a trading office, learning more about corporate training. Yet I was very unfamiliar with the visa system, so when I went through the agency in LA they arranged an E–2 visa for me. I thought that was a corporate training visa, but it ended up being just a teaching visa. That's how I ended up as an English teacher in Korea.

I supported my sister from the moment I arrived, sent her money for the baby, and started paying back my student loans. I've been working my ass off ever since to get back on track. I originally came here because I didn't know how to handle my situation anymore in the States, and I thought I needed a chance to breathe and still make money. It was the right decision. Having no time except to work and collapse at night turned out to be the best thing that could've happened to me. I didn't want to think about anything back home anymore.

I had actually been to Japan prior to coming to Korea, and I remember a Japanese friend of mine once saying, "Well whatever you do, don't go to Korea because the streets are dirt roads. You'll be robbed at the airport and everyone is poor." So when I did come to Korea I was surprised because it was quite metropolitan.

However, upon getting to the apartment the first night, I realized that things were not as rosy as the agency said. I was stuffed into a tiny villa with two younger roommates and a vindictive cat. My room turned out to be a cleared-out closet in the kitchen with a screaming freeway outside the window.

I was thrown immediately into English classes with no rest and no food. That was my start in Korea. The entire first month perpetuated the agony. I had but a few dollars to live on, and with constant strife with the girls, I looked to eating corn dogs at a 7–11-style store everyday. Work was pretty much slave labor, so you'd work early mornings till late at night, and they'd have you doing other work in between. I wanted to go home but my stupid pride got in the way. I had sold my car and quit my job before coming to Korea, saying to myself, "I going to go overseas and I'm going to be this wonderful international business person." I just didn't have the heart to tell my family what had happened, so I made it work.

The only reason I stayed in Korea after the first month was because my future husband happened to wander into my classroom. I honestly have to say it was love at first sight. I had never been attracted to Asian men, ever, and I never thought I would be with one. When he came into the classroom he was, frankly, a real jerk. He was late, very arrogant, but there was just something about him I had to pursue. He started bringing me canned coffees every day and made me paper origamis.

After a couple of weeks of class, he wrote "beer appointment" on the whiteboard and our whole class went out together. He sat next to me at the bar, we sized each other up, went out on a date soon after, and we've been together ever since. He said the M–word, "marriage", after the first week of dating, and I freaked out because I had just left my ex-fiancé to come to Korea. Yet there was just something about him that made me a better person. He strolled into my class some time in September 1995 and we've been an item since November 28th of that year.

Anyway, after that first beer appointment, we had many more beer appointments. We did a lot of shopping, took taxis to places by the water, went to the park, and just did a lot of walking, talking, and drinking coffee. It took until the end of February 2003, however, to officially get invited to my parents-in-law home in Mokpo (목포). They have known of me since December 1995, but my moniker all those years was simply "that woman." I was very welcome in the beginning because they thought I was his "English friend." Once his parents realized we were dating, though, I never heard from them again. The simple fact was that I'm not Korean.

It got even more severe when my husband stuck by me. They said, "If she just looked more Korean, we could accept her; if she had dark hair, was shorter, if she didn't look so Barbie-dollish, we could accept her." Actually, his mother insisted he go on "negotiations," *sun* (선)—blind dates—for a couple of years while we were dating and living together. Of course they didn't actually know we were living together because that was our secret. So he would go out on an arranged date and I'd be back at our place waiting in agony, thinking, "What is going on?" He would come back all sweaty and exhausted, saying, "I'm so sorry. I'm so sorry. I had to do this to make my mother happy."

I had a very big problem with that. He ended up going on three of those arranged dates before telling his mother, "No more. I'm dating an American and I'm very happy." After that, his relationship with his parents ended for a few years. He was willing to give it all up for me. He was estranged from his family for a total of five years. During that time is when we both decided that if everything ever fell apart we would both grow garlic somewhere on some island.

Just before we got married, about a month prior, he went to his brother and said, "I'm going to marry my American fiancé. I just want to let you know. I'm not asking for your approval, but I want to let you know. I owe you that much." Then it all started again. The mother started calling out of the blue saying, "You've got to marry somebody Korean. Don't marry 'that woman.'" But we got married anyway, just living our own lives.

The big change with the parents came when I got pregnant at the beginning of 2003, and subsequently lost the baby in a miscarriage. From that tragedy came this landslide of warmth and love from his parents. What an irony, huh? Now the mother calls all the time and asks about me through my husband. She even bought me a *han-bok* (한복)—traditional Korean dress—and some jewelry, so the next time I go down to Mokpo, I'll have a necklace and earrings and a ring that match my husband's.

The fact that this change came about because of the miscarriage made me feel bitter for a long time, until I finally got a chance to see what everyone talks about as Korean hospitality, the kindness, that Koreans can convey. I've known so many people who have married Koreans and they're so welcomed in the family. Now that I finally see that side, I can understand that it's a little bit of ignorance on their part, that they're too scared to have anybody different in the family.

However, this hasn't changed our plans about staying in Korea for the rest of our lives. In fact, that's been the other little heated part of my relationship with my husband: when we'll be leaving or when we'll have a second base. Korea is just too Korean. I want a balance. When I do have a child, we will balance it out. The plan now is to have a baby in a Korean hospital, because they know what they're doing and it's a lot cheaper. The first year of raising a baby here is no problem, even though I, as the mother, will miss out on all of the extra-curricular joys, like the baby shower. After the first year, though, we've got to make the choice: is our child going to be involved just on the Korean side of things until elementary school or not. I don't think that I want my kid to go to school here. I really worry about stigmas and I worry about imbalance of influence. I'm too American to have that happen.

SECTION III
PEOPLE OF KOREAN DESCENT

ANCESTOR

People of Korean Descent

When King Kojong (고종) formally approved the emigration of Korean citizens to the U.S. on November 5, 1902, it's unlikely he foresaw the effect this would have on future generations of Koreans. On January 13, 1903, the SS *Gaelic* docked in Honolulu, Hawaii, ferrying 102 Korean immigrants to the United States, the first of millions of other Koreans who followed in their footsteps.

According to the Ministry of Foreign Affairs and Trade, 5.65 million people of Korean descent were living in 151 countries around the world as of July 2001. (The countries where the majority of these people were living at that time are given in the table on the following page.)

There have been three major phases of Korean immigration to the United States: 1903–1950, 1950–1965, 1965–present. However, the bulk of today's ethnic Koreans living in the U.S. came in the two final waves of immigration. In the first, after the Korean War, thousands of Koreans, most of whom were orphans, students, or women married to American soldiers, immigrated to the U.S. to escape poverty. The second major wave came after 1965, when the U.S. eased restrictions on immigration. Millions of Koreans began arriving shortly thereafter. In fact, 78 percent of Koreans currently

Country	Number of People
United States	2,123,000
China	1,880,000
Japan	640,000
Commonwealth of Independent States	522,000
Canada	141,000
Brazil	48,000
Australia	47,000
Germany	30,000
Argentina	25,000
Indonesia	19,000
Mexico	19,000
Philippines	19,000
Britain	15,000
France	10,000
Thailand	9,000

living in the U.S. immigrated after 1980.[1]

Today, more than one-third of ethnic Koreans in the United States (550,000) are "foreign-born."[2] Of the more than two million Koreans in the U.S., only thirty percent are naturalized citizens. Seventy-eight percent of these Korean Americans speak Korean as their main language and 48 percent of them speak English "less than well." Nationally, a 1996 census revealed that Koreans rank ninth among communities with the largest "foreign born" population.

With respect to other parts of the world, the large number of ethnic Koreans living in China is not as recent a phenomenon as that in the United States. The two countries historically have shared very close ties, as well as a common border in the northwest of today's North Korea. In the modern era, though, Koreans only began migrating to China in significant numbers in the 1860s, in an effort to escape a particularly awful famine that gripped the Korean peninsula at the time.

The story behind the large group of ethnic Koreans in Russia today, along with other countries that today make up the Commonwealth of Independent States (CIS), is similar to their history in China. In an attempt to flee the Japanese occupation of their country (1910–1945), scores of Koreans migrated into what was then the Soviet Union, across the border the Korean peninsula shares with Siberia in the far north. Sadly, many of these same people were forcibly resettled to parts of Central Asia in 1937, when Joseph Stalin ordered their move, a bid to exploit their labor in places like Uzbekistan and Kazakhstan. In addition, there is a large population of ethnic Koreans still living on the Siberian island of Sakhalin because of resettlement by the Japanese who, during World War II, drafted 150,000 Koreans and sent them to the remote far east island to work in munitions factories. To this day, there is still a Korean language newspaper and radio station on the cold and barren island.[3]

Finally, a good deal of the Korean emigré in Japan are descendants of Koreans who were forced to move there during the Japanese occupation of the Korean peninsula, and again during World War II, when thousands of Koreans were brought over to work at factories in support of Japan's war efforts.

On the opposite end of the Korean diaspora, every year hundreds of thousands of men and women of Korean descent who hold foreign passports come to Korea, some to work, some to study, and still others simply to explore a land their parents or grandparents left years ago. In 2001, for example, 287,000 people of Korean descent from around the world visited Korea. Not all of these *kyo-po* (교포)—overseas ethnic Korean—come to Korea just to visit the country on holiday, though. In 2002 there were approximately 19,000 *kyo-po* residing in Korea on one kind of visa or another.⁴

◗

Adoption has a rather long history in Korea, one that is inextricably bound up with Confucianism. As early as the second half of the Chosun Dynasty (조선시대 1392–1910), adoption became a common practice among families with no sons. During this time, mainly intra-lineage adoption took place.

The most common time for a man to be adopted was between the ages of twenty and thirty. Not only was it usual for males to be adopted late in life, but often they played an active role in the adoption process, talking with both families as the adoption process moved forward.⁵ Males were adopted in son-less marriages to fulfill two important Confucian goals: first, to preserve the marriage tie, and second to have a male offspring who could carry on the commemorative rites for family ancestors and retain the family name. According to Confucian tradition, daughters were never able to carry on a family's lineage; only males were sanctioned by Confucian law to carry on the family name. As a result, the custom required that a younger male sibling in a family provide a son for the elder male sibling if he had none. Even today, it is considered extremely important to have a son because Korea still has no adequate system of welfare to care for older parents, which is the duty of the eldest son. Furthermore, the eldest son still has the duty of performing *chae-sa* (제사)—ancestral rites for the deceased—which remains an integral part of Korean culture.

According to Holt Adoption Services, "Domestic adoption has usually been informal, with babies from relatives or found outside doorways cared for and then placed directly on the Family Registration as if born to the family. The custom is ... to protect the child from ridicule and being treated as someone shamed, a second-class citizen. Older children were often given to relatives or friends when a family could not care for them. Depending on the family who received them, these children could be treated well or poorly. Many lost contact with their families and some later lived in institutions."[6]

Although overseas adoption of Koreans was not common in dynastic Korea, it became the norm after the Korean War (1950–53). In 1954, with millions of Koreans displaced by the nation's civil war, and almost as many children in fatherless families, President Syngman Rhee (이승만) believed the solution for dealing with the country's staggering number of orphaned children was to create the Child Placement Service (CPS). The CPS later became the Social Welfare Society (SWS), which eventually incorporated another—department, the International Social Services (ISS), into its fold.[7]

In the roughly half century since the end of the Korean War, it is estimated that more than 200,000 Koreans have been adopted by overseas parents, predominantly Caucasian parents residing in Europe and the United States.[8] In 2000, the United States conducted its first government census on adoption, revealing that there were approximately 1.6 million adopted children living there. Of this number, nearly 13 percent, or 200,000, were born outside the United States. The Census Bureau also found that more than one in ten adopted children in the U.S. came from South Korea, more than any other country in the world.[9]

Although there are no exact records for overseas adoption from South Korea in the 1950s and 1960s, 140,735 overseas adoptions worldwide have been recorded since the Korean War, and 56,065 adoptions domestically.[10] Holt Adoption Agency, the agency that has assisted in more overseas adoptions than any other, is responsible for 69,307 adoptions, the majority going to the United States (43,519) and Europe (25,775). The number of Korean children being put up for adoption has subsided significantly in recent years, though. In 1975 there were 976 orphanages nationwide, with about 100 children at each orphanage, for a total of approximately 97,000 orphans. In 1980, the numbers fell to 891 and 80,000, respectively; and in 1997, 272 and 1,800, respectively, with about 2,000 adoptions by overseas parents in that same year.[11]

Early on, when the first overseas parents were adopting Koreans, the babies were referred to in Korean as *ee-byang-a* (입양아)—adopted child—but since then it has become somewhat politically incorrect to use this term. Arguing that they are no longer children, and should not be referred to as such, the first generation of Korean adoptees growing up in Europe and North America began referring to themselves in Korean as *ee-byang-een* (입양인)—adopted person—a term that has stuck to this day.

❒

In many ways, the five women and four men in this section are the hardest to define of all the interviewees in this book. Although all nine people in this section have some amount of Korean ethnicity, the quality that connects them to all other foreigners in Korea is their diversity. Where some cannot read or write Korean, others speak the language fluently; some are aware of Korea's long and distinguished history, others are just arriving and discovering the country anew; and while some prefer the company of Koreans, others only socialize among the rest of the foreign community. Yet the strongest tie each of them shares with everyone else in this book is the title Koreans inevitably distinguish them by—foreigner.

"I felt that my parents had no right to adopt me and that I didn't have to be removed from Korea. But then my parents told me it was Korea that sent me away, so it wasn't their problem."

Mihee-Nathalie Lemoine (35)
Belgium
Multimedia Artist and Social Activist
10 Years

Nathalie is, and continues to be, one the most instrumental voices in the adoptee community in Korea. She is co-founder of the support group that eventually became the Global Overseas Adoptees' Link (G.O.A. 'L.). Adopted by a Belgian couple, Nathalie was brought up until the age of 23 believing she was three years older than she actually was, one truth among many revealed to her upon returning to Korea.

ORIGINALLY, I thought I was born in 1965, what was written on my birth certificate. Only afterwards did I find out that I was born in 1968. I always thought I was maybe one or two years younger than I actually was, because I always had something a little bit different about me, yet for I years thought it was just because I was retarded or slow.

I was born in Busan (부산), technically in 1965, and was with my birth mother for two months before being given up to orphanages for a year and a half, two in Busan and one in Ilsan (일산), at Holt Adoption Agency, where they sent me to be adopted. I was sent to Belgium in October 1969 after three months of check-ups and a quarantine. I was only a year and half old at the time, but my birth certificate said I was four and a half years old and though that's a big difference, they never noticed, even on the airplane. When I arrived in Belgium, they had clothes for a four-year-old, but they had to change them to that of a one-year-old when they saw me. Even still, my adopted parents never questioned what was written on my papers because they believed what was written in English and translated into French; they totally believed the system. Later, in the 1970s, other people would check the forms in case there was a mistake, but I was in the first group of adoptees, when people wouldn't question the forms. When my birth mother orphaned me, she left a note on me with my lunar calendar birthday, but the year was erased somewhere along the way.

I think my first memories are really from when my "adopted" sister arrived in Belgium, me being the first of four adopted children from Korea in the family. My adopted parents didn't have children of their own. They were a young couple, just on the border of thirth years old—the age you can adopt from—so they made a request for an "older orphan, not a baby," and within six months they got me. Now, the thing for me was that my adopted mother's mother tongue is Flemish. She always knew that I knew she was different, not physically, but linguistically she had to make an effort. There's this language war in Belgium—French versus Flemish—so I think it was a very strong contrast in my own life because my father didn't want us to speak Flemish at home, yet my mother was a native Flemish speaker. Until I was a teenager, I think it was the language issue that influenced me more than my physical looks with my identity.

One of my other first memories is when I was seven and my adopted sister said to me, "I'm not Asian, you are Asian. Look! I have normal eyes and you don't have normal eyes." That really shocked me. After that incident I never talked with my sister about that again. My sister was one year younger than me—or so I thought at the time—and it was always a tricky thing because she was more mature than me. That's why I always felt that I was more retarded or slow because we always compared ourselves with each other. With our older—officially younger—adopted brother we didn't know; we thought it was maybe the fact that he was Asian that he acted the way he did. I felt he was a year or two older than me, but with my adopted sister, I thought she was her real age because many girls were abandoned in 1966, the Year of the White Horse and the year my sister was born. That particular Chinese zodiac sign has traditionally been very bad for a girl to be born under, something that only happens once every sixty years. Koreans felt it would be too hard for girls born in that year to live normal lives in Korean society and eventually get married, which is why so many girls were abandoned in that year.

Anyhow, later on, when I was officially 16—but really 13—I left home. I was pretty mad at my parents because they didn't understand me. I was the eldest sibling and so I felt I had too much pressure, even though my parents didn't think so. When I ran away I didn't want to get in contact with them and so I got many part-time jobs and went to school.

I had a very strong position about my adoption when I was younger and I was the only one in my family that felt strongly like that; my three other siblings didn't talk about it. I felt that my parents had no right to adopt me and that I didn't have to be removed from Korea. But then my parents told me it was Korea that sent me away, so it wasn't their problem. The main thing, I think, is that I always said that I had a biological mother. For an adoptive mother who doesn't have her own children it's a very big issue, so my Belgian mother would say, "Well, anyway, your mother is a prostitute. She just got together with a GI and the GI ran away and she didn't know what to do with you." On my adoption papers, it was written that I was a mixed-race child and that my father was probably a GI. Of course that's a good excuse to be adopted because I had no place in a society as racist as Korea.

When I was 13, but officially 16—the legal adult-age in Belgium—my grandmother said that because I was the eldest child I could go with her anywhere in the world, and I said I wanted to go to America. The reason I wanted to go to America was that I dreamt I was going to find my father there, just waiting for me, even though I didn't even know his name. I was expecting someone to come up to me at the airport and say, "Hey, I'm your father." The thing was, I had to find my mother to find my father, which was really difficult because she was the one who gave me up. Every time I would break down and cry and say I had to go back to my country, my mother would tell me, "Your country is here," which was true. She would then say, "What are you going to do in Korea? You don't speak the language and there's nothing there for you." Growing up, I had a lot of trouble with my mother because I think adoption was more of a sensitive issue with her. My adoptive father, on the other hand, was very distant and didn't talk much; he was an orphan himself. He said it was not to be discussed, and that we four kids were lucky and he was not.

It was some time later, after I had run away from home, that I wanted to make a film, and there was a competition to write a screenplay, with the first prize being awarded a small team to make the film. I put the screenplay together at the last minute—like a good Korean—and it ended up winning. It was at that point that I had to make my movie, when I was still going to school and working part-time. We shot for only two half days, once at night and once during the day at school, and it was basically about a letter I wrote to my birth mother and how Asia was perceived in Europe. Not just about adoption, it was more about being Asian. I later showed my movie at the Brussels International Super 8 and Video Festival, and it won the first prize for all of Europe. It was because of the award that I suddenly became a Korean for Koreans. The Korean attaché at the Korean Embassy in Brussels then called me and said, "I know you're Korean, but your movie is very bad because you say bad things about Korea," and so I said, "Yeah, because people think that Koreans eat dogs and they only think about taekwondo." The attaché then replied, "Well, you have to see the real Korea!" They had a program for adoptees then, and I got invited. I had to pay for my ticket, but everything else was paid for. This was back in 1989.

The next thing I knew, I was off to Korea with a bunch of other adoptees from Europe and a few from the States. The trip was very boring for me, though. Everybody was trying to show what was great about Korea. They were also telling us how much everything cost, like our meal, our room, and our transportation. It was kind of a pain, I think, and not very nice, so I said I would never go back to Korea. It was on that first trip, however, that they told me if I wanted to find my birth mother, I could apply and they would find her for me. At first I didn't understand what they were offering because I didn't speak English or Korean, but even later, when I did understand, I wasn't so sure that I wanted to do that. I was the only one from that trip who in the end didn't sign up for that program. A few people ended up finding their birth mothers, but I was not really paying attention. I did, however, happen to see one meeting between an adoptee and her birth mother and sat there thinking, "What would it be like if I found my birth mother?"

Anyway, three years later the same attaché from the Korean Embassy asked me again if I wanted to go to Korea because there was some kind of Olympic reunion of *kyo-po* (교포)—overseas ethnic Korean—and overseas adoptees. I, in turn, then chose another female adoptee I knew and we went back to Korea together. That trip was a better experience than the first time and again they said, "If you want to find your birth mother, we'll help you find her," which we believed, the other girl from Belgium and me. But it turned out to be a big show. Some people ended up calling my family but they never showed up. My friend and I had one more week in Korea after the Games were over, and so we decided to search by ourselves. It turned out that my friend was from the same orphanage as me and born in the same year.

When we went to Holt, they gave me some papers, and that led me to the orphanage in Busan, the place I was at after my birth. Unfortunately, the orphanage was no longer there. I then went to the other orphanage I stayed at in Busan and that led me to City Hall, where I found a letter from my birth mother without a date. At that time I felt a real connection through that piece of paper. The people at City Hall later told me they could show me where I was abandoned, but nothing more than that, so I had no real way to find my birth mother because I had no name or anything else to go on.

I was really lucky, though, because at the time there weren't a lot of adoptees back in Korea, and so one day MBC (Munhwa

Broadcasting Coporation) put me on TV, explaining that I was looking for my birth mother. The day after that, someone called up and said, "I think I'm the best friend of the birth mother of this girl, but the only problem is the date of birth—it's three years different." And because the birth mother was not in Busan, this woman had to check with where she was living and make sure of some details.

I then went back to Seoul and got a call not long afterwards, telling me my birth mother was waiting for me. I met my birth mother shortly afterward, but I couldn't speak English or Korean, so I wasn't able to actually talk with her. I was actually in the same room as my birth mother for an hour before someone said, "This is your mother. Say 'hi' to your mother." It turns out my birth mother didn't even know I was adopted because she thought I grew up with the family she left me with in 1966. Then I found out that my father was not American, so I asked if he was Korean, and my birth mother said "No," so I said, "I don't look black, so I know I'm not African. Was he Chinese?" and she said, "No." I then asked, "Was he Japanese?" and she didn't say anything. We went out to eat soon after that and my birth mother didn't want to talk about that issue anymore, so I thought perhaps I was half Japanese. This all happened in 1991, when I was 22.

Emotionally I think I was at a good age to deal with that. I thought it would be the only time I'd get to meet my birth mother, but we met again twice after that and she told me more and more about her story. As a Korean woman, there was a stigma of being a single mother. She was only 16 years old when she had me, and the eldest of five daughters in her family. If I had been a boy, they would have kept me and they would have passed me off as one of my mother's brothers so at least they could have had a boy in the family; my birth mother's father had already died by that point. When they found out I was a girl, however, it was like I was useless. My birth mother wanted to keep me, but after two months, her own mother pushed her to send me away because I was just wasting my birth mother's time. I couldn't be mad at my birth mother since she at least had told me the real story. That was the reason I went searching for her in the first place. By the way, in 1999, when I went to Busan to visit my grandmother, she told me once and for all that I was part Japanese. Somehow it was good to know that I was not fully Korean.

After this episode, many people asked me how I found my birth mother. A lot of Korean adoptees were asking me and my adoptee friend from Belgium this question, and so we thought, "Why don't we make an association in Belgium?" Actually, when I was looking for my own birth family in '91, one Korean family asked me to help them find their son, who was adopted in Belgium. That was the first case I took on, and I was lucky because I knew people who knew him, and with a lot of guesswork, I ended up finding him. It was because that first time went so well that my friend and I decided to form an association in Belgium. The main thing was to introduce Korean culture to Belgians because there was no cultural center in Belgium at the time.

When I came back to Korea this last time in 1993, I thought I'd be here just a year. It was then that we made the association branch in Korea and I thought everything would be fine and I'd be able to save some money. I was studying Korean and also volunteering at Holt to learn more about the Korean system of adoption. I slowly started to make connections to start my own association, because before then this concept of a Korean adoptee association didn't exist, so I was like a pioneer.

After my first class, I moved over to another university and there was an adoptee from Sweden in my class. At first she wouldn't talk to me, and it wasn't until the end of the course that she finally did. I mentioned to her that I might be able to find, or at least guide her, towards her birth family. When I eventually helped her find her birth family, she was very surprised. It was after that she said, "Okay. I'll help you form this association you've been talking about." That was in 1994.

We put some ads out and got some volunteers and started an English club, for Koreans to learn English, where, incidentally, I would end up learning English myself. It was at this same time that I met a very nice businessman who lent me his office, where I had a desk and computer and could use his phone and fax machine. This was not enough for our adoptee association, though, because the volunteers always expected me to pay for the food or drinks.

After a while I was kind of burned out with all that. I understood that the volunteers didn't want to spend money, but I couldn't keep paying for them. I understood that they were giving their time, but there was a fine line between what I could give and what I could not, which is why in 1995 I started working by myself. I called this group the Euro-Korean League, Korean Branch (EKL-Korea). In the first year, I had maybe 100 or 200 members, mostly from Europe, particularly Belgium. But after 1996, people started to hear about me in the States, and so I got more requests from there, which meant I had to speak better English. That's when I changed the name to Korean Overseas Adoptees because it was no longer just European. The main thing was to keep up with the searches and the support, working together with other agencies and trying to make a network out of it all.

This was also at a time when we were trying to fight for the fact that we were no longer children, *ee-byang-a* (입양아), but adults now, *ee-byang-een* (입양인). In Korea, people would sometimes treat adoptees as children, and so I thought it was important to bring awareness to all Koreans. There was also the problem of the visa status for adoptees, in that we couldn't stay here for long periods of time. We were not considered any different than other foreigners, which was unfair, I thought. We started a campaign because of this and, along with the Korea International Network, an NGO, and alongside Koreans who believed in our cause, we got more than 1,000 signatures.

By 1996, though, I was really burned out and fed up with Korean adoptees. For them, they came over on vacation and expected certain things from us. We told them that they had to understand there were certain limitations to what we could do. As an artist, I always continued to paint, right from the beginning. I was doing exhibitions at this time and thinking about doing a show with other Korean-adoptee artists. We had a very good response from companies like the Chosun Ilbo and Samsung, so we ended up putting on the show. There were eleven of us who participated in the show—adoptees, *kyo-po* and foreign students, under a group named KameleonZ.

Now, after all my experience with this issue, if I were to offer advice to other adoptees, I would say take your time. It's about you, because adoptees are each individuals. It's not because you're adopted that everyone has to think the same way. Many adoptees have this feeling that because they're an adoptee they have to act like every other adoptee, which is wrong because we all have very different backgrounds and points of view, even feelings about Korea, feelings about our adopted family, feelings about our birth family. Understandably, a lot of adoptees are concerned for their adopted families, as they don't want their adopted families to feel bad because they're searching for their birth families. If you don't feel ready, you can discuss the issue with your adoptive family.

If you're planning on coming back to Korea to work or to live, though, I would say come with some money. Don't expect to get rich in Korea in the first few days. Only Korean Americans can make any serious money here. Also, don't expect Koreans to see you as a full Korean. You might even feel rejected in some situations because you don't speak fluent Korean. But I think if you're very positive and realistic—don't come thinking Koreans are going to help you all the time—you'll be okay in Korea.

The thing is, a good deal of adoptees grow up trying to forget about Korea, only to have their own children years later thinking about Korea more than they ever did. These people need to be ready to answer their children's questions if they want to be good parents. There are now adult adoptees throughout the world who are having to deal with their teenagers' and young children's questions. I have a friend whose daughter said she wanted to meet her birth grandmother, and so my friend said that the next time they come to Korea she's going to meet her birth grandmother. I'm just thinking of that generation of children who perhaps don't have the stigma of pain or suffering and so they just want to embrace Korea. And why not? It's another generation.

"Being of a multi-ethnic background can be difficult. However, it can also be rewarding. You open your mind to two different ways of thinking and learning. Today, I'm open to other cultures and I never think there's only one way of at looking at something. I like to think of it as an advantage."

John (29)
America
Captain, U.S. Army
11 Years

The son of a Japanese Korean mother and an American father, John had a tough upbringing in an American neighborhood he says was predominantly non-Asian. Having learned to overcome fear and racism while growing up, he is now an officer in the U.S. Army, and has served in Korea on two different missions.

BORN IN SEOUL to a Japanese–Korean mother and a Caucasian American father, I spent the majority of my life between Korea and the United States, with a few years in Europe. While in Seoul, early on, I went to Seoul American High School, and as an elementary student I was at Seoul Academy for a couple of years.

My mother speaks Korean and English, but she seldom speaks Korean—only English. The only time I would hear her speak

Korean when I was younger was on the phone with Nana, or if she were upset. My mother grew up in Korea and after she got married that's when she started going to the States and traveling around with my dad to different countries. My dad doesn't really speak any Korean, though, just some words here and there. However, I took a personal interest in Korean early on and decided to take it in class because I wanted to communicate with my family. Some of my relatives couldn't speak English and they were older than me, so learning Korean seemed to be the only logical solution. I wasn't fluent growing up, but I was comfortable. Today, to say that I'm fluent would be incorrect. I can communicate, yet not at the level of a Korean national. I can read, write, talk to people, understand things, and be understood, however. My job now requires me to do translations, in fact.

When I was younger, I always identified myself as an American, yet if I was asked about my background I'd tell them. I rarely talk about my Japanese background because it's something that I had little exposure to. After my grandfather passed away you couldn't see any indication of Japanese heritage in any of our homes. I don't know why, but we view ourselves as Korean Americans and that's it.

In Korea, I was just another guy. There are a lot of kids on base in my situation in Korea: Korean mother and American father. In the States, however, it's different being "different." I went through several spurts in my life with friends, for example. One time I spent hanging out only with Korean Americans. This would have been my first year of high school in California. Other than that, the majority of my friends have been American people. When I say "American" people I mean no Asian background whatsoever, or knowledge, or familiarity. It was those friends who always found me as being the "different" guy. Whether my friends were Korean friends or Caucasian friends, however, they judged me only after socializing with me.

At the same time, in my earlier years my background was sometimes a problem, not as much in Korea as it was in the States, though. But, depending on the type of neighborhood you're living in—whether there's one predominant race or not—people may not like you for whatever reason, and in my case it was because my mother was Asian. With racism like this, it wasn't so much physical violence that we experienced. We were living in a lower income neighborhood, where the majority of people were black and my mom and I were the only two Asians. People didn't like that, and so we'd find rocks thrown at our door, or the public laundry room, which we shared with other tenants, would be filled with sand. You know, if your eyes are slanted in America you're Chinese, so there would also be a lot of name calling back then. That was tough to deal with at the time. My mom and I didn't talk about it much. She was a tough lady and I was a tough boy. Things have gotten a lot better over the last couple of years. She started going to church and it's given her the ability to talk more about what was going on when I was growing up. She's apologized and that's a step, but it's been so long. Don't get me wrong, when I go home, I show her respect and I do things to make her happy. I bury my feelings deep inside. It's a personal thing for me.

Essentially, though, as a kid I just wanted to keep my parents happy—do my homework, etcetera. When you have a Caucasian American father and a Korean mother you're always going to have two cultures when you're dealing with issues. A lot of the time they didn't agree on how kids should be raised, and that's because of their respective cultural upbringings and backgrounds. So I did have problems with trying to please both my parents because what may be right for one wasn't necessarily right for the other. It was hard to please both of them and so I had to search for that neutral territory. That was probably the most difficult period. Being the first child and a male was pretty tough, too. I think that my parents learned from me and that made it easier on my sisters.

To be honest, at times I was embarrassed having parents of a bicultural background. Through their actions—whether they were American actions or Korean actions—people who don't know you automatically kind of point and say, "You guys do this?" or "You guys have done that?" I've been embarrassed by things like that. I didn't necessarily have anything to do with those things, but it was a part of having the two backgrounds I'm from. Being of a multi-ethnic background can be difficult. However, it can also be rewarding. You open your mind to two different ways of thinking and learning. Today, I'm open to other cultures and I never think there's only one way of at looking at something. I like to think of it as an advantage.

Eventually the decision to come back to Korea was my own. This is the second time I requested to be posted in Korea, actually. I chose Korea for a couple of reasons. One, I'm comfortable here. I know the culture and I have friends here. I know how to live here. The second reason is that I chose to go to the most difficult assignment, and that's Korea, which is why it's a one-year tour. They call it a hardship to work and that's because your learning curve is so high. You get here and even as a second lieutenant, you don't know anything. This is a real-world mission. The training is intense and long, but it's been good.

My first time serving in Korea I was up in Area 1, and that was really difficult because we trained all the time and that's the front line of our defense. Professionally, coming back this second time and working in Seoul hasn't been as satisfying as Area 1. I think that's because I've always been on the move and coming to Seoul has been a shift down. I'm doing great and important work in Seoul, but it's not what I really enjoy doing.

Since returning here to work, I wouldn't say that I'm necessarily drawn to other people of Korean descent. In fact, I think I pull myself more towards Americans in the U.S. Army. In my section of the office, there are only Koreans who work there. I have no problem communicating with them if we work together, but as far as my personal time, even at work I'll bond towards American soldiers. However, having a Korean background and seeing another Korean is kind of like—how do I say this without offending anyone—being a brother. You recognize them and you try to help them out any way you can. I do, however, get the same feeling with an American officer.

One thing that I've noticed since returning is that it's really a shame what's been going on in Korea with all the anti-American sentiment. I am a United States serviceman and I am part Korean. I come back here and it feels like my second home. It's sad that Americans come over here to protect this country and there's so much anti-Americanism in Korea these days. I attribute that to people just not understanding and not knowing; people don't understand our presence here on the peninsula and its history. We're viewed as bad people. We've been working here for fifty years, and if you've ever been to the war memorial here in Seoul you'd know just how much blood Americans have shed for Korea. This anti-Americanism is coming mostly from the younger generation, I think. It seems they're being taught to lean this way as well. That really hurts me and saddens me when I see these Koreans doing this. Coming back to Korea and wanting to connect with this country and its people, with whom I share blood, it just hurts when I see these people trying to spread hate. People don't want to go where they're hated! These Koreans could be throwing rocks at me, for all I know, and my mother's Korean!

"When I was a kid I considered myself Korean, but I wanted to be Canadian—to be white, blonde, and blue-eyed."

Julie Kim (35)
Canada
Businesswoman
18 Months

How to describe Julie Kim? Fun, talkative, and outgoing is just the start with this extremely lively and gregarious woman. Her story is a great window into the kyo-po *(교포) —overseas ethnic Korean—experience in the West.*

I WAS BORN in Seoul. My family decided to emigrate to Canada when I was a year old. We moved to a suburb of Vancouver called Penticton, which is in the Okanagan. My grandfather, who passed away before I was born, had traveled to Canada and he was ranting and raving about it, saying all these wonderful things about Canada, so my father decided that was the country he was going to emigrate to. He wanted to be able to provide a better life for myself and for my brother, who was later born in Canada, and give us a better education. My father got a job working in Parks and Recreation for the city upon arriving, and my mother was a homemaker.

We lived in Penticton until I was four years old and we were the only Asian family there. I don't recall there being any racism from what I heard from my parents, just because it was such a small town and everybody there was so nice to us and was so helpful towards us. When we moved into the city, to a suburb of Vancouver called Port Coquitlam, that's when I sensed a lot of racism. I started hating myself and hating the fact that I was Asian; I hated the fact that I was Korean; I just hated looking Asian. When I was a kid I considered myself Korean, but I wanted to be Canadian—to be white, blonde, and blue-eyed.

When we moved to Coquitlam for the second semester of grade nine, it was a really tough transition for me because I'd already established friends at my old school. I had this group of girlfriends and they were pretty popular and I was kind of proud of myself that I accomplished getting into this group. And then all of a sudden my parents decided to move. At first I was commuting to my old school, but it became too tedious, so I decided to go to the local high school that was close to our house, and that was tough because again it felt like I was starting all over.

I remember growing up with a big chip on my shoulder, trying to do everything possible to change the way I looked, to make myself look Caucasian, from my clothes to my hairstyle. I wasn't allowed to wear makeup and a lot of the Caucasian girls were allowed to as early as grade seven, just because their parents were more lenient and my parents were more strict. When I used to wear eyeliner, I'd go into the girls' washroom and put it on, only to take it off before I went home after school. I just really went overboard trying to fit in.

There was a period of time when I really resented my parents and I resented being born to Korean parents. That was mostly when I was in elementary school, up until about junior high. I couldn't deal with the pressure of my peers. I wanted to fit in with the popular crowd because I always felt they were ostracizing me because of the way I looked. In junior high it changed, though. I finally learned that the best way for me to fit in was to excel in sports. When you excelled in sports you were representing your school, so it didn't matter what color or race you were, or even what you looked like, because you were winning for the school. I decided that was the route I was going to take, but I had to practice a lot because nothing came easy. My father always wanted me to concentrate on studies and be a straight-A student. One time when I was younger, I asked him if I could join the baseball team. He said "No," so I went down and used my allowance to join the baseball team. My mom always knew but my father didn't, and then when he did find out he made me quit. It was tough.

Another problem I had growing up centered around the fact that I spoke English. Actually, Korean was my first language, because when I was young that's what I spoke, and when I started school that's when I started learning English. My parents wanted me to be able to keep Korean as a language, so they sent me to a Korean school on the weekends. Eventually, though, I dropped out and they just kind of gave up. I kind of regret it now, because if I had kept it up I'd probably be fluent right now and not just speaking survival Korean. Today, for example, I cannot read and write Korean. I can write my name, and that's it.

My mother and I do manage to speak Korean these days, however. I speak to her in English sometimes, but my mother always speaks to me in Korean. She's taken ESL lessons, which I'm very proud of, because my step-father's Irish and he adores my mom, and so I just have to commend him because I don't know how the heck he understands her sometimes. With my father, he actually tries to speak in English with me more. I think it's because his English level is a lot better.

And so, because my Korean's not fluent, my mom and I mix English and Korean. It's frustrating at times, but then, she's my mother and she gave birth to me and nothing will change that. She'll always be my mom. Even though we do have communication problems—and believe me, we do, and we don't see eye-to-eye on a lot of things—she's still my mom, and she'll always be my mom, just like my father will always be my father. There were lots of times it frustrated me that I couldn't tell my parents exactly what I felt. When I was in my teenage years, hitting puberty, I had a lot of questions in my head and I wanted to ask my mom, but because she was so Korean it was almost like it was taboo. I didn't know how to ask her, so I learned a lot of things from my peers. These are things that I felt your mother should be teaching you and explaining to you.

At the same time, having said that, despite the fact that I don't really agree with how my parents raised me, they did the best they could. They were two Korean parents who had immigrated to Canada, trying to deal with children who were being raised in North American society. They wanted us to hang on to our culture and be Korean. Basically, that was the problem, and it causes an identity issue for a child growing up because we end up getting confused, and it took a long time for me to get rid of that chip on my shoulder. I went through a lot of fights growing up in school, and it's made me a very strong woman today. I'm able to hold my own because of it. When you're called every racist name in the book, there comes a point where either you get beaten up or you learn to fight. And I learned to fight.

University was a whole different ballgame, though. Because there were so many Asians there, I completely fit in. When I moved to Vancouver to go to school at UBC, it was like, "Why didn't I grow up in Vancouver?" If I had gone to high school in Vancouver I never would have had to deal with all the issues I did. It was because I was living in the suburbs that I had to deal with all these issues. In Vancouver, there were so many Asians. I met lots of Asian friends and I kind of found my niche, because I first hung out with the Korean group of students at UBC, which soon after I decided to stay away from because they were just too gossipy for me. The Korean community in Vancouver is very small —everyone knows each other—and so whatever you do, it reflects upon your parents. You can't take responsibility for your actions. As much as I wished I could take full responsibility for my actions, it was my parents who were getting the blame. If I did something wrong it would make my parents look bad, and I decided that the best way for me to avoid that was just for me not to have anything to do with Koreans, so I decided to just hang out with Caucasian friends.

To be quite honest, I've always been aware of the racial split between friends. I have Asian friends, but I can't relate to them. The only reason why I'm close to friends is because of communication, because we share the same language. For me, I have Korean friends that are Korean-Korean, but I feel that I can never get 100 percent close to them. They'll never be really, really close friends because I can't share that communication level with them where we can have in-depth conversations. I don't want to explain myself all the time, I can't be bothered, and I certainly don't have the patience. For me, language is very important, so it just happens that I have more Caucasian friends because of the language barrier.

Anyway, it was right after the 1988 Olympics, when I was 21 or

22, that I returned to Korea for the first time since my birth. It was a culture shock for me; I was blown away. We stayed at my cousin's place and I remember thinking to myself, "God, this place is so cosmetic. They're so vain. The women are so concerned with how they look, their clothes. They're so materialistic."

The second time I returned to Korea was in September 2002 because my boyfriend, whom I was living with in Hong Kong, switched investment banks and his company hired him for the Seoul location. He had offers from an investment bank that was based in Taipei, Taiwan and one that would have kept him in Hong Kong, and he asked me where I would like to live out of the three. I was tired of Hong Kong, so I said, "Let's go to Korea." I'm here basically because of my boyfriend and I've just made the most of it.

At this point, how much longer I stay here really depends on my relationship. This has been a very great cultural experience for me, just to see my heritage. I find it really cute, for instance, when Koreans, especially taxi drivers, get very impressed when they hear me speak Korean. My students freak out when I speak any Korean. It's almost like they put you on this pedestal because you can speak English so fluently, but yet you're Korean. I always look at them and say, "But you guys speak Korean so fluently and so well and how awesome would it be if I could speak as fluently as you!" And they say, "But you speak English." Okay, touché.

I can't say that I've ever experienced any racism here in Korea. However, I've had one type of prejudice, that I've dealt with twice now, on two different occasions, which kind of shocked me because it would never happen in North America. It had to do with the fact that I'm 35 years of age. I had one taxi driver comment on how old I was and the fact that I didn't have any children and that it was probably too late. I've been called *a-jum-ma* (아줌마)—middle-aged woman—a couple of times when they find out how old I am, which irritates me because to me this *a-jum-ma* stigma is an unfair comment. I may be 35 years of age, yet I don't feel old and I probably have a hell of a lot more energy than most 23-year-old Korean girls.

On the flip side, one of the real positive things that's happened to me since coming back to Korea has been my relationship with my parents. My parents got divorced when I was 21 years old and my mother later got remarried to an Irish guy. My father remarried Korean. I have a bit of an estranged relationship with my father, actually. He's very traditional, and part of the reason we're estranged is that we're too much alike—we're both very stubborn. A lot of it has to do with the fact that when I was growing up he was extremely strict. I understand why he did it, because he was raised that way, but a part of me psychologically cannot forgive him. There was a time I hated him for it; I grew up resenting him and rebelling against him. But now, when I look back in retrospect, I realize that he did it because he loved us and that was the only way he knew how to show us that he loved us, as twisted as that may sound. We don't see eye-to-eye, but at the same time I love my father. I would be there for him. When it was his sixtieth birthday, *hwan-kap* (환갑), I threw a huge party for him, which I paid for. I didn't have to do that. I'm Westernized, but because I'm the oldest child I did that. It put me back six grand, but I did it. I'll always be there for my father.

After all my experience here, if I were to give any advice to *kyopo* who have never been to Korea and are thinking of coming, I would advise them to come here after university so at least they can get a decent job. To live in Korea, I think you have to be happy in your career and what you're doing because otherwise it's a tough country to be happy in. I would also suggest for them to stay here for the two-year term because they are entitled to the F–4 visa; take advantage of it. Stay here for two years, make some money, and then go back and experience your culture and your heritage at the same time.

"... I feel most comfortable when I'm with other adoptees because we don't have to explain a lot of things. We share one thing together: we are different. And how different and why we're different, we don't have to talk about, because that's personal. I'm always going to see myself as an adoptee—not Swedish, not Korean, but as an adoptee—one group."

John Hamrin (37)
Sweden
Volunteer and Teacher
16 Months

John is an inspiration. He is an inspiration to adoptees returning to Korea, but he's also an inspiration to anyone searching for their roots. He, like many other adoptees, has had his world turned upside down over the years by new information about his past, but he has succeeded in making it work out for the better. Today, he assists other adoptees returning to Korea through G.O.A.'L. (Global Overseas Adoptees' Link).

I WAS BORN in Seoul in 1966. I also have three older siblings from my Korean family. My two older siblings were born outside of Busan (부산) and my younger brother was born in Seoul. I'm actually one of the few adoptees who has full names for grandparents from both sides, and also addresses and birth dates on everyone, so it was very easy to find everyone.

The reason we were given up was because our mother died ten days after my younger brother's birth—she had stomach cancer—after which our house burned to the ground. My father was standing there with a newborn child and no wife and no house, so he gave the three older siblings to relatives and me and my younger brother for adoption. I stayed at an adoption house in Hongjae (홍제) for eight months and eleven days. I think my brother was given up before me. We were promised to go to the same family, but we didn't, and I think he got adopted almost directly overseas to Sweden.

When I was eventually adopted, I got a younger sister, who's also adopted from Korea, but she's not my biological sister. I grew up with a sister that's four years younger than me. Ironically enough, my birth brother, who is also four years younger than me, grew up with an older sister who's about my age, so we both have siblings. We also had similar environments growing up—our parents are both academics, and we even have similar names.

In my case, though, I grew up in a very small fishing village where some of the sailors had actually been to Korea before. For them I was nothing strange, with my black hair and brown eyes. Everybody in our village of less than 300 people knew me, so I was a person with a name and not just a little boy from another country. Even when I started elementary school and middle school there were no problems because I knew my identity. My mom never put me in front of a mirror and said, "You're blonde and blue eyed." She said, "You are from Korea and that's why you have dark hair and brown eyes." I had a strong identity from the beginning. Even so, after six months in Sweden I forgot all my Korean.

Growing up in Sweden I always felt like an adoptee. I knew that I came from another place and that I was born in another place. I've seen myself as John my whole life. I didn't face any discrimination in Sweden growing up, more just curiosity. Sometimes I would hear people talking, so I would turn around and say, "If you're talking about me, please do it directly." Then they would get embarrassed or they would deny talking about me. Sometimes people told me, "Hey, go back to your home!" and I would say jokingly, "Actually, I'm on my way back to my village right now!"

One good thing is that I've always known about my family. When I was 18, my mother said, "Here are your adoption papers, so if you want, you can look through them and I can describe the adoption process and other things like that." I saw that I had a younger sibling, but I didn't know if it was a brother or sister—it only said "younger sibling."

Several years later, I made contact with an adoption center in Sweden and they contacted SWS, the adoption agency here in Korea that dealt with me. At first they sent a letter saying that I had a younger sister. Then they changed it because they made a mistake, and in fact, I had a younger brother. He was twenty at the time and serving his mandatory military time in Sweden, so I wrote a letter and made copies of all my adoption files so he could compare them against his own adoption papers. The letter was addressed to his adopted parents and I explained to them that I didn't want to interfere in their life, but this was an opportunity for him to get to know me if he wanted. Later I received a phone call from his adopted father and he asked me, "Have you considered everything? This can change a lot," and I said, "Yes, I have. That's why I waited so long." I could have contacted him earlier when he was 18 but I waited a little bit longer, to be sure for myself. Shortly after that I got a letter from my brother and that was very positive. You know, it's not everyday that you get a letter from a "new" younger brother. We had good contact from the very beginning, though. We met for the first time in 2001. We decided to meet at my place because I live by myself in an apartment so that would be kind of a neutral place—not my parents' place or his parents' place—and it turned out really well.

I myself decided to eventually come back to Korea because I had gotten in touch with my oldest brother here in Seoul. He called me up one night and, though I didn't understand any Korean at that time, I understood his name and my name, so after something like half a minute I pretended there was something wrong with the connection and hung up. Later on, he called again in the middle of the night and an interpreter on the phone asked, "Do you want to talk with your brother?" I said, "Okay." My brother then said, "Can you come to Korea tomorrow?"

"No.

"How about next week?"

"No."

"How about next month? I'll pay for the flight."

"No, but I'll come later."

After that, in May 1998, I came to Korea for one month. I had broken up with my girlfriend a year before that. She actually forced me to go to Korea in a way, so I'm very thankful for that. I decided to come and my brother paid for the flight. I wanted to see my biological family and get to know more about Korea.

A friend of mine who was living in Korea at the time came to meet me at the airport, with my biological family. There was not a lot of hugging or any crying. It was more like handshakes. It was like we were strangers, but we had something in common. My two older brothers were at the airport. I met my father later in the afternoon and then we went to my oldest brother's house.

My whole family was very open about the adoption. They were not trying to hide me from people. My three oldest siblings all grew up with different families—cousins or aunts or uncles. There was a clash between my oldest brother and my father, actually, because he said that it was wrong to give up his children. They ended up reconnecting again after my eldest brother had children, though. My oldest siblings always had a really hard time understanding why my father gave us up for adoption, and also them, of course.

That first trip when I returned to Korea, my first impressions of the country were that it was hot and humid and there were a lot of people. I wrote a diary every day, so I recall these things. My family laughed, but writing in my diary was the first thing I did directly after we had been out for the day, and that was good because now I remember things. If I hadn't done that I wouldn't have any memory of that time.

Later on, when I decided to return to Korea in 2002, I did so to help other adoptees and also to change my life. I had been working for eleven years in an elementary school as a recreation leader and teacher in Sweden. I had begun feeling that nothing was happening in my life. I had no girlfriend, no love, and I wanted to do something new. I took some of my savings and came here. I got in touch with my biological family and met some of the G.O.A.'L. staff in Norway at a conference. It was there when I made a promise that I would work for them. I arrived on March 1 and said, "Here I am. I've kept my promise."

I've been in constant contact with my birth family since

returning, but they complain that I should meet them more often. They respect me for who I am and what I am doing, but we get to see each other only about four times per year. I should add that I've never, ever, ever held my father responsible for giving me up for adoption, not even when I was in Sweden and didn't know anything about him or the fact that my mother died giving birth or that our house burned down, because what you think a lot about as an adoptee is if you caused anything that led to the adoption: "Could it have been my bad behavior, no love—whatever?" The more I got to know about my family, the more I became concerned about their feelings.

Since I've come back to Korea, though, my relationship with my adopted family has not changed. I think my mother was worried that I would give her up and find another set of parents, so I said to her in an e-mail once, "You'll always be my mom." Right after that e-mail, she felt less worried. Nowadays, I write to her about three times a week. She also understands that because I've been working with adoptees for so many years that it's important for me, that I'm giving something back to other adoptees out there, so she can understand that. Today, when I see a Caucasian person or a European, I want to help them out if I see that they're adopting a Korean child or going to adopt a Korean child. I go up to them and talk to them. I don't tell them that the child will come back here to Korea and get really messed in the head.

When it comes to my personality, I'm open to get to know native Koreans and be friends with them. I have some friends that I've made on my own, outside of the adoptees' network. However, I feel most comfortable when I'm with other adoptees because we don't have to explain a lot of things. We share one thing together: we are different. And how different and why we're different, we don't have to talk about, because that's personal. I'm always going to see myself as an adoptee—not Swedish, not Korean, but as an adoptee—one group. And I know a lot of other adoptees who feel the same way. I was born Korean and grew up in Sweden, but if you asked me, "Who are you?" I would say my province name because I spent most of my time there. Now that I live in Korea, though, I don't see myself as Korean or someone from Seoul. I'm a Swedish adoptee born Korean.

As a result, if I were to give advice to an adoptee coming back to Korea, first of all I would say, think about your life situation. What's the reason you want to come to Korea? Is it to search for your family? Is it to escape something? Wherever you go, you can never escape from that. You have to solve some part of it in your adopted country or the country you're living in. You'll also have to bring a lot of savings because you might not get a job in the first month or maybe not even the first three months. Don't come to Korea and think that you can get everything for free because you're an adoptee, because you've been suffering for such a long time, or whatever other reason. Whatever you do, though, don't change your personality.

What I would say to the younger people is get to meet more adoptees and listen to them. Talk with them and then maybe you'll better understand yourself. There are a lot of associations and organizations concerned with Korean adoptees in many countries, so start with that. As well, try and make contact with people before you come to Korea so you have some stability when you arrive.

Equally as important, I think it's necessary for both sides to give their version of why adoption still exists. One thing Koreans have to understand is why we're looking for our birth families. In a lot of adoptees' papers, in a lot of files, it says "unknown," but that's not true. There are so many fake papers out there that should be open. Also, many more native families are looking for the children they gave up for adoption or to relatives, so it goes both ways. Adoptees deserve to know why Korean society is still giving up babies.

"My parents and the people around me taught me to believe that I was lucky, unique . . . I was too busy feeling almost indebted—to the world in general, really—to have time to worry about group identity or fitting in."

Maya West (20)
America
Translator and Student
14 Years

The daughter of renowned translator Chun Kyung-ja (전경자), Maya is the future of Korean literary translation. And Korean literature is in good hands with someone as intelligent and well-read as Maya at the helm, directing the way in which people around the world will read Korean fiction in the coming years.

MY DAD WAS a consultant with a Korean law firm here and my mom was already working as a professor at the same university she's at today when I was born. I lived in Seoul until I was 12. I went to Korean schools from nursery school through first grade, but I ended up having to transfer because of some racial tension with some of the older kids. I was actually pretty popular with the other little kids in my grade because I was considered *shin-gi-hae* (신기해)—novel/unique—but I had to take the bus to and from school. The older kids on the bus were probably just bored, but they heckled me a bit and I had a really hard time with that. I was basically just too young to understand what was going on. They'd tell me to go back to America, but I'd only ever been there on vacation. I might have understood a fair amount of English but I certainly wasn't fluent, not back then. Even so, transferring to a foreign school wasn't my idea. My mom caught me crying a couple times and just decided enough was enough.

That's when I entered Seoul International School. They set me back a year, because of the different Korean school year, so I was in first grade again, but I caught back up eventually and skipped up to third grade, with kids my own age. I was there through sixth grade. Around then, my mom was offered a position at Harvard University as the director of East Asian Languages and Civilizations, and so my family moved to Lexington, Massachusetts.

All in all, I think I had a really great childhood. The vast majority of my experiences while growing up here in Seoul were positive. There was a relatively large foreign community in my neighborhood, at least, compared to other parts of Seoul in those days, so I wasn't that unusual. It was a friendly neighborhood overall, and I got a lot of compliments on my curly hair and on how good my Korean was—it didn't occur to anyone that Korean might just be my first language. I think the discrepancy between my looks and my Korean ability made a lot of things easier for me —people wanted to know me and talk to me, so it was easier to make friends, whether it was in school or with shopkeepers. They loved the fact that there was no language barrier. Actually, that's pretty much the same even today.

With my parents, I had a really unique relationship. It was never really them and me; each of us had separate relationships with the other two. I had a great relationship with both of them and I never thought about the fact that one of them was Korean and the other American as being strange, just different or special. As a child, I never really mulled over the fact that I was bi-racial—there was no identity crisis. If anything, my identity was that much more firmly set than it might have been otherwise. My parents and the people around me taught me to believe that I was lucky, unique. Living in Korea and speaking English and Korean gets you an amazing amount of positive feedback from just about everyone you come into contact with. And, above all, my parents raised me in an environment full of advantages. That was always at the forefront of my mind. I was too busy feeling almost indebted—to the world in general, really—to have time to worry about group identity or fitting in.

Ultimately, it might have made a difference that my mom and dad didn't have any trouble communicating with each other—being bi-racial could have been more of an issue for me if my mom's English was poor and my dad's Korean was lacking. I know some people in my situation who have always had to act as the bridge between their parents, but I was spared that experience. It wasn't until I moved to America that I actually started to identify myself as half Korean.

Moving to America was definitely a big change in that respect. For one thing, I could go out in public without people turning around to stare at me. I didn't stand out in a crowd anymore, and for a little while, that feeling was almost intoxicating. At the same time, though, I began to feel my Korean-ness a lot more. It's strange, actually. Somehow my mom being Asian stuck out more in Lexington, Massachusetts than my dad being American in Seoul ever did. When I went to boarding school in the States, speaking Korean with my mom on the phone would draw much more attention than speaking English in Korea had ever done. In Korea, everyone expected me to speak English because I look Caucasian, whereas in the States, the Korean part of me came as a complete surprise to everyone.

The language stuff aside, my first few months and years in America were pretty surreal. To me, life in America seemed like I'd walked into some sort of movie. Scenes from American suburbia that I'd watched on my Korean TV set were suddenly my reality. On top of all that, I underwent a sort of passive culture shock: I could speak English fine, but I had huge gaps in my familiarity with American culture. I had no idea what people were talking about when they made pop culture references that American kids take for granted. "Snoop Doggy Dog? MTV? What's that?" I would say. The only musical group I knew at that point was the Beatles, because of my dad. When it comes right down to it, I basically missed the entirety of the eighties—not that that's necessarily a bad thing, from what I gather. And in the early nineties, just as Rap was getting really big, I felt so far behind. I just had no background at all. I actually remember watching TV in a conscious effort to catch up on my pop culture know-how.

It was the same thing with slang. I still remember the first time I realized that "cool" meant something other than not quite cold. I was nine or so, and I didn't even let on that I hadn't known its meaning before. That's how I learned most of my slang—hearing people say it in passing and making a mental note of it. There was a ton of *noon-chi* (눈치)—sly common sense—involved in the whole process.

Despite these little hiccups, though, I would say that I really embraced "Americana" with a vengeance during those years in Lexington. I think everyone tries to create a persona for him or herself when they're in middle and high school, and for a while I pushed my Korean half aside and just tried to be as typically American as I could. The social structure of American high school life is really fascinating, and I loved being a part of it. I was completely immersed in that existence—going to the mall on weekends and worrying about prom dates—when my dad suddenly passed away while he was on a business trip back here in Korea. I was fifteen.

Coming back to Seoul for my dad's funeral was the first time I'd returned after we moved to America, not that it was much of a homecoming. After that, my mom moved back to Korea and I transferred to a boarding school called Phillips Exeter Academy in New Hampshire because I wanted to finish high school in the States. My father's passing and the two years I spent at Exeter following it—that period in my life made me who I am today. At that point, my priorities shifted. I became less interested in creating a persona for myself and more interested in just letting myself be me.

While I was at boarding school, I would come back to Seoul to visit my mom over the summer and winter vacations. That's when I really started to rediscover Seoul and remember how familiar Korea felt. Since then, I've chosen to spend more and more time in Korea. In 2002, after I finished my freshman year at university, I decided to take some time off school so that I could spend a longer stretch of time here in Seoul and really get back in touch with Korean life.

On a more personal note, another major reason I decided to take time off school has to do with the change in my priorities that came after my dad's death. It really made me realize that the future isn't something you should necessarily depend on—or in other words, I felt like I needed to recognize and appreciate and get the most out of the things that were most important to me while I still could. Right now, spending time with my mom while I still can is the most important thing in my life, and she's here in Korea. Every time I got on a plane to go back to school I would think about how I was going thousands of miles away, just to take some classes and eventually get a piece of paper that would make strangers think well of me and my so-called intellect. And all that when I could just spend what time I have with the people who are really important to me instead. The whole notion just struck me as both foolish and frightening.

My dad and I were incredibly close, but after he passed away my mom and I grew closer and closer, too. These days she is as big an influence on my daily life as my dad once was. I've been living in Korea as an adult now for about two years, and Korean people that I come into contact with day to day usually assume that I'm a tourist or an English teacher here for a year or two. After a great deal of trial and error, I've discovered that the easiest way to explain my heritage and my reason for being in Korea is to just say, "My mother is Korean." So, I'm constantly being reminded of my Korean half.

When I first started translating, this whole West-meets-East thing came to a head. My mom has been a well-established translator for as long as I can remember, but it never even occurred to me that I might follow in her footsteps, as it were. I always thought that I would be an English Literature major, and my dream was to write. It still is, really. I sort of fell into the translation field when my mom got this notice from LTI Korea (Korean Literature Translation Institute) about a competition for first-time translators. She suggested that I give it a try, especially since we both agreed that I should work on my Korean writing and reading, so I picked a short story and I translated it and sent it in. The short story I ended up selecting was written by Lee Man-kyo (이만교). I chose it because of its interesting format—prose written in verse form—and because I thought he captured the tone of the female main character's inner monologue remarkably well. It was interesting and very challenging to translate—and I was amazed at how much of a learning process it really was. Winning the award really shaped the rest of my time here a great deal. People gained confidence in my abilities and I started working quite a bit, on all kinds of different translation projects. Right now I have two novels and a book of poetry in progress, as well as another couple of novels waiting in the wings. It's difficult work, but I find it incredibly rewarding, not to mention educational.

"... I'm okay with being called a foreigner because I'm not Korean. I understand that now. I may have Korean blood and heritage, but culturally I'm not. To be Korean is to be Korean—there's no black or white about it."

Monica Montero Lim (25)
Spain
Student
4 Months

Over the course of three trips, Monica has spent a total of nearly four months in Korea. Inspired by stories her grandmother used to tell her, she originally returned to explore her roots, but now finds herself studying the Korean language full-time, learning about things she had never considered before arriving in Korea.

I WAS BORN in New York to a Spanish father and a Korean mother. I lived in New York until I was 18. I always spoke in Spanish with my dad growing up. With my mom, I spoke in Korean as a little girl. In fact, I didn't know how to speak English when I went to preschool, which was a problem. From then on I spoke with my mom in English, and forgot all my Korean.

We moved to Spain when I was 18, against my will, but my dad really wanted to and my mom was into it. Since then, I've lived and studied in Spain. I've always been interested in my Korean roots, as it was really difficult to find out about them. My father being Spanish and having closer ties with Spain than my mom does with Korea meant that I spent all my summers in Spain. With the Korean side of my family, because of the politics on the peninsula when they were living here, they were dispersed. When someone tells you twenty percent of a story, you want to find out about the remaining eighty percent, so I've always been interested in Korea for that reason.

My mom was raised by very strict parents and she was never fully comfortable with that. She wanted our relationship to be more open. Today we're actually each other's best friends. She knows everything about me. I don't think our situation is that common in Korea. Most Koreans hide a lot from their parents, I think. Sometimes we may have to repeat ourselves, but it's not awkward or anything like that. My mother's English is quite good because she lived in Hong Kong. It's inconvenient at times, I guess. For example, if I'm talking with them and I realize that what I have to say is more important for my dad to hear, then I'll say it in Spanish; if it's a priority that my mom understands, then I'll say it in English; if it's important that they both know what I'm talking about then I just have to make sure I get my point across.

Personally, identity was a major issue for me growing up. When I was a little girl living in New York, I was American. When people would asked me, "What are you?" I would tell them I was American. It was easy. When I got to college in Spain, everyone was Spanish. I felt American, but also Spanish and Korean. When I moved to Spain, I switched to Spanish. As a little girl, I'd go to Korean houses and feel comfortable taking my shoes off and bowing, for example. Yet when I moved to Spain I had an identity crisis. By the time I was in college I'd call my mom up and ask, "What am I?" She tried to calm me down, explaining that I was

American. I said, "Yeah, but I'm also this, this, and that!" and she replied, "Don't worry about it." Then I took a course at college on multicultural literature and I was exposed to authors that were just as whacked as I was, and I realized I wasn't alone. After that course, I stopped crying. That helped me a lot vis-à-vis understanding who I am.

I never had any guilt or anything about being Eurasian, because I grew up in New York, and I'm normality there. I don't know what it's like to live in other parts of the States, but in New York it's a given that you're American. You eat, sleep and breathe America. New Yorkers are always curious of where you come from. People in New York aren't afraid of their ethnicity or how mixed their blood may be, so I would say confidently that I was Spanish and Korean. The only issue that concerned me was that people would assume I meant Puerto Rican or somewhere in Latin America and I'd say, "No, no, Europe!"

When I came back to Korea in the summer of 2002 the trip was completely orchestrated by me; it wasn't my mom or my Korean family. I was studying Korean in Pamplona and the town is so small and no one spoke Korean there, so it made my studying all the more difficult. I arrived in Suwon (수원) and spent two weeks there, which was a really good introduction to Korea for me, as I went to different places from there and met some of my family for the first time with my mom, who was here because I knew she wanted to come. It was a great first experience.

I had no expectations before I came here. The impression of Korea that my mom had imprinted onto me was that it was a very austere, patriarchal place: you must respect your elders and don't dare to eat, drink, laugh, or cry in front of them. That may still be true, but not to the extent that my mom had prepared me for. So, when I saw that young people here were normal—they wore short skirts and dyed their hair like anywhere else—that was a fun discovery.

I think what caught my attention the most was Korea's hospitality. It was overwhelming and actually uncomfortable. I didn't know how to take it because I'm partly Korean. When I was in New York, I'd go to get a manicure at a Korean nail salon, and if I'd say two or three words in Korean all the ladies in the shop would run over and treat me like a queen. If I hadn't said anything, they'd have treated me like anyone else. The fact that I'm partly Korean had everything to do with it.

Later on, the second time I came back to Korea, I was killing two birds with one stone. I'm interested in diplomacy and international relations, and so I did an internship at the Ministry of Foreign Affairs and Trade. It was a perfect opportunity for me. The other thing is that I was in Asia, more importantly, Korea. I know America and I know Europe, but not Asia. So, personally it was important, and professionally, I was gaining experience in Asia, especially for a country like Spain, and Europe for that matter. Their involvement is still in its infancy in this part of the world.

That second time back it was okay. I found that it was easier to get used to living here than it was getting used to living in Barcelona. When I first went to Barcelona to work I still wasn't integrated after working there for four months. It was more difficult to make friends. People in Barcelona weren't worried about whether you were going out to lunch alone, for example. They weren't worried about whether you had friends. They'd ask you, but in a very Western way. They might say, "Oh that's good for you. I hope you make friends." Here, it was the opposite. The first day at the ministry, a top official and his colleagues took me out to lunch, which was really sweet because I was just this rinky-dinky intern working here for three months. They treated me so well and I didn't expect that. If I was cold, they'd give me their coat. I didn't ask for a cell phone but they gave me one anyway. It was these small things that meant the world to me, so it was much easier getting comfortable living in Seoul than in Barcelona. Koreans show true, genuine concern for your well-being. The thing is, once it's your turn to return the favor, you should appear as overwhelmingly kind; kindness, but with a modicum of self-interest. They expect the same from you. When I go back to Spain, even now, people are normal and kind, but not that kind.

Anyway, the third time I came back to Korea I returned because I have a to-do list for my life, and one item was to live in Asia and another was to learn Korean more, which is why I'm studying Korean at Yonsei University (연세대학교) now. I never felt pressure to learn Korean just because I'm half Korean, which is why I can compare myself to other people in my program. I think the fact that I don't look Korean is a blessing because people don't have the same expectations. If you're a foreigner here, nobody expects anything of you. There's nothing written about how you're supposed to act or what you should say, and that's wonderful because it's total freedom. If you look Korean, of course, you won't have that same freedom. Some of my classmates complain in class that their families are so impatient with their progress with the language, thinking that their progress is a failure. For me, I don't have any kind of pressure like that and I think my learning the language isn't viewed as a necessity but more so a bonus. When I tell Koreans that I'm half Korean and I came to study my roots, they just start to cry.

More than just studying Korean, though, I'm also volunteering at Korean orphanages. I realized that my chance in life to experience those two things was right now. I didn't have to give up a very important job; I wasn't leaving a boyfriend; I don't have a husband and kids; my parents are both healthy—I have no reason not to do this now! I'm not sure how much longer I'll be here, though. I came here with the idea that I'd be here for three months this time, but if I find something interesting to do here I'd love to stay. Yet if I was ever to work in Korea over a long period of time I don't know how I'd do it because I don't like the way that Koreans work. This is definitely my Spanish-ness influencing me, but I don't think your job should dominate your life. In Spain it's so different. You have your life and you have your work, but you work to live, not live to work. In Korea, free time is a waste and happiness is equal to how busy you are. For my Korean class at Yonsei, I once studied this conversation:

"Mr. Kim, where is your wife?"

"She's on vacation with our child."

"Why aren't you?"

"Well, I'm very busy at work and I take English classes at night; I'm too busy to go."

Now, the next sentence, instead of saying, "Oh, I'm sorry to hear that," said: "Wow, you're such a hard worker. I'm so envious of you."

I couldn't believe it! I mean, you live seven decades on earth to want to work like this and not spend time with your wife and child, Mr. Kim? Come on! You have a wife, you have a kid, and when you die, what's going to be more important? The honor of having worked so hard? I don't want to sacrifice my life for work. I want a job, yes, but I don't think it should take away that much from your family.

When I was here doing the internship I started to look around me and I thought it was so sad to work that way. If I had to do that, I could maybe do it for a year or two but I know I don't share that mentality. I sympathize with the Spanish way of living. After five years of living in Spain, I'm more European that way.

On the other hand, in some instances I really feel Korean. I'm really different from my friends in the West, both from New York and from Spain, for instance, in the way that I look at older people. I've always been more affectionate to seniors, more understanding, whereas my Western friends tended to make fun of them. I could never understand that. Also—and this point has been crucial in my life—when I was told as a child not to do something I would always obey my parents, whereas my friends would chide me, and attempt to persuade me that it was okay to disobey my parents because they'd never find out. My feeling was that I was aware of that possibility, but if my mom asked me not to do something I wouldn't do it. Now I realize that my choice of obedience has always come from my instinct to respect my elders. And in Spain or New York, believe me, that doesn't exist.

To be sure, when Koreans call me a "foreigner" I'm cool with that. When I was here for my first visit last year, I think I was hoping that I'd be thought of as at least partly Korean; I was hoping that people would recognize the Korean in me. But after living here for four months I'm okay with being called a foreigner because I'm not Korean. I understand that now. I may have Korean blood and heritage, but culturally I'm not. To be Korean is to be Korean—there's no black or white about it. It's a society that's so old and set. Thought and behavioral patterns are very clearly defined: the way people date in Korea, the way people work in Korea. It's not how I would like to live my life. I realize I'm a foreigner, but I am tied to Korea in some way.

In terms of advice, I'm not sure telling someone they should return to Korea or not is a subject you can advise someone on. I can, however, warn people who come from Korean parents to Korea for the first time that much is expected of you, as opposed to someone with mixed blood like me, for example. I find it strange that people with the same blood get treated worse than the rest of us. At the same time, I find it really interesting that Koreans are moved by their emotions, as opposed to the other cultures I've been exposed to. In these other cultures, I think most people are moved by ambition or material interests, such as money. In Korea, it's different. I think Koreans will forego their own benefit if something moves them emotionally. If you touch a Korean's heart, they'll move the world for you. It amazes me how Koreans are moved by emotions like love and hate—and they love to cry!

"My thinking is still almost completely Japanese, yet my heart is Korean."

Son Sang-kyun 손상균 (24)
Korea
University Student
4½ Years

Japanese Koreans, or jae-il kyo-po *(재일교포) as they're known in Korean, are one of the most misunderstood mixed ethnic groups in Korea, if only because of the two countries' violent history. Sang-kyun, born of a Japanese Korean father and a Korean mother, grew up in Japan his whole life before coming to live in Korea for university, an experience that has helped change his views on many things.*

MY MOTHER was looking to get married, as was my father, so my mother's cousin introduced my parents to each other about thirty years ago. My mother is from Seoul and my father is from Chiba, Japan. My mother was a high school teacher at that time and shortly after getting married she got pregnant and had my sister, my only sibling. My father, a Korean Japanese man with a Korean passport, had his own transport business. My grandfather had moved to Japan at a time when many Koreans were doing so—during the Japanese occupation of the Korean peninsula—so I'm the third generation to grow up in Japan.

When my father was growing up in Japan, it was very hard for him—much different from when I grew up in Japan—so he used to get into fights with other Japanese kids sometimes. When he was trying to get a job later on in life, people would occasionally tell him that they couldn't give him the job because he was Korean. There was racism like that in the workforce back then. For my generation, though—and especially in my case—I experienced very little discrimination, and so I had no trouble growing up. In fact, I had many Japanese friends when I was younger, and was very active as a child. The truth is that Japan has changed so much since my father's childhood. It's become a lot more international, a lot more globalized.

My first language was Japanese and Korean was my second language. As a child, I felt much more comfortable in Japanese. I could understand some Korean words, but I couldn't speak Korean. When I was in high school, I used to go to a Korean school, a Korean *min-dan* (민단) that was set up for the Korean community in Japan. I went there once a week and learned the Korean language. I learned how to read, write, and speak Korean there. Fortunately, though, I could use Japanese at home because my mother's Japanese is so good that it's like a native speaker's. Yet even though my mother could speak Japanese, it was a little bit hard on me as a kid because she always acted like a native Korean. So sometimes I couldn't understand the way she behaved and her habits and her education. That was difficult for me because my mother was always saying, "You have to do this and you have to do that!" something Korean mothers do a lot, not Japanese mothers. She even hit me sometimes!

When I was younger, I always considered myself Korean. People like me are foreigners in Japan, but we're special foreigners;

we're different from regular foreigners, *gaijin* (Japanese for "foreigner"). For example, I never had a Japanese name, even though I grew up in Japan, and so I always said, "I'm Son Sang-kyun and I'm Korean." You have to understand that the relationship between Japan and Korea is very special. If I was born in America, for example, I'd be American. But because there is a special relationship between Japan and Korea, I'm a little different. Many Japanese Koreans think that they're kids are Korean so they don't give their kids Japanese names or Japanese citizenship. I could get Japanese citizenship if I wanted to, but I've chosen not to. It's not that I want to keep my Korean citizenship; it's more that I don't need to change it to Japanese for any particular reason. Japanese Koreans have very strong feelings about remaining Korean. For me, it was because of my parents, and the fact that I was ethnically Korean. For example, when I was younger I performed ancestral rites, *jae-sa* (제사), and the family memorial services, *cha-rae* (차례), every *Sollal* (설날)—Lunar New Year.

Nowadays, even though there are a lot of Japanese Koreans in Japan, they're not necessarily close with one another. It wasn't until high school, for instance, that I made my first Japanese Korean friend, and even then I wouldn't say we were close just because were both Japanese Koreans; I never felt closer to him because of our ethnicities. Although you have two kinds of Japanese Koreans, technically—those like me whose parents grew up in the country but are ethnically Korean, and those that have one parent that is ethnically Japanese—we're both just *jae-il kyo-po* (제일교포), and so there's no difference in my opinion.

Truth be told, though, growing up as a Japanese Korean in Japan, I did face some prejudice. One time, for example, I was applying for a job by phone and they asked me if I could start from that very day. I said that was no problem and he said, "Great. What's your name by the way?" I told him my name and then he said, "Your last name's Son? Are you Chinese?" I told him I was Korean to which he then said, "Oh, I'm sorry. Our company only hires Japanese people." I tried to tell him that I was Korean Japanese, but he wasn't listening by that point. From that time on, I used a Japanese name when applying for jobs. I didn't have a Japanese name, though, so I used my father's surname, Ishigane, and I converted my name from Chinese characters to the Japanese pronunciation, not from Korean as they usually are, and so my name became Ishigane Shoking, from Son Sang-kyun.

Unfortunately, I think I'll continue to face some problems in the future. I feel Korean Japanese, separate from Korean and separate from Japanese. I'm very different from native Koreans in my habits and language. For instance, Koreans are extremely conservative whereas I'm not. When I first came to Korea four and a half years ago, I would shake people's hand with one hand. I did that until my sister told me that was wrong and said I had to shakes people's hands with both hands. Also, I used to use a lot more *ban-mal* (반말) —informal speech—with Koreans when I spoke until people told me I should use *jon-dae-mal* (존대말)—formal speech—when talking with strangers or older people.

The whole reason I came to Korea in the first place, actually, was because my sister was going to a Korean university and I heard so many stories from her that I thought it a really good idea to come here. That wasn't my first time to Korea, however. When I was younger I'd come to Korea every year for around a month. When I visited Korea on those trips growing up, I thought it was a developing country. Many Japanese people think that Japan is number one and that Korea and China are developing countries.

They think European countries are industrial and everything, but Japan is still the best. I thought the same way at that age. My thinking is still almost completely Japanese, yet my heart is Korean.

Anyway, I came to Seoul four and half years ago and had to study for one full year to take the university entrance examination. When I first got here, my Korean was not fluent; at best, it was so-so. I could understand most of what Koreans said to me, but I couldn't speak very well. Studying for the entrance exam was tough, as a result. However, after studying day after day my Korean improved a lot. Still, when I took the entrance exam, which consisted of three parts—math, English, and Korean—it was really hard. The English was fine, the math was fine, but when I got to the Korean section ... Wow! It was really hard.

Thankfully, since starting university I've started to feel more comfortable with the language here. At first, it was so hard understanding any of the lectures in Korean, but now it's much better—but still hard. The problem is not Korean necessarily. Business is fine, for example, yet something like politics is so hard for me because it's not just the language but the history and the specific knowledge associated with the subject. I don't know a lot about Korean history, so that's a problem for me.

Four and a half years ago, students at my university were really surprised when I spoke Korean, making me really feel like a foreigner. Now, however, people don't usually make a big deal of the fact that I'm Japanese Korean. I do, however, still have trouble with my pronunciation and accent. People double-take with me all the time. "What was that you said?" they ask me. I'll say my name, Son Sang-kyun, and Koreans will ask me, "What was that? Song? Sun? Seong?" The Japanese pronunciation of my name is very similar to Korean, but still Koreans can't understand it most of the time. My alien registration card is also a little different from other foreigners. Koreans have one ID card and foreigners have another, but Japanese Koreans have another ID card altogether called *jae-wae-koong-min-deung-nok-jeung* (재외국민등록증), which has your birth date as the first six digits, and then 1000000. So, if I buy something like a cell phone, I need to show my passport, unlike Koreans who just show their regular ID card.

Right now, my plan is not to stay in Korea once I graduate university. I'm going to move back to Japan. If I don't move back to Japan I'll have to serve the mandatory 24 months in the military here in Korea. At present I'm a student, a kind of exchange student, so I'm exempt from serving in the military. However, if I stayed in Korea after graduation I'd have to go to the military, and I don't want to do that.

Essentially, the reason I'm studying here in Korea is because I think Japanese universities are not difficult to graduate from. Many people don't study hard in Japan and I thought that if I came to Korea I would not only get a university education, but I'd learn a language as well as every other good part of going to a Korean university. Also, if I went to a Japanese university, I think it would have been really tough for me to get a good job right out of school, because I'm not Japanese.

I've learned a lot about soccer while I've been in Korea, too. Four years ago, I rooted for Japan because I knew a lot about Japanese soccer players. I didn't know much about Korean soccer players at the time and so I wanted Japan to win. These days, though, I don't know much about Japanese soccer players anymore and know a lot more about Korean soccer players. During the 2002 World Cup I was so happy because Korea did well; my favorite player was Cha Doo-ri (차두리)!

"I think my relationship with my mother is now the best we've ever had it because she's become more American and I've become more Korean."

Susan MacDonald (31)
America
TV Personality, Cross-Cultural Awareness Lecturer, and Interpreter
12 Years

Born in Virginia of a Scottish-American father and a Korean mother, Susan spent part of her childhood growing up in Korea before moving back to the United States to continue her education. Fluent in both English and Korean, she is truly rare in that she understands both cultures and languages on an intimate level.

I'VE BEEN IN Korea exactly twice. I was in Korea from when I was four and a half to nine years old, and the second time was after graduating from university and coming to Korea in November 1995. I've been here since then. As far as my language speaking abilities are concerned, to my recollection, I spoke English first, but I believe my mother spoke Korean to me as a baby because that was her stronger language. My parents were both bilingual, my mother's Korean being stronger and my father's English being stronger. My mother spoke Korean to me, but in the house with my father we always spoke English. When I came home from school as a child I would speak to our maid in Korean. All the kids I played with were Korean, too. I'm an only child so I didn't have any siblings to speak with in English.

Since I had gone to an American school in Korea, my parents didn't think that it was going to be a big change when we moved back to the States. But in fact, it was a big culture shock because in Korea at that time there were few Americans going to the American school. There were maybe 10–15 kids per class, and half of them were foreign. As far as American culture, I didn't know what McDonald's was and I didn't know what curse words were. There was really no AFN (American Forces Network) in Korea at the time, and I think Beta videos were really popular then, so I watched a lot of videos with my father and mother. Other than that, I just really learned American culture from my parents and through my Korean American cousins, who were more American than I was then.

When I was young, I don't think it really occurred to me that my mother and father were different from each other ethnically, because for someone who comes from a bi-racial background that's their norm. You realize that your mother's English is not as perfect as your father's, but it's just something that you learn to accept. It's not something that I really thought of. I think in many bi-racial marriages there are certain cultural differences. Culturally, I think my father made more of an effort to assimilate. I think my father was very Korean in the sense that he respected my mother's family, maybe even more than his, and really put them up on a pedestal. He was a really great son-in-law to them.

There were, however, two incidents in my life when I realized that my experience was maybe not the norm. The first experience was when I came to Korea right after my first year of college, when I was an intern at Samsung. Someone at the program said to me, "Wow, you're half and half. You must have had a really tough life."

I looked at her and replied, "What the heck are you talking about? Why would you assume that I had a hard life because I'm mixed?"

"Well, all the friends that I knew who were mixed, they've had really rough backgrounds. One, because their father was in the military, enlisted, and their parents got divorced, or two, they mainly had parental problems, so the kids went in a bad direction," she said.

"Well, I don't know about other people, but I've had a really good upbringing."

"Have you had any problems here in Korea?" she then asked.

"Actually, no," I answered.

"Well, a lot of Koreans, they don't like *I-nohkohs*," *I-nohkohs* meaning half and half, but a Japanese way of saying it.

"Anyway, I never had any problems."

Personally, I never experienced any racism until high school prom came along. My mother never let me date anyone, so I never really had a boyfriend. But I did hear from my best friend growing up in school that someone that we mutually knew said to the guy I was going to prom with, "Why are you going with Susan? She's Asian, or part Asian." The guy then answered, "Well, we like each other so we're going to go together." I had no idea that anyone had even considered me anything other than just American. And so when my friend told this to me, I thought, "Who could possibly say this?" That made me feel sad for that person. I never felt bad about me because I always felt privileged to have both cultures. In a strange way, I tried to tell myself not to become too arrogant with the fact that I had two cultures to draw from, because I always felt like, "Wow I'm so lucky—I have a Korean and an American-Scottish background to draw from: two great families on both sides." I had both languages, whereas other people only had one. Honestly, I never felt like it wasn't anything but a privilege.

Anyway, the year before I graduated in 1995, I thought that Asia was really opening up. My concentrations in political science studies were North Korea, South Korea, Japan, and China, so I wanted to be here. It turned out I knew someone from my alma mater, Columbia, who was living in Seoul at the time, so I told him my situation and that I was looking for something. I came here for an interview with an investment bank, a joint venture, and never left.

I started working as a junior equity analyst and editor. I was there for a year and a half. Although I came to Korea for work, the other reason was to get the "Asian experience" because I wanted a challenge. I wanted to see how tough I was, and I knew that coming here as an adult, without as great a set up as when my parents were here, would be an experience. I also wanted to do some charity work in Korea in hopes of later, with reunification, being able to do something in North Korea.

Coming here was a big adjustment. Korea in '95, as developed as it was then, didn't have everything that it does now. With the language there was no problem, except I didn't speak the Seoul dialect, I spoke the Busan (부산) sa-too-ree (사투리)—dialect—first of all, and second of all, I spoke like a kid, even though I was 23. Something else that actually happened to me all the time was when someone who could barely speak English would insist on using their English with me, even when they knew full well that I could speak perfect Korean. Most of the time I didn't get angry, but I got very annoyed and I would use Korean and continue to speak Korean. Usually, if it was just a one-on-one thing, I knew that they would use Korean, but if there were other people there, they were just trying to impress their boss or their friend or their girlfriend or someone else, for example, and I felt it was offensive to use me as a way to promote themselves. I usually didn't say anything unless it really happened so often that it was just unbearable to be with them, which happened once or twice. That's where I would say, "Listen, when we're in your country why can't we speak your language?"

Anyhow, after arriving in Korea in 1995, I lived with a friend for the first four months I was here before moving out on my own. Now, even though I had my own friends and friends of my parents here, I still experienced a little loneliness those first few months in Korea. I didn't really want to go to those people with my problems because it seemed they had bigger problems to deal with. One such problem, for example, was dealing with Korean men. Although we were in a foreign investment banking-house, most of the people were educated in Korea and Korean through-and-through, just with nice pin-striped shirts and suits. I had to deal with a lot of problems on both ends. I don't want to say it was racism, because I never really felt that they didn't like me because I was American or mixed, yet I did feel the ageism because I was younger than they were. I knew I was talented, and maybe pointed out some things that I shouldn't have as a young person to an older person, not understanding the hierarchal situation—pointing out Korean men's weaknesses is a big no-no for a young, aspiring analyst.

As far as dating is concerned, I used to say that ethnic background didn't matter when looking for a partner—who this person was, what background he came from—and to some extent it still doesn't matter. However, because of my varied experiences, to find someone who could understand me may not be as easy. To give you an example, most Korean men do not like a woman who has traveled more than they have, who is more educated than they are, who is independent, who is more liberal in her views, who's patriotic and yet critical and is a multi-colored person. I think most Korean men traditionally have a problem with that, even for people who are Korean American, unless they've only lived in the States. So, that would seem to exclude those who are just pure, native Koreans, because I can't see myself as a sit-at-home wife who makes my husband's meals and takes care of the kids, because that's just not me.

Coming back to Korea has, I believe, also changed my relationship with my mother. I think my relationship with my mother is now the best we've ever had it because she's become more American and I've become more Korean. One of my personal reasons for coming to Korea was to indeed understand my family and my, what I sometimes considered "crazy," mother. In high school there were so many restrictions she put on me that naturally I felt that she was restricting my freedom, as does any teenager whose parent is a good parent. Yet being young, and thinking that you know everything when you're 15, you don't really think like that.

When I used to listen to rap music as a teenager, for instance, she would ask me to turn it down, and maybe not so nicely. However, when I came to Korea she was listening to Run DMC on her own and enjoying it—singing along even! She loves that stuff now. Aside from those things, though, I've seen a lot of my Korean girlfriends deal with their mothers and, just seeing how they are with their parents and how they are with each other, I see why my mom was the way that she was, and my mom can understood me. I think it's that mutual understanding. I realized my mom wasn't being too overprotective; that's just how Korean moms are, or that's just how moms are, I guess. Part of it, I think, comes with maturity. But part of it, I think, is her and my simultaneous experiences away from each other in our non-native homelands, so that we've grown to care and understand each other's situations better. I think that it's a really beautiful thing for me to understand her more because I do appreciate her more.

    I should add, though, that even though I've been living here for quite some time, I still consider myself first and foremost an American. The word "American" encompasses so much, really. It encompasses all kinds of races, creeds, backgrounds, and religions, so being an American enables me to have a very strong Korean culture within me. On the opposite end, I don't think that I would ever consider myself Korean, partly because, though I've mastered the Korean language and though I even teach classes on cultural awareness and understanding, and all of that, the Koreans themselves don't embrace anyone else who doesn't have pure Korean blood. Because Koreans themselves determine what is Korean—and they have full right to, I guess—I can never be Korean. So, because I'm aware of that, I wouldn't ever consider myself Korean.

"I was always proud to be Korean."

Toney Dong Yul Shin (34)
America
English Teacher
8 Years

Toney was born in Korea, but spent only three years in his birth land before moving to Los Angeles with his family. Growing up in a rough area, Toney admits to struggling through much of his youth. He returned to Korea in 1993 to work at the Daejeon (대전) Expo for a short time, and the country left a lasting impression on him. Two years later he returned to teach English, eventually marrying a Korean national with whom he now has two children.

I THINK IT was American movies that made my parents move to the United States. Seeing what America was like, my father wanted to go. He hated Korea. At that time, in the fifties and sixties, Korea was very poor and America was the land of the free, opportunity, and hope. My father explained to the family that he was moving to America to give us more opportunity for a better education. He didn't like the institutions in place in Korea either. At the time he left, Korea was being led by a dictator, freedom was repressed and all the politicians were corrupt. Compared to the Korean system, America seemed like a dream.

When I was growing up, I used Korean at home but we spoke English outside. My parents wanted me to learn Korean, so they made it a rule to speak Korean at home because my Korean was pretty bad. My family life in general was very strict. My father was a very rigid man and a very strict disciplinarian, so it was very difficult, actually. It was like being raised in a free country, but in a prison environment with no freedom. I didn't like that environment so there were a lot of problems between me and my parents. In many ways, it was a real culture clash. I had a lot of difficulty adjusting because all my friends had a lot of freedom. For example, they could stay out late but I had to go straight home and be in bed by nine. I couldn't watch TV, I had to come home, do my homework, and I was really upset about that. I used to find myself lying a lot to my parents and tricking them so I could have some freedom. It was also shocking because some of my friends in high school smoked cigarettes in front of their parents or they'd cuss at their mom. I found those things really shocking because Koreans can't smoke in front of their parents, nor can they cuss or use foul language in front of them, let alone at them. So it was shocking to see those different types of attitudes.

I guess I had a chip on my shoulder as a result. It just seemed that when I was younger everyone else around me had so much freedom and I didn't. I liked sports, for example, and my father was dead-set against me playing any sports. My father was an athlete in Korea and if you're an athlete in Korea, you don't have any choices. They just force you down one path and you don't get any education. He was afraid that might happen to me, so he didn't let me play any sports at all.

As I was growing up, I got hit up a lot by gangsters and they'd say, "Where're you from?" and I'd say, "Korea. I'm from Korea, man." People would laugh at that. They just thought it was funny, because most people claimed to be from a neighborhood. Actually, if a gangster hits you up and you're not from a gang, most would say, "I'm from nowhere." I didn't like saying I was from nowhere so I'd say, "I'm from Korea, man. What's up? Where are you from?" All the gangsters respected me for that, thinking that I was proud to be where I was from; I was always proud to be Korean. As I got older, I'd either say I was from Korea or Southern California. That changed, though. Now I say I'm from America because I'm living in Korea.

I eventually came back to Korea because I had some problems in the States. I had a lot of sorrow because I had a friend who got killed in LA and I had some pain from an ex-girlfriend. I got sick of America, actually. I had to get away, more or less. Also, my father wanted me to leave. There was a lot of friction between me and my father, a lot of arguments. We just couldn't live in the same city together because we were very angry with each other. However, I also came back because I like Korea and wanted to learn a little bit about the culture, seeing as it's my heritage. I mean, I couldn't read or write Korean when I first came—my Korean was terrible. My speaking ability was pretty bad, so I wanted to polish that up, too.

In 1993, when I first came to Korea, it was really hard to adjust, though. I really hated it here. Making friends was very difficult at first. It seemed as if Koreans were all users; the people who wanted to be your friends were the user-type-of-crowd. I felt they were really selfish. A lot of them were students and they didn't have much money, so they didn't mind spending my money, but I did. I didn't mind treating them but I expected to be treated in return. They never intended to return the favor, and so I knew I was being used.

I came to Korea on advice from a close friend who told me that I could be an English teacher or he could get me a job at the Daejeon Expo. He made some promises, telling me to come to Korea because I would make a lot of money if I did. This got my attention, and so I came. Yet when I arrived, my friend just totally flipped out on me. I couldn't get a hold of him so I called my uncle who helped me out and let me stay at his house. At the time, I thought that I should learn a little bit of the language and culture but I found it difficult to adjust. My Korean wasn't very good and people would give me some pretty hard stares. I look Korean, but I speak like a fool. In the beginning, people would look at me and wonder if I was retarded or something. "Why do you talk like that?" they'd say. I was resentful of that. I found some of the older Koreans to be very rude and disrespectful, and I was a little angered at that. In the States, I'd slap people around if they didn't use polite or good language with me, but coming here and having total strangers treat me as a child—I didn't like that.

In the end, it took me about six months to a year to make my first good Korean friends. It was still difficult to adjust, though, because they couldn't speak English and my Korean wasn't all that great. It did, however, make my time here a lot easier because Korean friends get so close. They were very nice, always thinking of me and my feelings. That's a nice thing about Korean friendships—Korean friends are very considerate. They make the best of friends, I think, better than American friends.

Even with my Korean friends, however, I still felt a lot of discrimination, especially from my *hagwon* (학원)—private academy. For example, non-Korean foreign teachers got two weeks vacation and paid airfare and I didn't. Non-Korean foreign teachers received housing allowance, which I also was not given. I'm a U.S.

citizen but that didn't matter. When I asked the people at the *hagwon* about it they said they wouldn't do that for Korean American teachers. I couldn't believe they were prejudiced against me. Their point was getting non-Korean foreign teachers to work here is more difficult. There are many *kyo-po* (교포)—overseas ethnic Korean—in Korea, but not that many non-Korean foreign teachers. My director's other point was that foreign teachers only get an hourly wage, whereas I could get a percentage and make more money than foreign teachers, which was true to a certain extent. Regardless, though, the foreign teachers had more benefits, like their own conference room and computers, and I didn't like the double-standard. Another thing was that I wanted to teach the advanced English learning classes but those were reserved for non-Korean foreigners only. I was left to teach the most basic English classes for Koreans who couldn't speak English. Their reasoning was that Koreans pay money not only for an excellent English teacher, but also for a person that "looks" American, too. I found that highly offensive. I really got turned off after that experience, realizing that *hagwon* are just there to make money, use and take advantage of you, and so I quit. That was back in 1998. After I quit, and went home briefly, I came back to Korea from New York. I was planning on leaving Korea for good but then I met my wife. One thing I promised I'd do was to stay in Korea if we got married.

Nowadays, even though I've lived here for years, I don't think I could live here indefinitely with my family. I have children and I don't like the education system in Korea and the side education where the children are forced to go to a *hagwon*. I'm totally against that. I want my children to have a more liberal education so that they're not just sponges in school, having to memorize everything. I want them to be more creative. I want them to go to an American school in the States. Right now we're raising our children ninety percent Korean and ten percent English. I've got a three-year-old son and one-year-old daughter. My children understand a few things in English, and I read English books to them whenever I get the chance. My son, he's at nursery school right now, and his English skills are pretty good for his age. He knows his ABCs plus a few American songs.

I'm not raising my kids the way my parents raised me. I'm trying to raise my children with a little more understanding than my parents did, I think. I read up on how to raise children because I want to be a good father. I don't want to make the same mistakes my dad did. I try not to scream or hit my children, and I try to be more compassionate. I'm not really raising them the Korean way. I want them to know their culture with proper manners, education, the polite forms of language, and things like that.

Actually, now that I have a family of my own, my relationship with my own parents is much better. I understand them a lot more. I was very resentful of my parents when I was young, but now I've realized that my parents went through a lot of sacrifices, especially my mom. She came from a very rich family here in Korea, but when she went to the States she had to work in a sewing factory. It was a tough life. My father, he came from a good family with a good name too, even though his wasn't a rich family. My parents went through a lot of hardship in the States and I'm very thankful for that. They immigrated to the States so that I could be afforded a good education, and because of that education I'm able to make money just by talking.

If I were to offer advice to other *kyo-po*, I would say remember your culture and take pride in learning about where you come from. Try and understand where your parents are coming from.

Don't forget that your parents' guidance is what's best for you, even if it's difficult and confusing. The path your parents are guiding you along may be hard, but the harder path is usually the better one. One of my regrets is that, maybe if I had listened to my father more instead of concentrating on rebelling against him, I probably would have turned out a much better person.

Section IV
Teaching in Korea

SCHOOL

Teaching in Korea

ALTHOUGH PEOPLE from the West have been teaching foreign languages in Korea since the Chosun Dynasty (조선시대 1392–1910), it wasn't until after the Korean War (1950–53) that English teachers arrived in any significant numbers to have a meaningful impact on the country. Indeed, the bulk of the country's foreign language teachers today are English teachers. Early on it was the Americans, working under the auspices of the Peace Corps, as well missionaries from different churches, who did the majority of teaching of English as a second language. But after the Miracle on the Han River, the name for Korea's launch into one of the Asian Tigers in the 1980s, everything changed, and English education exploded as a result. Since Seoul hosted the 1988 Summer Olympics, the number of English teachers from Western countries has increased steadily, alongside teachers and professors from countries all around the world teaching in a wide array of fields.

As of 2002, there were 9,390 teachers and professors living and working legally in Korea, with the great majority teaching English as a second language or English literature. Of the nearly ten thousand teachers and professors in Korea, most hail from five countries: Canada (3,150), U.S. (2,728), New Zealand (694),

United Kingdom (604), and Australia (538).[1] However, these are not the only teachers working in Korea. There are presently teachers and professors living in Korea from a total of forty countries, with a significant number of teachers working illegally in Korea.

The phenomenon that is English education in Korea has been the impetus for more than a few people to come and work in Korea over the years. And though some people come to Korea with qualifications like CELTA (Certificate in English Language Teaching to Adults), TESOL (Teachers of English to Students of Other Languages), ISA (International Studies Abroad), and RSA (Royal Society of Arts), there is an army of young men and women in Korea today that came with the prospect of making it big in the Land of the Morning Calm, some seeking adventure, others fleeing peril back home.

Geographically, English teachers are perhaps the most pervasive group of workers throughout Korea. From rural hamlets and small towns to the megalopolis that is Seoul, today English teachers—more than any other group of teacher, instructor, or professor—are everywhere in the Republic of Korea. Yet the teachers that are here do not come only from English-speaking countries in the West. These days you are just as likely to find an English teacher in a large *hagwon* (학원)—private academy—or university as you are a Japanese, Chinese, or Russian instructor.

❡

The four men and four women in this section come from eight different countries, teaching languages as diverse as English, Japanese, French, and Russian—Korea's thirst for foreign languages is growing and the teachers have come as a result. The stories in this section will, no doubt, remind many teachers here now of what it was like to teach those first classes way back when, adjusting to a system of education so different from many of our own. And for those reading this section with the hope of one day coming to Korea to teach, they will provide much needed insight and information about the day-to-day realities of getting by in a classroom in South Korea.

"English is not learned here for joy or pleasure. English is approached as a weapon, giving a competitive advantage to those who have it over those who do not."

William* (32)
United Kingdom
Hagwon Teacher
4 Years

In a country where very few English teachers take the time to learn the local language and the culture on an intimate level, William is a rare exception. Regardless of his ability to speak Korean, William still faced many of the same challenges and frustrations that countless English teachers before him have dealt with.

I WAS AT a crossroads, not unlike many people who come to teach English in South Korea. I'd previously been working and living in Canada. Work over there kind of dried up and I noticed an advertisement in a newspaper for teaching jobs in Korea, and that was it. It was kind of a weird destiny, I guess. I didn't have any teaching experience before I came to Korea. However, after my first teaching stint here I did return to England and obtained the RSA Cambridge Certificate to teach adults.

When I first arrived, I was teaching in a *hagwon* (학원)—private academy—located in the Gangnam (강남) area of Seoul. I was working in what is known in TESOL parlance as a "split shift."

There's nothing more exhausting than working one of those. You wake up at some ungodly hour, using toothpicks to prop your eyelids open, scarcely washed or fed, and turn up in front of a gaggle of blue-collar workers/housewives/students who are hungry to suck every syllable of English out of your brain. In my case, because of the location of the *hagwon* vis-à-vis my apartment, I had nowhere to go during the interim before the next shift. It's a wake up call for anybody who thinks that teaching—specifically in South Korea, where the demands and expectations of students are probably greater than any other country in the world—will be some kind of relaxing, recreational job, because it ain't. You'll sweat blood and tears. Make no mistake of that; it's hard work

On my first morning, I overslept. My housing had not yet been properly arranged so I was staying in a *yaw-gwan* (여관)—traditional inn. The walls in most *yaw-gwan* are paper-thin and so it's quite difficult to get any sleep. My neighbors blared their TV to mask the sounds of their lovemaking the night before, and so I think I was actually hauled out of my *yaw-gwan* by one of the *hagwon* employees, arriving to my first class five minutes late.

As far as the mood, well, at all times it's difficult to gauge just how Koreans are feeling. They tend to hide behind this inscrutable Asian mask of embarrassed laughter, whether they're truly feeling angry, happy, frustrated or otherwise. I remember coming into my class, observing the embarrassed laughter, and then just winging it for two or three hours, devoid of a lesson plan. In *hagwon* that recruit unqualified teachers, oftentimes the directors bestow upon themselves these grand titles, for example, Director of Studies, or Director of Education. Beneath their title, however, they lack any kind of practical or concrete knowledge of how to interact with foreigners, let alone manage them. They simply enjoy their grand title along with their grand office, and if you come to them, especially as an inexperienced teacher looking for help, they'll offer fantastical, unforgettable advice. For instance, "Feel the impression of the students," or better yet, "Cheer Up!" Obviously, most rookie teachers are left to come up with their own solutions.

Regarding my the earliest challenges in the classroom, I could start by mentioning the obvious: the practical, the grammatical and the structural differences between English and Korean. But really, all that stuff doesn't matter a damn because fundamentally it's the relationship that Koreans have with English that's the real challenge. No other country goes as far, or invests as much money and energy, to prove to the rest of the world that they are able to communicate in English. Upon arriving here it began to sink in for me—English is not learned here for joy or pleasure. English is approached as a weapon, giving a competitive advantage to those who have it over those who do not. Simply put, being conversant in English opens avenues to the highest reaches of society, government, and the corporate world.

As a nation, Korea sees English as a way to maximize trade volume with the world. I wish I could say that English is studied idealistically, as a way of enhancing relations with other countries, improving communication, and sharing knowledge and culture. Yet anyone who believes that to be the case is deluded or simply naive. Koreans approach languages in a very empirical, scientific, detached sort of way. Sentences are broken down into units of grammar and syntax. To the detriment of a lot of foreign English teachers, many have been in awe of Koreans' knowledge of how the present perfect is formed by adding the past participle to the verb, for example. After a while, you begin to understand that there is next to no cultural content in their approach to the English language. When I say "cultural content," I mean that Koreans have no appreciation of the culture behind the English language. They regard English as a skill, like playing the piano or riding a horse. What I've tried to impress on Koreans over my time here is that English isn't a skill; it's a way of life. While Koreans are pouring over their "English Grammar, Volume 2" textbooks, there is a total detachment from the culture behind the language. I'll be more specific: if we compare the English and Korean languages, we see that they are languages of diametrically opposed values.

English is the language of Western individualism and so it doesn't fit very comfortably next to a language such as Korean. English is the language of independent thinking and volition. Moreover, it's the language of intellectual democracy. When two Westerners speak English, *yoo-gyo* (유교)—Confucianism—does not influence the discourse. People are free to express an opinion whether it clashes with majority thinking, regardless of a person's age or social rank. Korean, on the other hand, places certain constraints on the speaker. It is a language of deference and obedience, a language that demands conformity of behavior and speech, and is built on the idea of deferring socially and mentally to "elders" whose age automatically confers great importance to opinions. It's a totally different mindset. And that's the dilemma: English and Korean just don't mix and are the most unsuitable bedfellows. It's a strange paradox—while Koreans profess to love English, they are completely at odds with the culture that moves it.

In my own case, I tried to stress the contrasts of culture more than anything else in the classroom. When we engaged in a dialogue or role playing, I would spend time breaking the dialogue down and pose comprehension questions, such as "Who are the people?" and "What's the relationship?", etc. This deductive methodology simply does not exist in the Korean education language model. Instead, it's repeat-learn-repeat-learn-repeat-learn. I would try to illustrate the context very clearly and bring imagination into the classroom so that when they left my classroom, they had learned a language point and managed to relate the language to the cultural content.

Maybe because of this, I always got along with my students. Korea is a very uniform society, but beneath that there are individuals with different characters and temperaments. Generally, the more difficult students to deal with were the older *a-jaw-sshee* types (아저씨)—middle-aged men—who had very fixed, prescribed notions on what good teaching was. The younger university student, for example, was easier for me to get along with and relate to. And, if they had had some kind of experience in a Western country, then opportunities for misunderstandings and friction were reduced even more. The most important thing in dealing with all of them was always to just keep a cool head, be patient, and not take things personally or get emotional.

Also, to interact with your students outside of class is expected of the teachers working in a Korean *hagwon*. If it's not expected by the students, it's almost certainly expected by management to keep the students sweet and give them opportunities to practice their English. Remember that when you're talking with Koreans in English, you have to simplify your language. If I tell Korean elementary English students to "take a seat," as opposed to "sit down, please," all that will produce is confused looks and embarrassed smiles. Being around that environment for prolonged periods of time does become mentally taxing, and you do need to break away and speak with other native English speakers after a while.

In my own case, I ended up teaching at that *hagwon* for about one year before doing the infamous "midnight run" (leaving the country in the middle of the night, before anyone is able to find you). I should mention that I wasn't the first person to do this, and that this is a common occurrence. It's when all your options have run out and you find yourself backed into an impossible corner. You have to remember that in Korea there is no distinction between professional and personal relationships; they mix them up here. You're professional skills aren't separated from your personality and whether or not someone likes you.

Not unlike thousands of other English teachers who have come and gone in Korea, I had performed a lot of duties or favors that went un-thanked and unpaid. And for what? A slap in the face, really. For a majority of *hagwon* directors, blatant lying and cheating are so commonplace that few teachers are surprised or shocked. When it happens the teacher will have very little recourse. Most likely, the English teacher can't speak the language and employing the services of a lawyer will be prohibitively expensive. In many cases, the midnight run is the only option for survival.

It was circumstances like this that led me to leave my job abruptly, and, might I add, I don't regret it one bit. I'm sure that the *hagwon* proprietors didn't give it a second thought after I left either. They probably just moved on and recruited somebody else —that's the nature of the *hagwon* business. Teachers coming here should bear this in mind and be very street-wise in their dealings with the *hagwon* owners who promise them the earth.

To be honest, I wouldn't recommend other ESL teachers come to Korea unless they want a pretty tough battle and have a kind of sadomasochistic streak; that, or are a glutton for punishment!

Korea wouldn't be the first place I'd recommend, not for someone's first experience teaching English abroad. I think to gain teaching experience, to understand classroom dynamics, to learn how to set up a class, how to motivate a class, to prepare a lesson that's simply flawless—all of these experiences and lessons maybe shouldn't be the foreign teacher's initial experiences, at least not here in Korea. European students might provide a safer, less challenging initial experience for the new English teacher. The dynamics of a Korean classroom make it a real challenge for a foreign teacher. The lack of class participation can also make for a very frustrating and potentially damaging experience for a new teacher.

I think I speak for a lot of foreign residents here when I say that my relationship with Korea is a love/hate relationship. Over time, as you remain here, you have to reach a stage of compromise and accommodation with things that will never change. At the end of the day, for better or for worse, for love or for hate, Korea has had an extraordinary impact on my life. Korea has brought me some truly amazing situations and introduced me to some truly amazing people, and I will never forget that.

"I don't think going and getting a TESOL certificate or a CELTA, or anything like that, is going to help in a Korean classroom. I think the only way you can learn to teach well in a Korean classroom is by experience."

Fairlie Atkinson (26)
New Zealand
Hagwon Teacher and University Instructor
15 Months

Adored by her students, Fairlie's story is only too common. A certified teacher with experience in Australia, she suffered through a rough ride at a Korean hagwon (학원)—private academy—before being fortunate enough to land a position at a reputable university. Since starting classes at university, her life has done a one-eighty, and she now finds herself happier than she has ever been.

IT WAS A COMPLETE spur-of-the-moment decision to come to Korea. I taught for two years in secondary schools in Sydney, teaching in the worst—absolutely worst—secondary schools there, the ones where there are guns and knives and drugs, and each day I would come home in tears; each day was a struggle. I was working full-time as a high school teacher and part-time as a debt collector for the Commonwealth Bank during the evening. One of my friends at the bank, whose Korean boyfriend's father was a recruiter, said to me one day, "You're not saving any money in Australia, so how about you go to Korea? You can earn a lot of money and save a lot of money there. You even get free accommodation." She outlined all the benefits of working in Korea and I just said yes. One week later I was having an interview on the phone with an adult *hagwon* who rejected me on the basis of my accent, but then the day after that, I was accepted by a children's *hagwon* on the basis of my teaching experience. I packed up my things and five days later I was in New Zealand, saying good-bye to my family. Two weeks after that I was in Korea.

I arrived in Korea and it was freezing cold. I walked out of the airport and there was a bunch of short Korean men, all in their fifties, holding little plaques with people's names. My name wasn't there, so I stood around for about twenty minutes, feeling the tears welling up, and I thought, "Oh my god, I'm in a country where they don't speak English and it's so cold and dry! What am I going to do?" Eventually, this scruffy little man with a real ill-fitting suit waddles up to me and thrusts his sign into my face—with my name all spelled wrong—saying, "Are you Pae-ree Ad-e-ken-sen?" I just looked up at him and said, "Yeah, I think I am. You must be Mr. Lee, my boss."

"No, no, I am Mr. Kim."

"Umm, okay, who are you?"

"Oh, I take you, I take you, I take you... "

The next thing I really saw was this huge Korean man with one of those mini-light sabers and a whistle wandering around, slapping tickets on people who were parking in the No Parking Zone. He was blowing his whistle the whole time and flashing his light saber around and all I could think of was, "God! Police state! Police state! What have I got myself into?" I had no idea what I was getting into. I had no idea about Korea; I hadn't read anything about Korea; I hadn't talked to anyone about Korea; I just had absolutely no notion whatsoever.

My first impression of Koreans was that they were friendly, though, because as we were driving along Mr. Kim kept on looking in the rear vision mirror, saying, "Your students, your students like you. You beautiful. You very, very beautiful." And I hadn't heard that kind of compliment in a long time so I thought, "Wow, Koreans are nice."

I remember being so shocked when we were driving through Seoul. All these beautiful, sweeping bridges and the lights—Seoul is beautiful when the sun's coming up, absolutely beautiful at dawn. By the time we arrived in Bundang (분당) I thought, "Oh my god, it's just row upon row of box apartments. Is there any greenery? Is there any foliage?" because Seoul in the winter is just so stark, so absolutely dark. I remember thinking, "I have never been in such an ugly place in my life."

Anyway, the day after arriving I had my first class. I've never liked children and I realized, as I was sitting amongst a bunch of four-year-olds, that I in fact hated children. After teaching really, really, really rough teenagers, having to teach really spoiled pre-school kids was ... I just hated it from the word "go" because I'm a bit of a control-freak in the classroom. I like to have control over everything in the classroom and when you've got four-year-olds you can't, and you can't hold their attention for forty minutes when you're supposed to be teaching one page of the book, which happens to say, "Hi, my name is Bum-suk."

My recruiter lied to me from the beginning about my situation. My director were also a conniving, lying piece of work. There was mention when I was hired that I would be teaching adults, but when I arrived there was absolutely no adult classes. The oldest kids I taught were about twelve years old. They said, "Well, you're here now, so get on with it. You're a teacher, you can teach. You've had experience. You're the only experienced teacher we've ever had, actually. Go on." I always tried to communicate with my director about any problems that I had and he just refused to be accommodating. He just kept on saying to me, "Why don't you lose some weight? Have you started a diet yet? Are you exercising?"

As a result, I really wanted to leave that *hagwon*. Actually, I knew right away I wasn't going to get on with my workmates, so the first weekend I was in Seoul I jumped on the subway and managed to somehow navigate my way into Itaeweon (이태원). I then grabbed a guidebook and made my way up to Hyehwa Station (혜화역), in an attempt to try and find the Seoul Old Fortress Wall (서울 성곽). I walked up past Sungkyunkwan University (성균관대학교) and then got completely lost. I ended up in the university looking at the old Confucian shrine. They happened to be having a ceremony while I was there and a Korean guy walked up to me and said, "Hi, I'm looking for a native speaker to teach on the weekends to my Chinese philosophy students. Would you be interested?" I said, "Wow! Yes!" knowing full well it was illegal. The weekend after that I started teaching university students. My boss gave me legal permission with the stipulation that I work extra hours at the *hagwon*.

So, that kept my sanity the first six months I was teaching at the *hagwon*. Every weekend I was teaching the university students and socializing with them as well, which allowed me to make so many friends and contacts. It was great. I didn't spend any time in Bundang on the weekend. Six months into it I simply couldn't work for the director any more, though. He was just such a pig. I was working ten in the morning through ten–thirty at night. The money was terrible, no better than anyone else. On top of that, the director was in the process of selling the school, but we weren't supposed to know about it, so our contracts were going to be taken over by someone else and we were going to lose all our severance pay and he didn't care. Plus, he had been taking tax from us but not paying it to the tax department, and he refused to refund this money to us, which just added to all the other drama. I finally said to my director, "I want a letter of release." I ended up having to pay five million won to get my letter of release, just to get out of the contract. Fortunately, my boss in the Chinese philosophy department at the university then set me up with another *hagwon* job and also set me up teaching part-time at Sungkyunkwan University in the mornings.

The biggest difference I noticed when I began teaching at university is that your students sit and listen. God knows whether they're actually absorbing anything you say, but you have their attention. I have control over my classroom, which suits me perfectly. I walk into a classroom and everyone goes, "Today, you look beautiful, teacher," or "Great sunglasses, teacher," or "Teacher, today, great color coordination." I now get along with my students really well. Loving the attention is one thing, but the other thing is that teaching a class is so rewarding when your students actually start using the information that you've been giving them and you've been pounding into their heads for weeks. I love it when a student suddenly corrects something that they've been saying wrong for weeks or uses a phrase that you've given them. Socially, I do get on with my students, too. The ones who are around my age, we tend to go out and drink.

However, the biggest challenge about teaching in Korea—

whether at a *hagwon* or at a university—is keeping the students' attention, because there are always students who do not want to be there. Reaching those students and keeping them interested and committed is really difficult, a real challenge, especially when they tend to be the ones who have a lower ability and who have no respect for Western culture.

The other challenge I find about teaching in a Korean classroom is (a) I'm a female, and (b) I'm from the West. Some of the non-credit classes that I teach, where I have men or women older than me, we may disagree on a point of culture, or even grammar, and walking the fine line between showing them respect, but also pushing or putting forward my point of view, is really difficult without causing them offense or causing them to lose face. I always have to be aware of that when I'm teaching older people.

And being a woman in Korea, I've definitely had a different experience than the men I know here. The fact is, my student body is generally male, as are the people who elect to take my non-credit classes. One thing I would tell other women is to be careful of all the flattery and the adulation, as it can definitely go to your head. Every Korean thinks you look like a movie star simply because you've got white skin.

I must say, though, I really, really love my job here and it's not just the attention or anything like that. It's because the students have an opportunity to have so much fun in my classroom because there aren't any control or discipline issues. The students are so well-trained and conditioned already that we can have a lot of fun and not worry about things getting out of hand.

There was one time, however, the second week I was teaching my freshman classes at university, that things got a little crazy. It was White Day, March 14, and I had a boy at the end of class stand up in front of everyone, holding a rose, and say, "Teacher, frankly speaking, I love you. Frankly speaking, I would like to practice kissing with you. Teacher, it's White Day, here." He then thrust a rose in my face. By that time, I had backed myself up against the door and sort of grabbed the door handle and I ran. So every day is interesting, but that's not always a good thing because then you have to regain your status as a teacher in the classroom, which can be difficult. I had to go into the next lesson, for example, with that boy sitting in the back, a big grin on his face, and I had to be all business. The students certainly don't have the same level of respect for women as they do for the male teachers.

One thing I can say definitely about students who have studied with me is that I think every single one of them, whether it be after six weeks or twelve weeks, feels comfortable; they lose their fear of using English with a native speaker. Whether they have improved or not is difficult to know, because when they walk into my classroom they're petrified of using English, absolutely petrified, so you can never gauge exactly their level. But when they leave they're completely comfortable, so in that sense there's definitely been an improvement.

On another level, being from New Zealand has proven difficult in its own right. Something I hear all the time is this: "But teacher, your pronunciation is very bad," and "But teacher, your pronunciation is not American style. You have British English. Not good. We don't understand." The university administration, when I was applying for a full-time job, actually said, "We'd really prefer to have someone with a North American accent." You can't argue about this with Koreans. They have a set way of thinking. If Koreans think that the American accent is the right one to have then that's the way they think. At first it really offended me, but now I've just become completely and utterly accustomed to it.

To someone coming to teach in Korea in the near future, I would recommend that you seriously consider all your options and that you understand your situation. Whatever you do, though, try not to teach at a *hagwon*. If you do eventually land at a *hagwon*, you should read your contract through and realize that in the end the contract will be absolutely worthless, and that your school director will, in most cases, not hold to the contract. The contract is not respected at all in this country. Korea is a completely different place, so if you're going to come, you've got to be open-minded. Be prepared for anything. For every negative thing, try and find one good thing, because there's going to be plenty of negative things. Many foreigners who end up in Korea say nothing but bad things about Korea. As foreigners, we all have issues and things that we find really upsetting or disturbing about living here. But it's not our country. It's not our culture. Who are we to criticize? We would be offended if a Korean came to our culture, our country, and started criticizing things.

The thing that has helped me the most is starting to learn the Korean language and understanding Korean culture and why they say things the way they do. Other than that, I don't think going and getting a TESOL certificate or a CELTA, or anything like that, is going to help in a Korean classroom. I think the only way you can learn to teach well in a Korean classroom is by experience. I think my first six months of teaching children I was a disaster as a teacher. I think the second six months those kids taught me how to teach them. At school today, having taught absolutely the worst teenagers in Sydney, and now Korean kids, I have no problems with control over my classroom.

"The simple truth is that where you work greatly influences the time you'll have in Korea. In fact, I would say it's eighty percent of the experience."

Craig Service (32)
Canada
Hagwon Teacher and University Instructor
5 Years

Like many before him, Craig had no background in education or teaching English as a second language before arriving in Korea. Still, his hard work over the years seems to have compensated for what he lacked in formal training, as is evident from his infectious optimism and perpetual good mood.

THE REASON I came to Korea is very simple: I had a friend here. He was a friend I knew from university. He'd come to Korea just to pay off his student loans because he had heard from a few friends of his that it was a good place to go. I was finishing up with my undergraduate degree when he gave me a call. We had been talking back and forth when he told me that he was getting married. I would be finishing my degree in April and he was getting married in May so it seemed like a neat idea to possibly go out to Korea for the wedding. When I found out the price of the ticket I was a little more intimidated, though. It was going to be about $1,500, and that was more money than I had, coming right out of school. When I told him that that might be the barrier, he said, "Well, have you thought about working in Korea?" to which I said, "No, I hadn't thought about it." After thinking about it, however, I realized that it really fit in with what I wanted to do. Graduating in anthropology, especially in cultural anthropology, I was interested in seeing another country, something very different from Canada, and Asia definitely qualified. So, Korea seemed like a good idea. My friend in Korea seemed to be enjoying his time, he spoke very highly of it, and in this case it was also a matter of convenience. He was the academic director at a relatively large *hagwon* (학원)—private academy—and so I knew I'd be getting a fair contract, a good contract, and I would have an interesting position: I'd be able to pay off some loans and save some money within a year.

Before I got to Korea I always pictured it at night for some reason. Also, I didn't know whether or not the country was going to have running water in the buildings; I didn't know if the buildings were going to be clean; I didn't know what kind of food the people ate. When I first arrived, though, I was pleasantly surprised to find that things looked so good. All the cars looked so new! When I finally arrived downtown at my hotel, I was surprised at the fashion, at how well people were dressed. I mean, the people we would see on the street in Canada would be a variety. You'd see business people dressed up in their best clothes and you'd see students dressed in sandals and shorts. Here, all the men were wearing either suits or formal short sleeve dress shirts, and the women were dressed to the nines. They looked very attractive.

Anyway, when I first got here, I was teaching at a *hagwon*, one of the larger ones in Korea. In fact, it's a chain, and like I said before, I had a friend here, so I was much more fortunate than a lot of other people. So, for example, my first day I went with him into work and that's where my training began. Training basically was sitting in on other teachers' classes and observing how they did it. I can't say there was a whole lot of formal training because basically it was observe, follow suit, and learn from a new experience. Mostly I'd say what I learned is that the teaching style is a lot more relaxed than I had envisioned it to be. It was a lot more casual. There was less expectation and demand than I thought was going to be placed on the teachers.

Training lasted two days, and that was a day more than most people got, because I was here early. Actually, before my contract started, one of the other teachers was sick and they were stuck for people, so they stuck me into a class that was on its last day. All the students were comfortable with one another, and when they put me in this class they just said, "Okay, here you go. This is yours." That was my first teaching experience, which was nice because it allowed me to catch my breath at the end of it and then go in to the next day as a full teacher.

However, I definitely held insecurities about not being qualified and not feeling like I was willing or able to do a proper job because I didn't feel like I had enough skills or qualifications to do this. Getting the kinds of questions I got from students, it was difficult, and I definitely felt uncomfortable. Yet going into the second month, where I was starting everything fresh, I had come to realize that the questions my students had about English were things that I could answer, and I did know the answers to, which made me feel more comfortable. From the second month on, when students made a mistake, I could tell it was wrong and I could see where the error was and I could give suggestions on how they could say it properly. Once I was comfortable with that, it was easier going into the classes, knowing that I did have enough of a background in English to be able to explain to them what the correct answer was.

I was very fortunate at my *hagwon*. It was definitely not run in a Western style, but just like the West, you get good owners and bad owners, and you have certain expectations of how employees should or shouldn't be treated. Working in Korea was simply different. For me, I would say that the treatment I received was fair. To give an example, I never had a problem with wondering whether or not my paycheck was going to be deposited in my account. And I think that's kind of a telling statement in itself, the fact that I count that as a good thing rather than something taken for granted, because a lot of people in a lot of *hagwon* cannot take that for granted. In other *hagwon*, it's sometimes questionable whether or not they will be paid.

Anyhow, I eventually moved to a university because it was a much better deal there in terms of money and hours. Right now, I'm under contract for 18 hours. A typical day in my life starts pretty early because early morning classes in Korea are very popular. The students always seem to be very highly motivated to get in before work or before school to learn English. My first class, a conversation class, will start at about 7:50 in the morning, running until 8:40. We'll have any one of a number of textbooks that are available, with these textbooks working towards developing listening skills, speaking skills, some reading and writing skills. Usually the conversation books are more just listening and speaking. I'll start a class with a group of people ranging anywhere from five to 15 students. My job, as I see it, is to get them talking, to get them comfortable with communicating in

English, to correct the mistakes they make, to introduce new vocabulary, to introduce new terms they might not be familiar with, and to have them practice those terms. I'll introduce them to situations where they'll need to be speaking English and teach them how to respond to questions and situations that they might face in a foreign country or when speaking with native speakers.

My particular emphasis is business, and in those classes the students have expressed an interest in discussing current events, so for that class each student will bring in a topic or an idea that they wish to discuss. Our group of about five people will then sit down and talk about it and we'll go through different terms. When somebody makes a mistake, we'll discuss as a group what was wrong with that and then offer suggestions and work on improving it. Terms that come up I'll write down and work on building vocabulary for.

With my afternoon classes, I do more structured courses where we have a particular group and, like I said, it's business. So in one class the main focus is presentations: what are the elements of a good presentation?, for example. We'll practice English and we'll practice presentations, as well as have group discussions, on top doing job interviews. In another class we'll practice negotiations and what the terms and phrases are that you can use for different styles of negotiations, as well as the terms that people might use in business. In that class we also work a little more on writing, so we'll go through business letters, learning everything from how to write and design them, to how to choose vocabulary for business letters, to the styles of letters themselves. We'll practice writing memos and faxes as well as going on the Internet to do research, looking through different websites and the language that's involved with that so that basically these students have skills to work in the business world in English.

The greatest challenge I face in a Korean classroom is getting past the barrier that quite a few people have of feeling that just by appearing in class they can learn English. Some students believe that simply by showing up they'll learn English and that they might not have to practice or put the effort into it and to do more. They seem to think that just being in a classroom will do it. Now, granted, somebody that comes to class each day and talks and practices and makes that effort will improve. They can improve a great deal more, however, if they review information from the class afterwards and if they read it before coming to class the next day. You can give the students this information, but unless they use it and practice it, they're not actually going to learn it, and that tends to be one of the biggest problems.

Actually, quite often I'll see students diligently write down all of the words mentioned in class in their book and that's where it stays, never to be looked at again. In class, we'll go through unit one at the beginning, students will underline words and circle words that they don't know, on the understanding that they're going to go back and review it and learn it. On the last day of class, however, we'll go over some of these things, and I'll make a point of using those words in the class, and many people might not know what they mean, which is why I'd say definitely there is a problem with retention. A lot of students don't want to put the effort in; they're looking for a quick fix. They're looking for the English to just come to them so they show up to class thinking this will happen. So, for instance, you might see a student for six months, who shows up every morning at 7 o'clock, and I'll say, "How are you?" and he'll say "Fine, thank you, and you?" And I'll say, "I'm good." Now, you can say, "Fine thanks," I tell the student, but how about, "I'm good" "I'm great" "I'm all right" "I'm okay." instead? The student in turn will then reply, "Ah, yes. You are right!"

Next day...

"How are you?"

"I'm fine thank you, and you?"

"Okay, now remember what we talked about yesterday?"

And the next day...

"How are you?"

"Fine thank you, and you?"

So, if I can offer advice at all on working in a Korean classroom, I'd say be prepared to be flexible. It is a different culture here; it's not the same. The people who I've seen have the most difficult time here are the ones that are rigidly trying to follow their own ideas and expectations, who are not prepared to be flexible and roll with a whole new culture and a new set of ideas. The people who have been very successful are not even necessarily easygoing, but more accepting. They don't stick to their set views and set principles.

The second thing is, do your research and make sure that the place you are going to work has a good reputation. Any decent *hagwon* will provide you with contacts of people who have worked with them before, and they can give you a true-to-life recommendation. Also, try and find people that have worked there before and have left, because somebody working there at the moment might be under some pressure to give a better than average response.

The simple truth is that where you work greatly influences the time you'll have in Korea. In fact, I would say it's eighty percent of the experience. If you're working for a good place you'll probably have a good time. If you're working for a place where you're worried about your paycheck and you're worried about your treatment—whether or not you're going to be ripped off or taken for a ride—you're not going to enjoy your time, and in each case it's going to influence your thinking of Korea.

"... it makes me feel terrible, just terrible when someone thinks I'm a prostitute. I was in complete shock the first time someone approached me under that assumption."

Gumennaya Svetlana (26)
Russia
Hagwon Teacher
3 Years

Brimming with charm and charisma, Svetlana is an oddity to the Korean mindset about the average Russian. Well-spoken, highly educated, and fluent in English, she has unfortunately had to put up with many Koreans' negative stereotypes of Russians on more than one occasion.

I CAME TO KOREA three years ago, not to teach, but to work as a broker in a shipping company. My friend, he's Korean, came to my place back home in Russia once and asked me about my salary at the time. I told him I was making about U.S. $100 a month, which was pretty good for Russia. He then told me that I could make much more in Korea and promised to find a job for me. Although I was only qualified to teach, he found a position for me at a shipping company as a broker and subsequently trained me.

When I came to Korea they gave me some pocket money and paid for my ticket. I had to work from 8:00 a.m. to midnight, six days a week, because that's the way things work in Korea. I made U.S. $800 a month, which was substantially more than I could make in Russia. Officially, we finished work at six o'clock but no one really paid attention to that. It was a private company, and as long as the president remained at the office, so did everyone else—or else! Usually around 8:00 or 9:00 p.m., the president would emerge from his office, as he was feeling peckish, and announce that we would all be having dinner. We would then go to a restaurant all together and eat and drink. This would last until 11:00 p.m., at which time we'd all go to sing karaoke until about 2:00 a.m. We were usually allowed to go home around that time. I ended up working at that company for six months, and in this time I drank more soju than I ever care to remember; every night, except Sunday!

My first impressions of Korea were really positive. I liked it, especially during *Chusok* (추석)—Korean Thanksgiving—when Seoul would empty out. I really enjoyed that, as I come from a small Russian village. At first it was really hard because I was 22 and away from my family and friends, and I didn't have time to make friends here. All my friends and family wanted me back home. My decision to leave my comfortable life was very surprising to my family and friends. In Russia, when you have a good job, you hold on to it with all your strength. Canadians, Americans, and Australians, for instance, leave their countries for adventure and exploration, but we Russians don't do that. My mom has been working the same job for thirty years, not because she likes it, but because she has it. I would have stayed in Russia if my friend hadn't convinced me I could have more opportunity in Korea.

Anyway, I quit that shipping company simply because I

couldn't do it anymore. I had been in Korea for six months, yet I hadn't done anything; I hadn't been anywhere or made any friends. I didn't even know what Itaewon (이태원) was! Go to work. Go home. Work. Home. Work. Home. That was my life. The thing is, office work for a man in Korea is relatively okay because if you say something people will listen to you. However, office work for a woman here is very boring, just paper work—sorry, paper work and coffee work! My job was to sort paper and to serve coffee to people. Not very fun! The company was so small, and so when things were going badly, if we were facing bankruptcy, for example, it wasn't very pleasant in an office of six people. My contract was for one year but I decided to get out of it and found a teaching position in Ilsan (일산).

I don't know how I got that teaching job in Ilsan, but I think it was just good luck. I was surfing the Internet and I found an ad for a new kindergarten there. There were not many foreigners in Ilsan three years ago. Anyway, I told the owner I was Russian but that I could speak English and that I was qualified, with a teaching degree from a teacher's college in Russia, trained to teach English and German. The only question the owner had for me, though, was "Are you white?"

When I started work at that kindergarten, I was working five days a week from 10:00 a.m. to 1:00 p.m., entertaining children. The truth is that it was more entertainment than actual teaching, actually. I was jumping around and singing for the kids and trying to make them laugh. The kids liked me, therefore the parents liked me, and therefore my boss liked me. It was a great time. I was making twice as much as I did in my shipping company and, just as important, I wasn't drinking soju anymore. I was so happy! The kindergarten didn't set me up with an apartment, but by that time I had made some friends so I stayed with them. I was living in Seoul and had to commute every day to Ilsan, but it didn't matter. I liked everything about it. The teaching experience was still so fresh, so traveling for three hours a day was such a small sacrifice.

In the end, I taught in Ilsan for about four months and only left because the monsoon season arrived and I began to die! Russian girls and humidity don't mix. I was packing up to go home but before I went back I accidentally found a *hagwon* (학원)—private academy—where they were looking for English, German, Spanish, Chinese, and Russian teachers! I called the *hagwon* and the owner told me I should go to his office to discuss a contract. When I went to his office, he gave me all the documents for my contract and my visa. Everything happened so fast that I was very impressed.

So, I went home that summer and returned in September on an E-2 teaching visa. I immediately found an apartment, and then started work at my new *hagwon*. My schedule back then was crazy. In truth, I was supposed to be teaching Russian at the *hagwon* but there wasn't enough interest, so I taught elementary and middle school kids English. Also, because I'm a blonde girl with long legs, people wanted me to teach them privately. Even though my accent is not American, Koreans just wanted speaking practice. Koreans know how to speak English, they're just too shy, so my job was to make them speak, which I did. I worked at that *hagwon* for nearly nine months and then when summer came around again, I left for Russia once more.

When I got back after the summer, I had a visa from the same *hagwon*, but I didn't only work there; I also taught Russian privately. The English market is much larger than the Russian market here, and so when people want to learn Russian in Korea they don't really try and look for a *hagwon*. Rather, they try and look for Russians to teach them privately. If you go to a *hagwon* to learn Russian, you'll be taught by a Korean, and that's not what these people need. I mean, I've listened to Korean professors of the Russian language in Korea and they suck. The professors do! Their pronunciation, grammar, vocabulary—everything is bad. If you learn Russian privately from a native Russian speaker, you will learn the language and it won't cost as much as learning English. If you get 30,000 won for an English lesson, for example, you'll get 20,000 to 25,000 won for Russian. The Russian privates end up being less expensive than the *hagwon*!

I think there are different categories of Koreans who want to learn Russian. One may be Koreans who want to learn Russian because they're crazy about Russian girls. You know, for a Korean man who is well-positioned in society to find a beautiful Korean woman for a wife is not difficult. However, for men in Korea without a vast fortune, they may have to look elsewhere, and so may look for an international marriage. Maybe they want to show their friends their beautiful Russian wife because they feel it gives them status in some way. Russian women are white and they can be tall, blonde and sexy. I've had so many students who've just wanted to have a Russian friend. They're usually married, but they just want to have a foreigner to go out with. Maybe they don't want to go out with Americans or Canadians as much because they're so busy. I don't know.

Anyhow, Russians are always looking for private students. I had some students who were even looking to get married! Kind of like, "Maybe you can teach me Russian first and then marry me. Will you marry me?" You see, Korean women care more about money than Russians do. If you date a Korean woman, the first question she asks is "Do you have a car?" and the second is "What kind?" It's easier to marry a Russian because so many Russian women want to get out of their country. In fact, there are a number of Internet sites alerting Korean men to the thousands of hot Russian women who want to marry them! The Internet site should read "Desperate, uneducated Russian women with no way out want to marry your money and stability!" When these same women come here married to a Korean man, however, they usually end up being miserable. Miscommunication, different expectations, culture clashes—the list goes on.

However, it's only fair to point out that about twenty percent of Koreans who are learning Russian are doing it for business reasons. These people need to learn to read some Russian and learn common phrases because they're often in Russia on business. Russia is a good business partner for Koreans, if for no other reason than proximity. Koreans can export many things to Russia and import many things from Russia—not only women! There are other Korean students who want to go to Russia, say Moscow for example, to attend university, and that's why they need someone like me.

I must say that I really do enjoy seeing the results of my teaching efforts. If a child on the first day of class says to me, "*An-nyeong-ha-sae-yo, sun-saeng-nim*,"—Hello, teacher—that's fine. However, if on the second day they come to class and say "Hello, teacher," then it makes me feel wonderful. You can't make a lot of money teaching kindergarten, so it's seeing the result of my teaching with the kids that means the most to me. With high school students and university students, I love their crazy stories. When I ask them why they want to study Russian, some of them give me the most ridiculous reasons: "I love Russian music" or "Russian history is so fascinating" or "I respect communism!"

These kinds of students give me energy because they genuinely want to learn so much, so fast. On the other hand, with business people, you never really know what you're going to get. When you meet them for the first time, they all seem as if they honestly want to study. Then, maybe by the fourth class, you're trying to deal with two separate marriage proposals! It's crazy. Private classes all go for an hour, but the total duration is different, depending on who I'm teaching. With students, I teach them for three or four months, but with business people it can last for two months. Part of this is because Russian is really hard. If you live in Korea, where nobody speaks Russian, then it's useless. For the most part, people's interest in the language lasts for two months; once the language becomes really difficult, the interest disappears.

On the plus side, though, I've never faced any discrimination from my students. Once, however, I was looking for students to teach privately, back when I was still working at the shipping company, and I put on ad on the Internet to see if I would get any responses. I was very new to Korea. The same day, a man called me and asked me what teaching methods I used. I told him very innocently that if you're having fun, then I'm having fun. He was fine with that and asked me all the necessary questions, such as what qualifications I had, and so on. Finally, after I was sure I had impressed him, he asked, "Oh, by the way, where are you from?" and I told him I was from Russia. At that point I could feel in my bones that he'd changed his mind. "Russia?" he said, "How can you possibly teach English, then?" This guy had spoken with me on the telephone for over half an hour, and everything was fine, and then he asks me that, so I asked him "How can you teach English properly if you're Korean?" and then I hung up. I was proud of myself for saying that, but still cried for some time after that experience. Another time, there was a very funny reply to an ad I put on the Internet for teaching English and Russian. This guy wrote me and told me he was really interested in studying Russian, but that he knew very little about the language. He asked me how I taught Russian and if I used any special equipment! He then wondered if I guaranteed satisfaction or if I gave "oral instruction." This is a good indication of what we were talking about earlier, that is, what Koreans think of studying Russian. I mean, oral instruction!

Now that I've worked in Korea for a while, I've come to realize that for every *hagwon* owner or private lesson that refuses my teaching because I'm Russian, there are five others who will happily accept me. There aren't enough native English speakers to go around here in Korea so I know that I can always find work. Mind you, Russians don't have the luxury of being picky the way native English speakers do. We do our best within those limitations.

The thing is, with Koreans, they all think that Russians—every last one of us—are prostitutes. I hear this all the time from them. I think, with Koreans, about ninety percent assume I'm a prostitute if they know I'm from Russia; that's why I don't tell anyone anymore. I tell people I'm from Hungary, Bulgaria, Canada—wherever. I tell my employers I'm Russian before I sign a contract, but for random encounters on the street, for example an *a-joom-ma* (아줌마)—middle-aged woman—selling me something and telling me I'm beautiful, I never tell her I'm from Russia, because then she'll stop telling me I'm beautiful! The truth is, it makes me feel terrible, just terrible when someone thinks I'm a prostitute. I was in complete shock the first time someone approached me under that assumption. I'm not a prostitute and I can't understand women who sell their bodies. Thankfully, I do feel more in control of those situations now than I used to. I know how to answer those questions now.

If I were to give personal advice to people coming to Korea to teach, I would say, just be crazy and be prepared for craziness. Be patient and be creative. With *hagwon* owners, you have to respect Korean culture and customs while you live here, and part of the culture is respecting your boss, whether you like him or not. The people I've met here have come from their cozy homes in Canada or the States and upon living in Korea for a while they've realized that they don't really like it here, but they can't leave because they like the money. These people stay here even though they hate everything about Korea: the food, the culture, the people—everything. I think that's wrong. If you're living and working in a country, you should try to enjoy yourself. You know, kimchi is actually really cool! Now, we all know vodka is much better than soju for many reasons, but if you mix soju with Coke, they go well together. Oh, and soju and plum juice–nectar of the Gods!

"At first I was really scared to death because I thought that Koreans would hate me; I thought that they would reject me; I truly thought that they would dislike me. Yet they really liked me. When I realized that they actually liked me it was very strange. I was quite moved, actually."

Samantha Hanratty (29)
France
Hagwon Teacher
3 Months

As a Korean adoptee, Samantha's time in a Korean classroom teaching English and French has been very different from other Westerners who come to teach in Korea. Adopted by a French family at the age of five, it took her almost twenty-five years to return to her birth country. Now, after three months in Korea, this alluring young French woman is discovering that there is life here in Korea after adoption.

I WAS ADOPTED in April 1979, when I was five years old. I had been in the orphanage since the age of two, at which time I was found. I went through three different orphanages, the third one being Holt Adoption Agency. I've made attempts to find my birth parents, but I know I'll never find them. That doesn't bother me, though, because what is that going to change? It's not going to change my life; it's not going to change anything; it's not going to change me.

It was an ordinary French couple who ended up adopting me. I was adopted on my own, but I had a brother and a sister from my adoptive family. We didn't get along very well, though. It was very difficult, actually. I think one of the reasons my parents adopted me was because, at the time, adopting a child from Korea was easiest. It was easier to adopt children from Korea than from anywhere else; it was easier to adopt a child from Korea than from even Vietnam or from India. Korea was a country that didn't exactly "export" children back then, but that's the closest word I can think of.

The reason I chose to come back to Korea after all these years is that I had always wanted to come to Korea. Not too long ago I had thought, "I'm getting older and I should come before I get too old." I had to give up everything when I made this decision, but when you're 29 you can give up things; you can always return to your normal life afterwards. If I were forty, it would be more difficult, so I thought it would be better for me to come back now. I had memories of Korea, incredibly vivid memories, and I wanted to come back and make sure that everything I remembered was true. When I got back, I went to the orphanages I was at as a baby and talked with the Koreans there. Of course, things were very different, but everything that I remembered came back to me.

Coming over on the plane, actually, I was sick as a dog; I was very ill. I was very, very scared of coming here. I was so petrified on the plane, in fact, that I was extremely sick. When I arrived, though, and saw Korean people, it was a very nice feeling. It was so nice because for the first time I felt like I could blend in. I kept staring at people and they would look at me as if I was crazy or something. I would just stare back at them because I looked like them. Something I didn't realize when I first arrived was that Koreans would talk to me in Korean and then realize I'm a foreigner. Then, on the other side, I would have Western people talking to me in Korean when they saw me for the first time. I was just like, "Go away! Leave me alone." It was all very strange because I got the misunderstanding from both sides.

Anyhow, I came to Korea with the intention to teach. I had actually been teaching in Europe before I arrived here. I was teaching French in England, at a secondary school there, for two years. I'm a qualified teacher, with a post-graduate degree in French. I gave up everything in Europe to come here. One day, I just didn't show up for work in England. Everybody was worried and wondering where I was. Not long after arriving in Seoul, I saw an advertisement for a teaching position and so I just applied while I was here. I had an interview over the phone and got the job.

Thankfully Berlitz, the school I'm now teaching at, is very good, because it's not discriminatory and is dedicated to very equal opportunity, so I wasn't discriminated against because I looked Korean. They're very rational. I'm now teaching mostly English and some French. It's been really good, actually. At first I was really scared to death because I thought that Koreans would hate me; I really thought that they would reject me; I truly thought that they would dislike me. Yet they really liked me. When I realized that they actually liked me it was very strange. I was quite moved, actually. Sometimes I get some nice letters from students and they invite me to go out. So far they've been very kind to me, telling me a lot about Korean culture because they know that I was born here. They even give me presents sometimes.

Within the classroom itself, the English is very good. My students are excellent. I can understand them and they can understand me and there are no problems. It's far more difficult for them to learn French, however, because of the fact that they don't have the opportunity to practice the language. In Korea there are lots of foreigners, like Americans, Canadians, and Australians, but not many French people. I think students have more problems with the syntax in French, but phonetics and pronunciation are not the problem at all.

The only challenge I face as a teacher is that every month we change groups, like this morning when they told me I would have a new group, so I wasn't able to prepare for it properly. My schedule is awful. It's terrible, really. I teach at six forty-five in the morning until nine o'clock in the evening. I have a split schedule and sometimes I don't even get chance to have a nap because I just work. I have very busy days sometimes.

With respect to Korean society, there are instances when people who know I can't speak Korean take advantage of the situation by taking me to the wrong place, pretending they're lost. That's happened to me a few times. Sometimes people even laugh at me because I can't speak Korean, which doesn't make me feel good. But all in all, I wouldn't say I've faced any real discrimination. The truth is, I now enjoy living in Korea. I discover new things everyday. I like finding out about other people and understanding more about them and why they do the things they do.

"The truth is that Korea's not for everybody. You have to be a very tolerant person. You're going to be banging your head against a wall because of school principals and *hagwon* owners, and you're not going to change them. Korea's funny that way. It can break your heart and it can also put you on top of the highest mountain."

Ted Gray (36)
America
University Instructor
8 Years

With so many awful stories surrounding English education in Korea, it should be comforting to know that there are some people who have had incredibly rewarding experiences in the country. Ted's easygoing attitude is proof that being flexible and open-minded goes a long, long way toward success in ESL classrooms in Korea.

THERE WERE different reasons why I came to Korea. One was I had never been to Korea before, and since I love traveling, any place I've never been appeals to me. Also, there was a Korean family that was close with my family when I was young. They had a daughter about my age, so we kind of grew up together, and I thought it might be cool to see what her country was like one day. So, when I finished graduate school, I applied to a number of different places in the world to teach English, and the best offer I got on paper was from Samsung's Human Resources Development Institute (HRDI), in Yongin (용인), just outside of Seoul. I accepted the offer and arrived in Korea in April 1995.

I still remember my first impression when I landed in Korea. Everything seemed organized, though imperfect in some way. It was kind of like Japan, minus 25 percent. I was met at the airport by the Westerner who was running our program and the Korean who was kind of in charge there. I wasn't overwhelmed by everything, and in fact, I remember feeling somehow comfortable, which might seem odd, considering I was in a country where I didn't know one word of the language. I guess that had something to do with the fact that when I got to Korea I had already done a lot of traveling, so I wasn't scared or in any way afraid of going out by myself. When you travel a lot you learn ways of getting around without a language. Up to that point, my traveling had included Southern Europe, Japan, Thailand, Singapore, Mexico, and the Virgin Islands. I had even lived in Taiwan for eight months by that point. All that traveling gave me a certain perspective. I don't know if this makes any sense, but Korea struck me as the kind of country where there is a connection between the people, more than we have in North America. In some ways, Koreans are all on their own page, but in some ways they're on the same page, which is different from North America where we're all on our own page.

After settling in at my place in Yongin, I began teaching at Samsung's HRDI. The teaching there was divided into four ten-week programs and the students consisted of mid- and high-level managers from all over Korea. For someone like me who was new to the country, it was a great way to learn about Korea, because I was meeting people that lived and worked in all parts of the country. I learned a lot about the geography just because I had variety in the classroom that way. My students were well-educated and really great to teach, in fact. They would all get up at five thirty in the morning and do some stretching before studying English all day. If they spoke Korean in anything but an emergency they had to write a letter of apology to their boss—in English— explaining why they had shamed the company by speaking Korean when they were supposed to be learning English. It was that intense. Yet the men—and it was something like 98 percent men when I taught there—did all this happily. They had a great spirit and they were very nice to all of us foreign teachers.

I ended up teaching at Samsung's HRDI for two years. Now, originally I had thought that I would spend a year, maybe two, in Korea, see how it went, and then go somewhere else. So after my two years in Yongin I decided not to renew my contract. I left Korea for about two and half months and went traveling elsewhere in Asia with the intention of coming back after my travels, and then, either leaving Korea, if there were no good options available, or staying if there was a good option open to me. My hope was to work in a university, and so I thought if I got a university job that I was happy with I would stay. I didn't want to work at Samsung or at a *hagwon* (학원)—private academy; I wanted something more academic, unlike Samsung, which is more geared toward business.

When I got back after those two and a half months of traveling, I was immediately offered a whole bunch of private lessons. I didn't have much experience with that kind of teaching, but they paid a lot so I gave it a try. Soon after, I was making almost as much in one week as I was making in a month for Samsung! I was teaching four to six hours a day, six days a week, and making a ton of money. That led me to stay for the whole summer, at the end of which I was offered a job at Hongik University's (홍익대학교) Jochiwon (조치원) campus, south of Seoul, near Daejeon (대전). I thought about the job offer for about a week and then accepted it. So, instead of leaving Korea I ended up staying, yet not in Seoul where I wanted to be.

Hongik University, or Hongdae (홍대)—the abbreviation used by Koreans—has two campuses, like many other Korean universities in Seoul: one in the city and one outside the city. When I was in the country at the Jochiwon campus, I kept telling myself that I loved it there: it's a nice, small town, there's hiking in the hills, fresh air, and great people. But the truth was that I wanted to be in Seoul. I was riding the train back and forth between Seoul and Jochiwon every week, so I eventually asked my school whether it would be possible to transfer to the Seoul campus. "No," they told me. "It's impossible to transfer campuses." So I said, "It's the same school, though. I can't transfer?" to which they simply replied, "No. It just doesn't work that way." When I asked them my options they told me, "Well, you can quit and re-apply." Up to that point, I had worked two years there, and so I said to them, "Look, if I'm going to work this far away from Seoul, where I'd prefer to be, three days a week instead of four would be much better for me." They wouldn't budge, though. They just kept repeating that everyone at the Jochiwon campus had to work four days a week. It was after this incident that I decided it was a good time to break off from the university.

Now, in Korea there's always two ways of doing anything: the polite way and the impolite way, and as long as you do things the polite way, things will work in your favor more. Knowing that, I went up to the administration and told them, "I love working here, I love the people, the students—everything. However, I'm going to go study Korean full-time at Yonsei University (연세대학교) and maybe after a year or so I can come back and work here." They thought that was a great idea and so I left on really good terms with them and went and studied Korean.

I ended up studying at Yonsei for a term and a half, but in that time the Seoul campus for Hongdae was hiring for the following semester. I applied there and ended up getting re-hired! The lesson here was, if I had said to the people in Jochiwon that I wasn't happy about the new schedule and quit due to that, I probably wouldn't have been re-hired at the Seoul campus, because it's kind of against the way they do things.

In my roughly four years at Hongdae's Seoul campus, and eight years teaching in Korea, I've learned a few things. The first thing is that there's a huge market for English education in Korea. The market's limitless, I think. One thing's that kept me here all these years, for example, is the variety of jobs available in Korea. There's more than just standing in front of a class lecturing. You can edit, you can write, you can do private classes, you can do voice recordings, you can do radio and TV work, Internet stuff—you can do all these things—as it's all English-education oriented stuff. Back home, if you're a teacher, you don't have access to all this other stuff.

With the university students themselves, you'll get a whole range. I have great students, but at the same time I have students falling asleep in the back of the classroom, drawing sketches on the desk, chatting with their friends about where they're going to drink soju tomorrow—you'll get every type of student at a university. The biggest problem I have at Hongdae is that, because the classes are so big, it's not oriented to a real conversational, interactive class. The average class will have between 45 and 55 students. You can't teach a conversational class with 45 students when you only see them once a week for one two-hour conversation class! You simply can't learn a foreign language living in your own country, speaking your language, two hours a week with only a little homework on the side.

From a teaching perspective, you're not going to get a lot of improvement. What you're going to do in 15 weeks of two-hour classes is hope that they'll maintain the level they're at, learn a few things and have them come out of it ahead in some way. But you're not going to change somebody from a basic speaker to even an intermediate speaker. There's no individual attention given to students because the classes are so big. You're basically "lecturing" them, instead of "teaching" English. It's not useless, but it's not the best situation.

I have a master's in TESOL (Teachers of English to Speakers of Other Languages), but not much about the degree prepared me specifically for Koreans, mostly because I studied in the States. It was more just general advice about what to do when a student does this or that. There wasn't a lot of cultural awareness, for instance. It was more bookish and less practical. The best thing I got while I was studying was the teaching I was able to do at the same time. My program had a language center for international students to learn English, and so I learned more at the front of the class teaching than I did at the back of the class listening during that year of grad school.

I should mention, however, that if you study English language teaching like I did, you will get a lot of theories, ideas and suggestions, and some of them will be good and some of them you will never use. When you go to Korea, or anywhere else in the world, there's something called learners' strategy, and with

Koreans you learn that you want interaction; you don't want a teacher-oriented classroom, but rather, the students doing everything. Now, that may look good in a textbook as a strategy, but it's not going to work in every country or every culture. You have to learn how they learn and teach to that. You can't assume that they're going to follow your way. If they want a teacher-centered class because they're comfortable with that, you have to be that way. You actually have to do that, because they're going to get more out of it since it's that style they're comfortable with. If you throw English at them, plus you introduce a whole different learning style, it could be overwhelming. It's not for us to tell them how to learn; it's just for us to teach them our language and in a way they can learn.

Today, eight years in, I feel I'm fairly lucky in a lot of ways. I've done several radio shows and TV shows over my time here, and I was lucky to get into that, because it's been a great experience. I play on a rugby team here and have made a lot of great friends through it. On top of that, the job I have gives me a lot of free time. I teach three or four days a week and have up to five months' paid vacation a year, which has given me a chance to do other work and to travel, one of my greatest loves in life. That's something I've appreciated the most, having the time off to do what I want. I've learned very clearly here that when things are going well, they're going very well. It's kind of the land of opportunity, especially in my field, because there's just so much going on. However, there are some negative aspects to living in Korea. I like to call this country the land of extremes: a bus driver is driving 100 miles an hour and then he slams on the brakes; you meet somebody and they become your best friend right away or they're never going to talk you again; the building is going to be built tomorrow or it's not going to be built at all. And that's hard to adjust to, because in our society the range is sort of a 40–60 range, not a 0–100 range like it is in Korea. But if everything that bothers you really gets to you and you can't deal with things—you find yourself kicking trees and wanting to run over puppies, for example—then you shouldn't be here. The truth is that Korea's not for everybody. You have to be a very tolerant person. You're going to be banging your head against a wall because of school principals and *hagwon* owners, and you're not going to change them. Korea's funny that way. It can break your heart and it can also put you on top of the highest mountain.

"I was really sad to be back in my own country. I think I hung on very strongly to Korea when I got back, and I think it was the friendship bonding that I had in Korea, but I never had in South Africa, that made me feel that way."

Nikki Berrington (26)
South Africa
Hagwon Teacher
6 Months

Nikki's experience should be a warning to anyone thinking of signing a contract with a hagwon *(학원)— private academy—in Korea. Misled from the start, she ended up teaching at a Seventh-day Adventist chain of schools, that not only crammed religion into an already hectic program, but forced class upon class on the teachers. The experience nearly crushed Nikki. Six months into her contract, she was forced to leave Korea after suffering an emotional breakdown.*

I WAS BUSY with archeology in South Africa before the idea of teaching English in Korea struck, and I think it boiled down to finances. I had no money and teaching English is considered a quick way of making a buck or two. I didn't actually want to because everyone was doing it at the time and Taiwan was the number one destination for South Africans. My mom said to me,

"Try Taiwan. You can't lose anything by it," and I said, "I refuse. Firstly, I'm not an English teacher; I don't know what I'm doing. And secondly, I don't want to be with a whole lot of other South Africans in Taiwan."

Then I gave it some thought. I was just reading through a newspaper one day and saw an advertisement to teach English in Korea, which is when I reconsidered. I knew Korea was in Asia, but I didn't actually know where it was. I thought it was a new culture—and I am a bit of a cultural freak—and that I had to experience some kind of new culture. That was my decision.

It was a very quick decision, actually, because I applied and the second day after putting in the application I was called. Five days later I went in for an interview. The director of the institute said to me straight away, "I want you to come to Korea." I said, "What? Are you joking? How can you just decide so quickly?" He then replied, "No, I really want you to come to Korea. When can you come?" so I said, "I don't have all the documentation. I don't have any working visa. I can't do that," to which he said, "I've been doing this for twenty years. Leave it up to me." And as true as that, I was on an airplane within the next three weeks.

It was November 2002, the start of winter, when I arrived in Korea. It was minus 15 degrees at the time and I was exhausted, jet lagged, and immediately I was really sort of overwhelmed by the busy-ness of Seoul and all the apartments. And there were so many Koreans! Although, to this day I still deny having total culture shock because there wasn't anything I couldn't deal with.

However, when I got off the plane and walked into the airport, it wasn't like, "Welcome to Korea!" It was, "Okay, here are your bags. Let's go." I came over with another guy from South Africa and we were both exhausted, both jet lagged when we landed. We got off the flight and there wasn't anybody there for us. The guy I was with started to panic, saying "We need to do something," so I went to the reception desk, but not one of them could speak English so it was sort of pointless.

When I returned to my friend, my director had found him and told us that we were leaving. To the guy I flew over with, she just said, "Okay, you wait here. Nikki is coming with me. You can't come with us. Your director cannot come today but you must catch such-and-such bus and go to so-and-so suburb and your director will meet you there." My friend then said, "You can't be serious. I can't read. I can't talk. I can't pronounce anything. You have to take me with you." The woman who picked me up made a couple of phone calls and then decided to take my friend with us, telling him we would drop him "somewhere." This guy I was with, though, couldn't stand the whole experience of being in Seoul, and so cried like a baby. He decided right then and there at the airport, in fact, that he was getting on the next plane back to South Africa because Korea was just such a huge shock for him. It was literally the next plane back for him, which was a couple of days later.

With me, however, I got along with people right from the start. Koreans are very generous and quite hospitable once you get to know them. I assume this must have been largely because I was a foreigner—I was something new and interesting to them. I had a lot of people approach me and say, "If you need help, I'll help you. Anything you need I can get you."

That being said, I nearly starved to death the first few days because it's terrifying trying to buy something when you've got no concept of the currency or the product you're buying; trying to ask for something was really intimidating! I think the first few weeks were tough for that reason. I was just starting to become familiar with the currency during that time. I was always learning, and the thing was, I was alone; I was the only foreign teacher at my institute. My school was part of a chain of schools, but only recently developed. The director who had interviewed me in South Africa had put up one school, I think, a year before I left for Korea, and since that time he had put up 15 around Seoul. It was incredible. Initially, I wasn't told the schools were SDA—Seventh-day Adventist—and was only told the weekend before I left for Korea. By then it was to late to do anything about it.

When I arrived at the institute I was told that they had been expecting an experienced teacher, which I wasn't. But that didn't seem to matter: they told everyone, including the students, that I was the best—guaranteed! That was disaster number one because it was very difficult for me to live up to those standards, as I had no experience. Also, I had been promised that I would be teaching kindergarten, but when I arrived I was teaching anything but kindergarten. I was teaching adults, high school students, and elementary school kids.

I couldn't believe the pace of it all. I was expected to open the school at half past six in the morning and teach until late at night. It was quite something. On top of that, I was expected to go to church on Saturdays and find my way there via subway. Now, there's no subway system in South Africa, so that was quite an experience for me; just asking for a subway map took me about ten minutes! Asking someone to then explain where I should go was another disaster. I gave the person the business card for my school, they circled it on the map for me and then I went through the gates and saw two sets of stairs. I thought, "Which way do I go?" I grabbed a young Korean woman, because that's one piece of advice

I was given—if you're not sure, try and find a youngish Korean that will be familiar with English—yet she couldn't speak a word of English. I showed her where I wanted to go and where I thought I was supposed to go and she led me down some stairs. I could understand that she said that I had to get off three subway stops later, which I did, assuming I was at the right place, which I wasn't. She had meant that I had to transfer at the stop. "So, here we go again," I said to myself, looking for another younger Korean who could speak English. Eventually I found someone who guided me in the right direction and I got off at the right stop, but it ended up taking about three and a half hours to get there!

When I got to the subway stop, I exited out the gate and looked around, thinking, "Now what? This isn't the right building." I was a little bit intimidated to get in a taxi then because I knew all I could do was show the driver my business card. That was when a Korean, who had been watching me out of the corner of his eye, walked up to me and said, "Can I help you?" I said, "I'm trying to get to this place," and he replied, "Okay. I'll take you in my car." Now me, coming from South Africa, thought you don't just do that; you don't just hop in a stranger's car. So I wasn't sure how this would work out, whether it was appropriate or not. He then tried to assuage my fear by saying, "Don't worry. I'll take you." So, the both of us got in his car and he took me to where I was going and I discovered he was quite a decent man. When I finally got to the church, three and half hours late, the person in charge there asked me why my director had made me come alone. They were really shocked at this and I was quite famous for some time afterward because of it.

That was just the beginning of the workload at my *hagwon*. It became ridiculous, actually, endless. I had three twenty-minute classes in an hour, alongside a Korean teacher, and this was supposed to go on for six and a half hours, which it didn't, of course. Sometimes it would go on for eight hours, and that's excluding the other classes I taught by myself, which were an hour long each. In the beginning, I'd have one of those hour classes in the morning before having a short break. After that I'd have to start teaching these twenty-minute classes where I was rotating every twenty-minute lesson. I'd go into the classroom with the Korean teacher and she'd tell me, "Okay, I want you to drill this," and it was terrible because the kids didn't aspire to anything and it was boring. Yet I was expected to do this, anyway. I also had one animation class which was a nightmare to teach and that I had to do all by myself, and it went on for an hour, too.

What's more is that my director tried to make me teach classes which were Christian-based, although I adamantly refused. Now, I had Christian kids of all denominations in my class, not just SDA, and so I asked the students if they wanted me to base the discussions on religion, to which they said, "No, we're here to study English." That was a big relief. I was really lucky in that sense. I didn't have to do it when I was there—although it was expected later—but they wanted us to base the whole of Friday classes around religious activities, praying, singing and playing all kinds of Christian games, which I was really dreading. Actually, right when I left the *hagwon* was when they started implementing that at the *hagwon*.

I guess in retrospect, things began going horribly wrong from the day I arrived, yet I was in total denial that anything was wrong because I really didn't want to go home; it wasn't a consideration for me. I had hair loss after one month, as well as drastic weight loss. I went from a GP to a gynecologist to a dermatologist and eventually I ended up with a dermatologist who really wanted to help. He then put me on cortizone, though I didn't know it at the time, the last few months I was in Korea. When I got back to South Africa I went to see a dermatologist and he said I was on cortizone. I asked why I was on cortizone and he said because I had exima on my head, a rash that is stress related, but it is also caused by environmental factors. They said my case was a multiple-cause case: stress, weather factors—the whole lot.

What finally made me make up my mind to quit was the fact that they were going to change *hagwon* directors at my school. The director that I had, a woman who had no idea what she was doing, started to stress me out because she was falling apart. She then decided to sell the *hagwon* to her ex-husband, also a Seventh-day Adventist, who was based in Bundang (분당), where he had another *hagwon*. I then heard from another colleague at his school that he was a terrible man, and so I said to myself, "I can't put up with this change right now." As well, the Korean teachers just kept quitting one after the other, leaving me with new teachers and trying to balance the classes. I got so tired of listening to teachers crying. Plus, the pay was bad and the director was awful, and I just decided that I had to leave.

When I finally left Korea, my first thoughts were of relief, but also great sadness because I had to leave my boyfriend and my friends behind. I felt like I failed in my attempt to explore a new culture. I wanted to live the culture and I think I failed in doing so, and that was really hard for me to admit. I think that was probably why I hung on longer than I should have. I think I should have packed up, gone home and returned to South Africa as soon as possible. But I hung on, hoping it would go away. It was probably guilt that kept me in Korea, because I had made the decision to go there in the first place. Also, my friends had given me this huge farewell party before leaving South Africa and six months later I returned, so I kind of felt like I had failed my friends, too.

Upon landing in South Africa, I didn't make contact with anyone for half a year. My best friend knew I was back; actually she knew before I left Korea, but I didn't get in touch with her when I got back to Cape Town. It was six months before I contacted anyone at all because it was the guilt, the pining to come back to Korea. I really did miss my friends and boyfriend in Korea, so I wanted to return. I must have enjoyed Korean culture because it was difficult for me to adjust in South Africa. I was really happy to be home, but things felt different, and they were different, so I didn't feel like contacting anybody. It took time for me readjust. These days, I never socialize anymore–never. When I was in Korea, I socialized all the time. I haven't been too much of a social butterfly since I got back to South Africa and my life has changed as a result.

The truth is, I was obsessed with Korea when I got back. I left Korea not hating the country, and that's part of the reason I stayed in isolation for so long in South Africa: in my mind I was missing Korean friends, I was missing Korean food and I kept in contact with all my Korean friends. I kept telling everyone I wanted to come back to Korea. I was really sad to be back in my own country. I think I hung on very strongly to Korea when I got back, and I think it was the friendship bonding that I had in Korea, but I never had in South Africa, that made me feel that way. Also, it took me about eight months to get over my physical ailments.

Today, I want to return to Korea, but not to live–definitely not to live. If I were to work, it would have to be short-term periods, maybe six months at a time. My boyfriend will influence my decision, though. It's a very difficult decision. It's really tough for me because he's saying, "If I can't live here for, say, four years or so, it's going to be impossible for our relationship to stabilize." And so it's my choice: if I don't come back to Korea, I probably won't carry through with the relationship.

"Actually, I would go so far as to say that I love Koreans. In some ways I think there must have been a Korean among my ancestors because I feel more comfortable in Korea than I do in Japan."

Fujiwara Yoshitsugu (34)
Japan
Hagwon Teacher and University Instructor
8 Years

Fluent in Korean like few others who have spent as much time in Korea, "Fuji," as he's playfully called by his students, provided wonderful insight about his experiences in Korea. Although there are Koreans who believe that Japanese people harbor some amount of bitterness towards them, Fuji's time in Korea has yielded mostly positive memories.

THIS IS MY second time living in Korea, actually. What's more is that I came here once in elementary school and once in middle school, and then several times when I was in university. After graduating university in Japan in 1992, where I studied economics and did some Korean as well, I came to Korea and attended Yonsei University's (연세대학교) Korean language program for one year. After that I went back to Japan for three years and returned to Korea in 1996. I've been living here ever since. I've been in Seoul since 2001 and for five years before that I was in

Cheongju (청주), North Chungcheong Province (충청북도).

    I came to Korea when I was younger as part of an exchange between Korea and Japan's Boy Scout Programs. In those days, it wasn't very common for Japanese people to travel abroad, so when I arrived here, Korea had a big impact on me. To be honest, the history between Korea and Japan has not been very good throughout history. However, older Korean men and women took great pleasure in seeing me and spoke Japanese to me whenever they met me. After returning to Japan, I thought about my experience in Korea and realized that all those older men and women had learned Japanese in the years when we were the colonial masters of the Korean peninsula. Even so, no one ever made me feel bad for being Japanese and that made me feel really good. At the time, I asked myself, "If I were them, would I have been able to do the same thing?" Asking this question over and over made me think more and more about Korea. Furthermore, my hometown is Shimonoseki, which is close to Busan (부산), so I could listen to Korean radio programs in Japan.

    When I came to Seoul in 1992 to live for the first time, I was the only Japanese student in my neighborhood. Right away I could see that there were many differences between Japan and Korea. For example, I bought a bottle of orange juice one time and put it in the common room refrigerator, as I was staying at a kind of dorm for students. The next morning when I went to go and have a drink of it, I noticed that half of it was gone. The day after that I saw another friend help himself to someone else's drink in the fridge and when I asked him, "Is it all right to drink other people's stuff without their permission?" he said, "We're all living together here. Mine? Yours? That has no meaning here." This was a great shock to me. We Japanese think that what's mine is mine and what's yours is yours. Anyway, it didn't seem so bad to live like that, so I started giving it a try myself, eating and drinking others' things. I also noticed this kind of sharing behavior when out with friends. One time I was walking down the street with a Korean friend and he had only one piece of gum. Now in Japan, the person would either eat it himself or not eat it at all, but my Korean friend took the one piece of gum and split in half. This kind of behavior that I saw in Korea was very different from how we act back home. In Japan, people have a strong sense of individualism. In Korea, though, there is a very powerful concept of "we" that people adhere to, so that things aren't necessarily "mine" or "yours," but "ours," and so everything is shared. At times, I think this way of living is good, but at other times I don't think it's so good.

That's part of the reason I like Koreans. Actually, I would go so far as to say that I love Koreans. In some ways I think there must have been a Korean among my ancestors because I feel more comfortable in Korea than I do in Japan. Every time I come back to Korea from Japan I think, "I'm home! Home sweet home!" I don't think there's a foreigner who enjoys life here in Korea more than I do. There are so many things I like here. For example, I like the way Koreans do their best in everything—working, having fun, studying. I think it's great. At the same time, Koreans can become so political and critical about their own country sometimes. They criticize their own country too much, like politicians do sometimes. Japanese people, on the other hand, don't really care about what goes on in politics. Basically, I think there are two groups of Korean people. On the one hand, you have the people who talk about the country in a negative way, and on the other, you have the group who view their country very positively. Some people in that negative group even leave Korea, emigrating to other countries. Sometimes it's these same people who say bad things about Japan while buying Japanese products, which I find ironic.

Anyhow, when I came back to live in Korea in 1996, I chose to live in Cheongju because I wanted to teach Japanese. I also wanted to study Korean more, but I needed to work and make money before anything else. I applied for a job at a school in Seoul as a Japanese language teacher, but I couldn't find any work in Seoul at the time. It was a *hagwon* (학원)—private academy—owner in Cheongju that first offered me a job. When I arrived there I didn't think the *hagwon* was that bad. The city of Cheongju wasn't that bad, either. It wasn't nearly as crazy as it is in Seoul, so I liked that part of it right off the bat.

I had a lot of fun teaching, actually. Of course, sometimes it was really hard, but there was another Japanese teacher at my school who was as inexperienced as me, so we could lean on each other. The two of us had a difficult time teaching because we were both starting from scratch, without teaching strategies or anything. Fortunately, my students were at the intermediate level of Japanese and could communicate in Japanese fairly well.

Teaching Japanese at that *hagwon* in Cheongju gave me a lot of chances to become good friends with Korean students. And because I was very young at the time—I happened to be the same age as many of my students—I went out drinking with them from time to time. In Cheongju, there aren't as many *hagwon* as there are in Seoul. In Seoul, students might go to a language school for a couple of months and then move on to another one without another thought. Yet in a smaller city like Cheongju, students would continue going to the same language school for a lot longer, if out of nothing more than circumstance, which allowed my students and me to become better friends.

When it came to "free talking" classes, where we'd talk about anything, students didn't want to talk about the same things over and over, and so I constantly needed to think of new things, which wasn't easy over a long period of time. Also, Korean students tend to be very shy, so they don't always like taking in new students to a class. I wanted all the new students to always feel as if they fit in, so I would try and have students mingle with each other. However, that became quite stressful for me.

In general, though, I felt a lot of good things were happening to me because I was a foreigner. Koreans helped me out on countless occasions. There were, however, some bad things that happened, too. I can't say I ever experienced out–and–out racism, but I did feel at times that my nationality was the cause of a problem or misunderstanding. For instance, one time when I was drinking with a Japanese friend, a Korean guy who was really drunk came up to us, trying to pick a fight, and he said, "Why the hell are you speaking Japanese here? This is Korea!" Fortunately, it's rare that Koreans try to pick fights with me because I'm Japanese, due in part, I'm sure, to the fact that I may look Korean to people.

Take immigration as another example. When I lived in Cheongju, the closest immigration center was in Daejeon (대전), and whenever I went there to renew my visa, some of the immigration officials were rude to me, doing things like ordering me to come back at a time that was suitable only for them. Thing is, though, it takes about an hour from Cheongju to Daejeon, so it wasn't like I could just come back any time. I knew they could process the visa that same day because there were times when the immigration official was from Cheongju and he'd say to me, "Oh, you're from Cheongju!" and then deal with the matter very quickly, that same day. As public officials, they should be doing things by the book; there shouldn't be special treatment for certain people. One time I even saw a person bring in a box of drinks so that he would receive special treatment! That really got to me. I thought, "Am I supposed to do that, too? Buy them off?"

On another level, there's a lot of Koreans who think that buying foreigners a meal will draw them closer together because it's not simply the meal they're buying, it's the money being spent on the foreigner. That's all it comes down to for a lot of Koreans. I find it extremely frustrating that Koreans can't just look at foreigners as other people. Obviously we're not Korean, but we're all citizens of the same world, and until Koreans recognize that, they'll continue to treat foreigners—even the ones they're close with—as nothing more than guests in their country. Koreans feel that foreigners who come to Korea to work are stealing jobs and money from Koreans, and even though Koreans could do the exact same thing overseas, most people never think of doing that. Koreans try and get close to foreigners, but most times they aren't able to do so. I think that by only being friends with other Koreans, people in this country miss out on a lot in life. On the surface, Korea's as developed as a Starbucks coffee shop, but deep down, a lot of people still think like they did hundreds of years ago in the Chosun Dynasty (조선시대). There's something really interesting to this kind of unbalance.

As a last note, one question that Koreans ask me all the time is which team I cheer for when I watch Korea and Japan play soccer. Actually, I've really changed how I think about that over the years. Originally, I was really scared to watch a soccer game between the two countries. I'd be watching the game by myself at home and be unable to move. One time I was watching a Japan–Korea game with a bunch of my students from Busan who were really getting into the game—so much so, in fact, that they kind of frightened me.

To be honest, I don't particularly like soccer all that much, playing it or watching it. But, if a game's on TV and people are watching it, I'll watch it, too. And because I'm Japanese, I naturally think that I should be cheering for the Japanese side, but there are times when I hope that the Japanese lose. I was always scared that students would come to class the day after Japan beat Korea and be all angry or something. On the two occasions when Japan and Korea played each other, Japan won once and Korea won once, and I was extremely happy that Japan didn't win both times! Of course Japan winning is in the interests of Japan, but when Korea wins it doesn't seem like it's just about that. When Japan wins, people in Japan are happy, but when Korea wins it's like there's something else at stake; Koreans aren't satisfied with simply winning.

SECTION V
LEARNING IN KOREA

WISDOM

Learning in Korea

IN 2003 there were 5,795 students from 28 countries[1] studying in Korea full-time at a total of 151 colleges.[2] The four universities with the highest enrollment of foreign students in 2003 were Yonsei University (연세대학교), Seoul National University (서울대학교), Ehwa Womans University (이화여자대학교), and Sungkyunkwan University (성균관대학교). The number of foreign students is only planning to increase in the near future, as local colleges are planning to accept 6,022 full-time students for the 2004 academic year.[3] What's more, students on a D–2 student visa are now given more flexibility to work legally in Korea while studying full-time. The new system in place as of March 1, 2003 for foreign students holding a D–2 visa is as follows:

> The Ministry of Justice is implementing [a] more flexible programme in order to meet foreign students' expectations. A D–2 holding foreign student who has completed the first semester of more than six months at university or college in Korea will be entitled to apply for part-time work ... [but] their jobs should be applicable to ones such as a translator, a librarian and a project researcher, which has much to do with what they are majoring in. Among other things, a

foreign student whose language is a native mother tongue will be allowed to get a teaching job as an instructor at an institute only if the applicant has an academic degree after college graduation in his/her own country. However, their work time must not exceed 20 hours per week per semester. In addition, one more place of work could be added on approval. Application should be submitted with a recommendation certificate from the full-time assistant professor in charge. A qualified student will be granted one-year's permission should he/she satisfy all the requirements.[4]

Full-time students currently study a variety of majors at Korean schools in all levels of study, from language certification programs, to Bachelor's, Master's, and Ph.D degrees. And while many students who study full-time at a Korean university do so in Korean, this is not always the case. There are programs which are taught entirely in English.

At the same time, there are estimated to be thousands of foreigners who study in Korea without a student visa. The vast majority of these students are learning Korean, and the places they study the language range from private tutors—*gwa-wae* (과외)—to local private academies—*hagwon* (학원)—to accredited universities.

❡

Today, there are students from all continents studying one thing or another in Korea. The two men and three women in this section come from four continents—Africa, Asia, Europe, and North America—and since their experiences in the Korean classroom are colored by their previous education, each encounter is unique. These five people have studied subjects as diverse as Korean traditional music theory, international relations, and the Korean language. As a result, their stories are a unique window into the learning experience here, with a great deal of insight on how to thrive in the Korean classroom and maximize the education available in a limited amount of time.

"When you develop a relationship with someone in Korean, and if that relationship is an intimate one, some of the things that get said are so beautiful and touching, and remain particular to Korean, that they can't be translated into English perfectly."

Ron Schafrick (31)
Canada
Korean Language Student
5 Years

Not many people have studied Korean as thoroughly as Ron Schafrick. On the surface his story resembles that of many who come to Korea to teach English, but five years on he is his own success story, and a good example of how far you can take the language if you stick it out in the trenches of language warfare.

I HAD PHENOMENALLY huge student loans in Canada and I was worried how I would pay them back. I had a desk job at Concordia University and wasn't making a lot of money. I wasn't happy and I was bored with my job, and I was worried about those loans. Through the Internet, and word of mouth, I heard about teaching in Korea and that you could make a lot of money here. At the time there were a lot of posters up at Concordia advertising Korea as a place to teach English. Not too long after noticing these posters around school, I went to go and buy a bike off some people who were having a moving sale, and found out they were selling all of their stuff because they were going to Korea to teach English! I thought that was so cool, exciting and amazing. I thought that I had to go and do that, too. A woman who worked in the graduate faculty at Concordia University hooked me up with an alumnus who had been to Korea. He said it was great and that he made a lot of money. The next thing I knew I was packing my bags for Korea.

I arrived here on November 5, 1997. Because it was also the time when the Asian economic crisis began, I thought that I was probably the last foreigner to come here to teach English! In any case, I remember my first year as very exciting, and I think that was the best time I ever had in Korea. With respect to the language, I didn't make any effort, actually, for about the first year, because it just seemed like this huge, time-consuming monster of an undertaking. I did, however, feel pressure to learn Korean in that first year. People would tell me all the time that I should learn Korean, at least some key phrases. Korean friends of mine eventually taught me the alphabet, and then the numbers, and then some basic expressions, such as "how much," "delicious," and "thank you." After about a year, I started learning Korean formally at Sookmyung University (숙명여자대학교) three nights a week, after which I went to YBM/Sisa in Jongno (종로) five nights a week, for two hours each time. I then moved on to Sogang University (서강대학교), then to Ehwa Womans University (이화여자대학교) and then finally back to Sogang University.

When I first started studying Korean, of course I thought it was difficult. When I was learning Korean for the first couple of years, I can easily recall all the frustration and anger I experienced trying to study the language. I remember asking various Koreans how to say "I don't understand" and I could never get a straight answer. I also remember wondering why there were two sets of numbers, and having great difficulty making sentences where the subject is "you." I didn't know where to begin. Actually, the concept of incorporating "you" into a sentence is not that difficult, but I don't think I was taught properly. No one teacher ever explained that a specific verb conjugation implies "you." Therefore, it took a while before I was confident with those sentences.

On top of this, just understanding the levels of politeness in the Korean language was a foreign concept to me. The expression "it depends on the situation" is an expression that you hear over and over again while learning Korean. In the beginning, I remember thinking that statement was so arbitrary. In fact, there are certain situational rules, and it's not as willy-nilly or arbitrary as some teachers make it sound. Another thing is that it's really difficult to translate one word into Korean from its English equivalent because the words don't always overlap perfectly. A good example would be emotion words. There's so little overlap between English emotion words and Korean emotion words. Some Korean emotion phrases translate so poorly into English, and often times sound cheesy in our language.

I find that Korean can be a very beautiful language, though. When you develop a relationship with someone in Korean, and if that relationship is an intimate one, some of the things that get said are so beautiful and touching, and remain particular to Korean, that they can't be translated into English perfectly. Another thing I've learned is that Korean is not as hard as people make it out to be.

To be honest, I've never been terribly satisfied at any stage of my Korean learning, except early on when I was studying at Sookmyung University. I thought my teacher there was excellent.

Her teaching method wasn't anything particularly special, but it was effective. For example, when I studied at the Korea Herald, the teacher didn't speak a lick of English, and as a beginner, it made it all the more difficult to progress. We used a lot of role-play situations, which I didn't find very effective. My teacher at Sookmyung University, however, gave us a lot of grammar and vocabulary to work with and we were able to go from partner to partner, ask the question, get the answer, and then move on. She had a wonderful way of explaining things so that we could understand.

At Sogang University, I felt the teachers were really good as well. I liked how they introduced grammar structure in the first class, usually the writing or reading class, and then that grammar structure was carried into the next class, the conversation class, and then into the video class. I thought it was well-executed and well-balanced.

One major complaint that I have had over the years—but one I've changed my mind about recently—is that I felt *ban-mal* (반말) —casual speech—and *jon-dae-mal* (존대말)—formal speech—were not taught in the right order. When foreigners learn Korean, it's the exact opposite from the way a Korean child learns the language, that is *ban-mal* then *jon-dae-mal*. Adult foreigners learn in the opposite order. We're not taught *ban-mal* until much, much later. The more I spoke Korean and listened to Koreans I realized that I was hearing *jon-dae-mal* very rarely and therefore I concluded the teaching method of *jon-dae-mal* first to be inappropriate. Recently, though, I met an American who had learned some Korean but was disappointed that he had never been formally taught *ban-mal*. We were at a party with some Koreans and he began talking to them in *ban-mal*. What a goof! I thought. Even though they were younger than him, he didn't know those people and shouldn't have been speaking to them that way.

On the opposite end, though, I find that with some Koreans, when they want to speak English, it can be a bit rude. For some of them, speaking English is equated with the opportunity to be rude or silly. That can be offensive. However, if I say, "It's okay to speak Korean," I find that they become so much more polite and I become that much more comfortable. For instance, one time when I went to Ulleung Island (울릉도) and I asked a man for directions, he said, "We go walking. Walking. Okay? Understanduh?" and I just felt like he was making a fool of me. I told him he could explain it to me in Korean and found that he was much more polite to me after that. I found then, and on subsequent occasions, that using Korean in situations like that has been very much to my advantage. It helps Koreans feel more comfortable, too.

Regardless, like many people who begin to learn Korean, I was scared of speaking in public early on. Actually, I'm still scared! There are times where I simply lack confidence, when I might not be entirely sure of the right vocabulary or expression, which can be nerve-wracking.

For people thinking about studying Korean formally, my advice would be that you practice and study everyday. I still keep a vocabulary and expression notebook, which I used to go through everyday. I think that if you're going to study Korean seriously, you have to use it in every facet of your life. If you have a daily planner, try writing all your appointments and things in Korean. Even messages to myself I write in Korean. I've also started writing a column in Korean for a newspaper and that's really helped my learning process.

I can think of two other things that really helped me. One was going to the gym and speaking Korean with people there, and the other was joining a mountain biking club. Both examples forced me to use my Korean and learn a specialized vocabulary related to those kinds of environments. Watching TV is also very helpful. If you're in Korea, try watching Arirang. I like watching Arirang because of the captions. The captions always surprise me as to what I'm missing.

Whatever you do, though, you have to remember that it's going to take a long time! But there's a light. Personally, I'm not nearly fluent; not at all. I've been studying for four years, and it's taken me that long just to get comfortable. These days, I've become a bit lazy, maybe because I'm comfortable on a very fundamental level. If I were to talk about photography, a specific novel, or politics, though, that would be too difficult for me at this stage. It still amazes me, for example, how I can watch TV, like the news, and I still don't understand what's being said!

One last thing I should mention, which I didn't believe when I first heard it, is that even Koreans have a hard time understanding other Koreans sometimes! Part of that, I think, has to do with *sa-too-ree* (사투리)—dialect—Koreanized English words, imperfect pronunciation, slang, new and/or unfamiliar vocabulary, generation gap, and so forth, all getting in the way of communication. It really blows me away how even two Koreans can have trouble understanding each other. In any case, if you're studying this language, and you're willing to put up with those initial frustrations, the rewards are well worth it.

If you only plan on being here for six months to a year, though, then it's fine to not learn Korean. However, if you do learn something like a language, how can it be a waste? Learning Korean in Korea is the ultimate skill. My Korean will always be my souvenir from here. My friends in Canada are all so amazed that I can speak Korean, and I'm proud of it. For those that end up staying in the country and living here for a long time, however, I find it both annoying and offensive when they don't learn any Korean. I had a co-worker who was married to a Korean and they had a child. This guy couldn't even read his students' names when he did role call in the classroom, so he gave everyone English names! He went about his existence in Korea without learning the most basic Korean expressions. I find that so offensive! I don't understand how someone can live, work, and get married to a Korean woman in Korea and not want to learn to say "I love you" in her language. He actually went out of his way to not learn the language of the woman he loved!

"I'm in the first semester, and the thing that I didn't understand was that first semester students should respect the older students a lot."

Fatma* (24)
Morocco
MBA Student
2 Months

Fatma has tried hard to make the most of her limited experience in Korea. Not only does she study in the MBA program full-time, but she also studies Korean three hours a day. In a country where her homeland and religion are often misunderstood, Fatma says that she has been extremely impressed by her time in Korea and by everyone that has helped her along the way.

THREE YEARS AGO I was in Japan and I met some Korean students there who told me about Korea. When I had a chance to choose between other universities and my present university, I contacted some old Korean friends of mine. I said, "What do you think? Do I have to choose Korea or not?" and they said, "Choose Korea."

I was excited to come to Korea because in Morocco we have heard a lot about Asian cultures, yet we don't have any idea what it's really like, because it's too far away and there's not a lot of Koreans or Asian people there. So when I had this chance, I really wanted to discover this new culture without any hesitation.

The two first days I was in Korea I was afraid because between the airport and Seoul there were many, many churches—more than France—and I thought, "Maybe they don't understand what Muslim people are." I thought maybe people would be uptight, more so than in other countries. Yet after my first contact with Korean people, I realized they knew more about my country than I expected, and about Muslim people in general. I stayed in a guesthouse near the university when I first arrived. There are many foreigners in the guesthouse, most of whom are Chinese, and so it's a good chance also to meet other Asian people and also to see the difference between the Chinese and the Koreans.

My courses are taught in two languages: Korean and English. Because we come from a French business school, they told us not to choose Korean courses. However, if I want to stay more, up to two years, I have to learn Korean and choose other Korean courses. Americans, Canadians, and also Koreans—Korean teachers who were in America before—teach the courses. Most of them have taught or studied at an American university before. The level of English of the Korean teachers is very high. They speak like Americans and Canadians, maybe because they spent a long time in America. For the students it's different. Students who speak English fluently were in America before, but the others, just like me, have some problems in English.

In terms of my schedule, I have three hours of Korean per day. I can't speak Korean fluently, though, because I can't manage my MBA classes and my Korean classes, so sometimes I can't do my homework, which is of course very important to develop your Korean. Also, even though the French and Moroccan styles of education are the same, Korea is more similar to America's. This means all that we learn is in the book and we have first to study the book and then discuss it with the teachers. In France, and even in Morocco for that matter, it doesn't work like this. Back home, a teacher first explains and talks about the lesson in general and after that they give us the name of the books that we have to read and study. There are some positive points here in Korea that are better than France, but the French education system is also better in some ways. For example, sometimes we can't learn alone before the explanation of the teacher, so I think that there's no reason to learn before, but we have to do it because it works that way here. The positive thing is that we learn how to study and how to analyze on our own, which I think is very good.

In general, I have a good relationship with Koreans, but I think that Korean people are a little bit shy. For example, in Morocco we touch each other easily; contact with people is normal. But here, in Korea, I think we have to keep a certain space between people. The first time I learned this I was frustrated, because it's not in my culture, but once we understand this it's easier because we find people very helpful and very kind. That's why I like Korean people.

Now, I'm from Morocco, so when I tell Koreans that, ninety percent of the time there'll be confusion between Monaco and Morocco, something I have to explain to them. Actually, sometimes Koreans are disappointed because they really wanted me to come from Monaco! Others, though, are really interested about Arabic people, and Muslim people in general, because they have an idea of what Moroccan people are, and I can give them another idea, another image. I think they really accept me, partly because there are not a lot of Arabic people in Korea, especially Moroccans, so they are curious to know more about me and my country.

Fortunately, I don't feel I've experienced any discrimination because of my color or because of my country. I had some discussions about religion because, with some Korean young people who are Christian, they believe that Muslim people want to hurt Christians and they want to know why. That's when I have to explain that it's simply not true that Muslims want to hurt Christians. Initially, Koreans didn't want to talk a lot with me just because I'm Muslim. After I explained that I'm fairly open and not an extremist, however, these people were okay. I think Koreans believe that when I say the word "Arabic" they think of all Arabic countries and don't allow for any differences between countries or cultures.

One way that this poses a challenge is with food. I think there's a little problem, not because they don't allow you to practice your religion freely in Korea, but because it's so different that they can't understand. For example, I don't eat pork and sometimes I say, "Sorry, is there ham?" to which Koreans will often say, "No, no, there's no ham. There's only pork." This can create some confusion among people. It seems as if some Koreans find it difficult to understand that some people don't eat meat which has been killed in a certain way. This problem is compounded by the fact that there are no restaurants in Korea that can understand this.

Another example of the differences in understanding between our respective cultures is the belly dance. In Korea, it's not wise to dance the belly dance. One time a Korean student asked me if we have a special dance in Arabia. I said that we did, but when I did it, some of the students really misunderstood what I was doing. They said it's disrespectful to do the belly dance when your parents and your cousins and your friends are watching. What they don't understand is that the dance is not sexual. It's really the way that we dance in Morocco! Also, Moroccan people—and Arabic people in general, actually—kiss each other when we see friends. For Moroccans especially, we kiss each other six times and with Korean people it's forbidden.

Within the Muslim community as a whole, we're not very close in Korea. However, that's just because we don't know each other and because this community is so spread out all over Korea. When Muslims meet other Muslims in Korea, though, at a market area, for instance, we talk easily about Islam, about religion, and about our countries.

Personally, I've spent only two months here and soon I have to go back to France. I'm very sad to think about the idea that I won't come back. I want to spend more time here because I think one semester is very short to know more about Korean people and about the culture in general. I really want to spend more time to discover the culture here, and maybe learn more about my own culture at the same time. That being said, though, I wouldn't consider working in Korea in the future. There are some points that make me afraid of working here. For example, in my MBA class there are eight Samsung men, and at their company they work from seven o'clock in the morning to normally four o'clock. But, they say, in reality they usually break at seven or eight in the evening before their boss says, for example, "Tonight we drink together," and even if you have something to do, you have to go with your boss; you have to drink with your boss because it's disrespectful not to. That kind of behavior scares me.

For people coming to Korea to study here, there are a couple of things I might suggest. In my own case, if I had bought just a simple book about Korean letters, I think my first Korean lesson would have been easier, and I think I would have had more chances to speak Korean than now, because I spent a lot of time just learning Korean letters. I should have spent time doing this in France or Morocco.

Also, studying in a Korean group is different than Morocco or France. I'm in the first semester, and the thing that I didn't understand was that first semester students should respect the older students a lot. We have to prepare schedules, and before meeting, we, the younger students, had to do this. I couldn't understand this at first and would say, "Why do we have to do this? We should do this all together." Also, students can't express their opinion. What the teacher says is right all the time, so the first time I learned this it was a little bit difficult for me. However, after attempting to understood the mentality here, it's become easier for me because I know what is expected of me and what the limits are.

"Only later did I realize that if I had studied something practical, and done the language on the side, I would have had a much bigger advantage and better chances in the business world today."

Nicole Risse (26)
Germany
Korean Language and
Korean Studies Student
(B.A. & M.A.)
4 ½ Years

Nicole is clearly an intelligent and hardworking young lady. Although she has only spent four and a half years in Korea, her time here belies a great knowledge of the country, its language and its people. With a bachelor's degree in Korean studies from a German university and a master's degree from Yonsei University's (연세대학교) prestigious GSIS, plus time at a different Korean university learning the language, Nicole is well versed in so much more about Korea and Korean than she learned formally through her schooling.

A FTER I FINISHED high school, I wanted to go abroad for a year. However, I wanted to do something besides the typical au pair thing that most of my friends were doing. From the priest at our church I had heard about the Berlin Missionary

Organization, which sends young people overseas to help in church communities. Originally, I wanted to go to Africa, and I went to many seminars that were offered by other organizations to help people prepare themselves for this unique experience. In 1995, though, I met a Korean man while I was leading a group from all over the world in an international work camp. The two of us ended up spending the summer together. By the end of the same year I was supposed to submit my application to the organization and, due to my relationship with this man, I became very confused regarding my future.

It was then I learned that the Berlin Missionary Organization also sends people to Korea. Even when we parted ways, I was still really interested in Korea, and thus I applied for positions in both Africa and Korea. Apparently, a lot of people were applying for the Africa positions, and only a few for the Asian ones, Japan and Korea. I was subsequently picked for its Korea mission, and in the beginning of October 1996 I landed in Seoul.

Upon my arrival, I was just overwhelmed because everything was so new. Someone from the Presbyterian Church of the Republic of Korea picked me up at the airport and we took a taxi into Seoul. There was a traffic jam into the city, so the first impression I got was of traffic jams, crowded streets, and high-rise apartments.

After we got into the city and I met everybody at the office, we decided to tour around the city a little. I remember thinking that the sidewalks were crowded with so many people! And I was shocked to learn that motorcycles could drive on the sidewalks. People pushing and shoving, I thought, "What the hell is going on here!" But it was exciting and I loved it.

That night at my hotel I wasn't really tired and couldn't sleep.

Suddenly, I started to feel lost and lonely. My first thought was, "If I start crying now"—and that was what I really wanted to do—"I'm going to have a horrendous time during my one-year stay in this country." I didn't cry; instead, I listened to music and read. After I finally did manage to fall asleep, I woke up every hour, partly because of the noise from the street in front of the hotel, and partly because of the jetlag. In my hometown, there's no noise in the middle of the night, but in Seoul it just never stops.

The next day was October 3, German Reunification Day, and so I went with a German priest to the German Embassy where they were holding a reception to celebrate the event. After the reception, we drove to Ilsan (일산), where the host family lived, and with whom I was supposed to live for those first two and a half months. My host mother was really nice, but of course everything was a little awkward. The father was the only one who could speak a little bit of English. The others tried, but communication was very difficult. Language school wasn't starting for another four days, so I had some time to get adjusted to the country.

After the priest, who spoke Korean very fluently, left, the mother came to my room and offered to show me the neighborhood. We were on our walk when she suddenly started pointing at things and telling me what they were in Korean. For instance, she would point at a tree and say *na-moo* (나무), or at a butterfly, and say *na-bee* (나비). When we arrived back at home later that evening, I sat down at the kitchen table and asked the mother to tell me once again everything we had seen that day. I made my own vocabulary list. Every day from that day on, I would add new words to that list and try to memorize them.

Classes at Sogang University (서강대학교) started the following

Monday. Because I was in the first level, we were learning the Korean letters. However, because my Korean friend—the one I had met in Germany in 1995—had attempted to teach me the Korean alphabet, I had an easier an easier time learning it. I used to practice by spelling out German words with the Korean alphabet. I didn't understand what the Korean words I would try to read on street signs when driving by on a bus meant, and my pronunciation was probably very bad, but I could already read a little before starting my language courses at Sogang.

At Sogang we had three hours of instruction in three areas: reading, writing, and speaking. They always had us interact with each other, which was very practical. In the speaking class, for instance, we would work in groups. Each time, we were given a situation that we were to act out. After practicing in our groups, we would give a little performance in front of the class. The way the teachers encouraged us was a great way to make the class more fun, and learning Korean became more interesting. I had never had a similar learning experience before in Germany when taking English, French, or Russian classes.

In the beginning, the pronunciation was the hardest part of the language. I think for most Western learners it's one of the hardest parts. Also, trying to overcome that barrier whereby you go out and speak Korean in public is very difficult and takes a lot of courage. Our language instructors encouraged us to practice everything we'd learned that day in class by using it with Koreans we met on the street. An example of this was when we learned numbers. Our teacher suggested that we phone information, 114, and ask for a random telephone number, and then try to write it down.

However, I wanted to learn faster than the school was teaching, so whenever I got home after my classes I would try to talk to my host mother, which improved my vocabulary. At the time, I had not yet learned how to make a sentence. Once I had learned how to do that, I would just try to say anything and talk about anything, mostly with my host mother, but also with my youngest host sister. Up until then, I had learned English, French, and Russian, yet learning Korean was different because learning it in-country gave me the opportunity to apply the language immediately. With Russian, for example, I learned it like Korean students are said to learn English in school: we just had to memorize the vocabulary and grammar. Our main activity in Russian class was translating things in Russian. A few times I had to memorize my CV or other texts, and then recite them in front of class. This is no way to learn a language. It might have worked for some students, but it did not help me. I don't speak much Russian anymore as a result. A lot of friends who received the same education do not remember much either.

I should point out that, while learning Korean, there was one thing that helped me very much. It was doing a language exchange with a friend of an acquaintance. He was majoring in German Literature and wanted me to help him improve his German. In return, he taught me Korean sign language. I'm not sure why, but learning Korean sign language helped me better understand Korean grammar. One day I suddenly felt like a light bulb was turning on. From that day on, I started to understand Korean sentence structure from a different angle.

After finishing my course at Sogang University, I worked at a church in Suyu-dong (수유동) for about two and a half or three months. It was there that I had my first encounter with *ban-mal* (반말), or informal speech. After Christmas one time, I went camping with a group of kids who taught me *ban-mal*. Up until then, I had only been able to speak *jon-dae-mal* (존대말)—formal speech—and so when I spoke to the kids in *jon-dae-mal* they informed me that this was considered odd because I was much older than they were. When I returned to Seoul, I was so proud of myself that I subconsciously used *ban-mal* with everyone. It only occurred to me when somebody said, "Did you know you're speaking *ban-mal* to the priests?" That was a real lesson in *ban-mal* and *jon-dae-mal* for me. In Germany, we have a concept very similar to *ban-mal* and *jon-dae-mal*. However, whereas I was treated like an adult in Germany, in Korea I was treated like a child again, which was reflected in how people would talk to me. In Korea, I—who already felt like an adult—was supposed to be respectful and polite to people who did not take me seriously and treated me like a child. Why should I do that? I asked myself. Why should I respect somebody who doesn't seem to respect me as a person. There were of course exceptions, but that really bothered me.

Anyway, after finishing at the church in Suyu-dong, I went to Mokpo, South Jeolla Province (목포, 전라남도) in March of 1997, where I stayed for six months. Yet I wasn't actually living in Mokpo, but rather with a group of nuns in a small community in the mountains outside of Mokpo. We worked a lot in the fields, planting and harvesting—whatever the season demanded. Because we sometimes had guests, we also had to take care of the rooms. I would occasionally join a group of nuns and go into Mokpo and give medicine and acupuncture to sick or poor people. During that time I didn't really have anybody to teach me Korean. However, I continued learning by reading the Bible. I also had some books in Korean, like *The Yalu River Flows* (압록강은 흐른다). Reading that book, I observed different grammar patterns. To find out what they meant and what kind of connotation they expressed, I would ask the nuns. Talking with them, I learned a lot about the language and the culture.

After those six months near Mokpo, I came back to Seoul for one month and then returned to Germany, to pursue a degree in Korean Studies at university. Yet just before leaving Seoul, I met my second Korean boyfriend. For the two years we were together, I only spent three months here in 1998 and another month in 1999. When I decided to study in Korea to be closer to my boyfriend, I learned of a scholarship program for studies abroad by the German government and applied. A month after getting the scholarship we broke up, but I didn't want the scholarship to go to waste. After deferring my scholarship for a semester, which was supposed to start in fall 1999, I came back to pursue a Master of Arts degree in Korean Studies at Yonsei University's Graduate School of International Studies (GSIS).

The courses at GSIS are all offered in English, and the entire program lasts two years, minimum. In class, the level of English used by the professors was good to excellent—nothing to complain about. One problem I had with some of the professors was that they never seemed to have time for their students—whether that was because they were too busy or because they didn't care, I don't know. I don't think that this is a problem unique to my Yonsei professors, as I have encountered the same phenomenon at other Korean universities, and even at German universities. Despite that, Yonsei gave me the opportunity to meet some of the brightest and most exceptional people and professors in Korea, and from around the world.

Regarding the classes, it was often the case that during our lectures and seminars only the foreign students were open for discussions, whereas most of the Korean students were rather quiet. I guess that traces back to the Korean university system. Still, it was a great experience to study in Korea with Korean colleagues, although it was so very different from my experience in Germany. Korean universities seem to be stricter and more restrained than universities in Germany. Another great difference is that in Germany you don't pay for education; it was quite strange for me to pay for school, especially when the school makes you pay for every single little thing.

I actually had the great opportunity to work for one of my professors, which on the one hand caused me a lot of problems and grief, and on the other hand taught me a lot about life. My relationship with my professor was much colder and more businesslike than my relations with my professors back in Germany. I learned that professors in Korea demand and expect a very different behavior from their students than their German counterparts. In Germany I get the feeling that the two people form a sort of equal partnership, whereas in Korea there still seems to exist a strict hierarchal relationship.

If I were to offer some advice about studying Korean, I'd say don't take Korean Studies for the language. That's what I did at first and I sometimes regret it. When I left Korea after my first year here, I was so afraid of forgetting the language that it became one of the biggest reasons I entered Korean Studies. Only later did I realize that if I had studied something practical, and done the language on the side, I would have had a much bigger advantage and better chances in the business world today. I know some people who made the same decision I made and I know others who chose to go the other direction, and they are much better off for it. In the end, however, I'm really glad I learned the language, and I'm glad I learned about Korea's culture and history. Unless you want to become a Korean or Asian Studies professor—which used to be my dream—learning Korean should be more of a hobby than an occupation.

"I would, however, like to continue studying in Korea, because I think schools here are better than Japan, and the students usually study very hard."

Yuki* (25)
Japan
Korean Language Student
6 Months

In the short time Yuki was in Korea, she managed to pick up the language to a very respectable level. Her secret? She learned to become fearless when speaking the language, and studied every single day.

WHEN I FIRST arrived here I stayed at my Korean boyfriend's house. Even though I couldn't speak Korean at all, his parents helped me a lot, so I didn't have any problems. I used to go out with Koreans because when I went out alone I felt scared at first. This was partly because I couldn't use English. Before coming to Korea, I thought Korean people usually had a high TOEIC (Test of English for International Communication) score, so there wouldn't be any problem communicating in English, yet when I got here I realized I couldn't use English with Koreans.

I was living in a *go-shee-won* (고시원)—student boarding house—near the subway station shortly after arriving. I lived there three months or so, after which I moved to a different boarding house—*ha-sook-jeep* (하숙집). This last place was nice because it was very clean—it didn't have any ants—and it included everything I needed: a desk, a chair, and a stand light. It didn't include meals, but I could cook anytime. The conditions at my boarding house weren't ideal, but it was cheap, and as I was supporting myself from money I had saved while working years before, that was a big consideration. Also, I could get breakfast and dinner served to me by the landlady. The landlady was very kind. When I became sick she was very worried about me and came to my room very often. At times like that, she would cook me a special meal and I had a little chance to talk to her in Korean.

Actually, although I've had to speak Korean almost everywhere in Korea, the only place I've really been able to speak Japanese is at the big markets, like Dongdaemun (동대문) and Namdaemun (남대문) markets. Both those places are very famous places to Japanese people, so many shop keepers speak Japanese. However, Koreans don't usually realize my nationality and so they speak to me in Korean anyway, so I also use Korean. When I first arrived, I didn't like it when Koreans mistook me for being Korean, because I couldn't speak the language, but now I can speak some Korean so it's no problem.

All in all, I enjoy studying in Korea, but I originally wanted to study Korean full-time, like at an English institute, from morning to afternoon. Yet all of the schools in Korea only have morning classes—four hours, or less than four hours a day. The school I'm at now is not famous among the Japanese, so it doesn't have a lot of Japanese students. And though that's very good for me to study Korean, there are too many Chinese students at my school; there's not enough diversity there. I'm studying Korean, but I usually listen to Chinese more than Korean everyday in class. Some of the teachers can speak Chinese, and some of them actually use it to explain things to everyone. I wish they spoke Korean all the time, though.

Actually, one time one of our teachers said to our classmates, "Usually Japanese people have a strong accent in Korean, like someone from Busan (부산)." After that I didn't want to speak Korean; it made me feel very self-conscious when I spoke Korean. Another thing with the teachers is that, when I first got to Korea, I was studying level two and I couldn't understand what my teacher was saying at all. She spoke too quickly, and when I had a problem and asked the teacher to explain something, she usually couldn't explain it so that I fully understood.

I think that's part of the reason I don't really get along well with the teachers here. I don't feel they are very friendly. They just think they have to teach us, so during the class they are in the classroom with us, but after that they usually disappear. I think the teachers should give us a chance to ask them something after class because, when I studied English abroad, the teachers usually helped us a lot, not only in the class. Korean teachers just aren't at school after class usually. I don't know where they go. As well, we never get to go out together as a class, which is something I wish we could to do.

I would, however, like to continue studying in Korea, because I think schools here are better than Japan, and the students usually study very hard. Most Japanese people usually go to university to have fun, to go abroad, or to hang out with friends. Yet I think Korean people really want to study. All of my Korean friends study from early in the morning to late in the evening. It's very different from Japan. If I continue to study here, I think I'll be encouraged to study as hard as them.

"Just forget about trying to build theories about Korean music, I thought. If there was one thing that I finally understood, it was that the power of change affected everything, including what seems to be a very ancient, intangible culture. It's changing all the time."

Jacques-Yves Le Docte (36)
Belgium
Korean Traditional Music Theory
1 Year

A philosophical man, Jacques-Yves is learning about a field that few people outside of Korea know about: Korean traditional music theory. In a world that is becoming ever more a global village, he is trying extremely hard to put Korean traditional music on the world map.

THE VERY FIRST time I came to Korea was January 1999. I was organizing concerts in Brussels—world music festivals—so I've always been confronted with various cultures and artists. Almost six years ago I happened to be reading a British newspaper, when I saw an article about court music in Korea. There was a beautiful picture and I thought to myself, "Gosh, I really don't know anything about Korean music." I knew a lot of music from Africa and the Americas, but I didn't know anything about Korean music." Just after reading the newspaper, I called the Korean

Embassy and I told them I was a concert organizer, and that I was looking for some information about traditional music in Korea. Three days later I received a box full of CDs from the embassy of Korea. It was an amazing answer to my phone call. I've never experienced that with any other country or embassy that I've been in touch with. It was very exciting. The first thing I did was open the box and listen to the music, maybe 15 or 16 CDs in total. It was really a panorama of Korean music, and I listened to the CDs one by one. It was strange music at first. I don't feel ashamed to say that, because I really did find it strange, or at least very different, different from everything I had been listening to.

One thing that was very striking was that all those CDs were in Korean—there was no translation—so I didn't understand what it was. I had a box with CDs and pictures and a leaflet, but I couldn't understand what kind of music it was, so I had to go and get a music dictionary, the Grove dictionary, and try and understand, step by step, what was happening. That was the starting point. When I listened to Sinawi (시나위) I thought, "There is something very strong here." I was very moved, and though it was my first time listening to the music, it was very powerful, so I said to myself, "I have to go further."

I started to have more and more contact with the Korean Embassy, but it took a long time for me to decide that I wanted to organize a festival of Korean music in Brussels, because I wasn't planning on leaving everything else just to focus on Korean music. However, there hadn't been any festival like this in Belgium before. I had a good relationship with the new cultural attaché at the embassy in Brussels and very quickly he said, "If you want to organize a Korean music festival there's one thing you have to do, and that's go to Korea. You have to feel what is Korea. You have to experience Korea one way or the other and meet the artists there." That was what led the Minister of Culture to officially invite me to Korea for ten days in January '99.

When I first arrived in Korea, I didn't know much, actually. I just had the CDs I had received from the embassy and some books I found on the Internet, but I was not devoting all my time to that. The interpreter was waiting for me at the airport and we went to the Hilton, where I was supposed to stay for those ten days. Shortly after landing in Seoul, I had a meeting with a famous artistic director named Kang Jung-hyuk (강중혁). From that moment, everything started to go very, very fast; it was all very intense. It was Kang Jung-hyuk who introduced me to a world of things about Korean music, traditions, shamanism, Buddhism, Korean mask dance—*tal-choom* (탈춤)—and many other things.

The next day I had an important official visit organized by the Minister of Culture because the first meeting, Sunday night, had not been official. We went to a French restaurant and we sat waiting there, the interpreter and me, for the Minister and his group. When they came they were serious, so serious, and there wasn't a smile on anyone's face—nothing. It was very official. We talked and exchanged presents and I didn't feel very comfortable. It was not a very pleasant meeting. I mention it because it's important in my experience in Korea.

The day kept up and I was very busy. In the evening there was the sixtieth birthday of a famous arts critic, and at the party I met Kim Duk-soo (김덕수), An Suk-sun (안석선), and some other very famous artists. I kept on meeting a lot of artists and decided on a program with all these people and others from the National Center for Korean Traditional Performing Arts (국립국악원). I was very enthusiastic about the idea of visiting schools, so I visited the

Center's high school affiliate in Yangjae (양재) the following day. When I arrived there with the chauffeur and the interpreter, there was a big board saying, "Welcome, Honorable Mr. Le Docte." I was not expecting that at all. We then went into the director's office and had some tea. All these things were new for me. I was discovering the culture step by step, day after day. They talked about all the activities at the school and then the director said, "We have a small performance we would like you to attend, so let's go to the hall to attend the performance." They gave me a piece of paper that said, "Welcoming concert for Mr. Jacques-Yves Le Docte." I opened it and there was this program for an hour and fifteen minutes of traditional dances and music. It was a very strong moment, and I thought to myself, "I want to do something with that school." Later on, I ended up organizing a trip with 15 students from that high school who played in schools across Belgium.

What I'm trying to explain here is that many important meetings took place during those intense ten days. I met key people with whom I'm still in almost daily contact. That gave me a very positive impression toward Korean traditional music, culture—everything—so I started with a very positive opinion; I had no negative aspects at all, and I think that's important for my experience. Now, even though organizing a festival takes months, I negotiated all the things in Korea for our festival while I was there for those ten days—choosing the artists, making the program, negotiating the budget, etc. Going back to Belgium, we chose the dates, and so on, and put it in the brochure and in May 2000 we had 55 Korean artists come to perform for a few days in Brussels. It was very big.

This kind of music was totally unknown to Belgians, however, so it was very demanding on the promotional fields. We had to make huge efforts in promotion, but I did consider it a big success. Brussels is a city of one million people, and there are a lot of artistic events happening, a lot of theatre, so there's a lot of competition. I think it was a big success that on two separate occasions we had 800 hundred people in a big venue, and that we had different ceremonies with people like Kim Duk-soo and his brand of music, SamulNori (사물놀이).

From that moment I decided to organize Korean music and dance festivals at least once a year, and to take part in the promotion of this music and dance in one way or another because I wanted to go deeper into it. I was really interested in it by that point and had met some very good friends. I kept thinking to myself, "I have to do something more. There's no book in French about Korean music. How come? How is that possible with such an amazing music culture?" That's when I decided that I was going to write that book.

So, I contacted the Korean Embassy again and told them I had a project. "Is there any support I can get?" I asked "Sure," they said. "The Korea Foundation." So I applied to the Korea Foundation and I received a fellowship for nine months to write my book. Before beginning, I went back, in August that same year. The artists had come in May, and in August I was back in Korea for my second time, backpacking around and staying at *yaw-gwan* (여관)—traditional inn—which made it a very different experience from those ten days at the Hilton with a chauffeur and an interpreter.

The Korea Foundation gave me money to do my field research in Korea, so my project was to write an introduction to Korean traditional music, starting with the point of view of those who are still playing and transmitting this music. I returned to Korea a third time, this time for nine months, and spent the whole time doing interviews. The idea was to give people basic keys to get inside Korean music, to discover the field. In my own experience I was confronted with some music and I had no element to help go further, just a few papers and some information, but no books, so I really thought there's something to do here. I thought I could do that because I really liked the music and I was fascinated by the culture, and there was support from the embassy, the Ministry of Culture, and The Korea Foundation. There was a good wave of support I could surf on.

For me, the most amazing thing about Korean traditional music is the combination between very refined aspects and very rough aspects. Producing this kind of energy is characteristic of a big part of Korean music because there are many different styles and many different genres influenced by many aspects. When people talk about Korean music, they always start with court music, and then they go to *jung-ak* (정악)—the aristocratic music—and then they go to some *nong-ak* (농악)—farmer music—after which they go to shaman music, Buddhist music—things like that. There's a hierarchy, a very clear hierarchy, which is also a way of classifying. Every book has a different system, but there's always high-class music and low-class music. Of course, what's characteristic of *nong-ak* is very different from the characteristics of court music, like the speed and the intensity, because it corresponds to different influences and the roles played by the music. So when I say they're "rough," and "refined" it's probably mainly concerning a certain part of Korean music. I do believe, however, that what Koreans love so much is that there's an amazing, fascinating connection with nature. They always talk about that. You'll be talking with Koreans about music and they're always talking about nature.

In a certain way, though, music is not the goal in itself; it's a tool. It's the tool to meet the people, and this is really what interests me. That's why I interview them and try to understand what they were doing and why they were so involved so much in traditional things and what they considered "traditional." What's traditional about music if it's created in 1978, like SamulNori, for example. I've learned a lot about my own beliefs, what I believed was traditional and what I believed was contemporary, especially in the context of change—it was perpetual change doing these interviews. I changed my thinking a lot, the way I can introduce traditional music to a Belgian audience, for instance.

While I was going through the process of discovering Korean culture, what was dominating was this idea of tradition. That was a thread in the process of discovering the culture. In the beginning I tried to understand it and to think, "Oh, it works like this... " and I was coming to a confrontation between two aspects. But I discovered that was much too simple in Korea. It was not working like that at all. It was so tempting to reduce it to two elements all the time: tradition and modernity, north and south, yin and yang. It's very tempting to start there. Actually, I decided to stop trying to understand it, but just witness it and hope that at one moment things would just appear and become clear. Just forget about trying to build theories about Korean music, I thought. If there was one thing that I finally understood, it was that the power of change affected everything, including what seems to be a very ancient, intangible culture. It's changing all the time. When you read a little bit more, a little bit further, you discover it's always been changing. You have something that's introduced to you as very traditional Korean music, but it's not that traditional in the way we would think traditional is, transmitted from one generation to another.

In Japan it's a lot more like that, transmission processes based on imitation, rigorous imitation, which makes it follow a certain line. Here in Korea it's very different, though. It's in the nature of Korean tradition itself, and it's very interesting to understand that it was changing even more so before the twenieth century, according to what I've learned. Before, for instance, the transmission process was based on imitation, like between master and disciple. A master would consider his student very good if the student was producing something different from what the master was transmitting. The change process was included in the transmission process. It's not like that in Japan, however, as a point of comparison. Of course, with the changes in the twentieth century and recording, things have changed, because the idea of preserving certain art was also based on the idea of producing the exact same thing.

This idea of tradition is very exciting because there have been a lot of things appearing in the twentieth century, like those fan dances. Wherever you go you can see traditional fan dances in Korea. Contrary to popular belief, though, it's actually a very recent tradition. It has almost nothing traditional about it. It was created by a dancer who was living in Japan and came back with this kind of show, which had very little to do with Korean traditions.

Another example is *san-jo* (산조), which was a new tradition that started as a genre in itself in the nineteenth century. Also, *pan-so-ree* (판소리), like the five repertoires, was set up in the 19th century. There was a lot more improvisation in the *pan-so-ree* practice, a lot more repertoire. But that's difficult to say with any amount of certainty because there's been almost nothing written about those folk traditions. All those things are linked nowadays with the promotion of Korea and that's another very interesting aspect: identity. You're showing Korean culture to the world, such as SamulNori, yet few of those artists have identified with what their tradition is nowadays; few artists have critical thinking about what their tradition is; many are confused and looking for something new, which has huge potential.

For the nine months during my last stay, I think I got a sense of the music of the language, which is really important. I couldn't understand a word of the language because I was not studying Korean for those nine months. I was with an interpreter all the time, or people who were able to speak English. I was quite frustrated. During the interviews I had a very good interpreter, but it was an interpreter nonetheless, so it was frustrating in a way. I thought to myself, "I know I can't learn the language to be fluent one day, but I should stay here and live here and really devote all my time." I couldn't do that then, however, because I had other projects. At the very least, I thought to myself, I wanted to reach a certain level of understanding with the reading and get something from it, something more than just the music. So that's the process I'm in right now, my third time in Korea. Now I can get another dimension from all those terms in music. I understand how they work and can take a dictionary and go through it if I want.

To my knowledge, there's no French–speaking person who's involved in the study of Korean music the way I am. I'm not a university student writing a PhD or anything, but I'm doing something that is open to a wider audience. Of course there are a lot of things to do and organizers are quite demanding in the venues in Europe. I've been working with the Festival d'Automne a Paris, writing the program book and things like that, so I'd be very happy to continue taking part in that and promoting it, because I like it.

For people coming to Korea to discover or learn about Korean music, I would recommend two places: Seoul Norimadang (서울 놀이마당) and the National Center for Korean Traditional Performing Arts (국립국악원). Seoul Norimadang is the only open-air performing stage. It's very interesting because they invite people from the countryside, less well-known artists as well as well-known artists, and there are a lot of older men and women, *a-jaw-sshee* (아저씨) and *a-joom-ma* (아줌마), dancing. There's something very Korean to it. It's something you can't find at more tourist-like places, which is why I think it's a good place to start. The second place is the National Music Academy near the Seoul Arts Center (서울 예술의전당). They have concerts every Saturday at five o'clock and they show several aspects, starting with *meen-yo* (민요), *san-jo* and *pan-so-ree*, and ending with a *pan-goot* (판굿), and things like that. From there you can go further.

Section VI
At Home in Korea

CHANGE

At Home in Korea

THE SELF-PROCLAIMED "heavyweights" of this book, the five men and two women in this section have made Korea their home—their permanent home—for one reason or another. It seems inconceivable to some just arriving in Korea for their "tour of duty" that anyone would choose to remain in this country for the rest of their lives, but then, a comment like that is often made in ignorance. The people in this section who have chosen to remain in Korea have done so for myriad reasons, with some going that final step by renouncing their citizenship to become a naturalized Korean citizen. What all of these people share in common, though, is the remarkable lives they have lived since arriving on these shores years, decades, ago, with the stories ranging from everything like the unbelievable—escaping the tyranny of North Korea—to the extraordinary—living through three generations of life in Korea.

The community of "foreigners" that continues to live in Korea after first arriving many moons ago is a unique one. Every person in this section is fluent in Korean and, from what I gathered in the interviews, fluent in so much more that makes up the fabric of this country. They are an eclectic group of people who clearly love this country and their time in it.

"... if people ask me where I'm from, I speak with great pride about my hometown. I don't think I've ever felt the need to be ashamed about where I'm from. After all, there are now thousands of people from the North in South Korea."

Moon Hae-sung 문해성 (19)
Korea (North Korea)
Student
4 Years

On a voyage that spanned almost two years, Moon Hae-sung's odyssey, from the tyranny of North Korea, through the poverty of rural China, to the freedom of the South, was life-altering. Today, in a home he was taught to distrust since birth, this polite and sincere young man is doing his best to make his family proud of him, as well as to educate others about what it was like growing up in the world's most isolated country.

I WAS BORN in 1984 in Jaeryeong-gun, South Hwanghae Province (제령군, 황해남도), the plains area between Pyeongyang (평양) and Gaeseong (개성). When I was young, until around the time I turned 13 or so, I grew up without knowing much hardship. I had no idea what it might be like to go hungry. But after 1994, the year in which Kim Il-sung (김일성) died, the government rations just disappeared. Adults were then given 700 grams a day of mixed grains or rice. It was originally rice, but now it's often mixed, so it was 700 of mixed grains, really. My mother was a working adult so she got 700 grams. The elderly got approximately 4–500 grams and students received 400 grams in total. Fortunately, because we were living in the plains areas of the southern provinces, and it was the harvest season, we were able to obtain a decent amount of food. We certainly had it better than those who lived in the northern provinces, for example. Actually, the really tough rationing began about four years later, in 1998, yet people didn't begin starving to death in our area until about six years after the rationing began. Even so, right from Kim Il-sung's death in 1994, my mother began to have trouble feeding us and going out to make money. Around this time there were virtually no jobs to be had, and so people were unable to find much work. It was then that we first began to go through some rough times. Up to that point, I think I'd been pretty carefree and happy.

My mother was a chemistry teacher at a school, and had been so since before I was born. She majored in chemistry, and she was teaching at middle and high schools until she got pregnant with me. She quit because of the pregnancy and after I was born she got a job at a mine in Jaeryeong, where they mine iron. My mother's job was to analyze the metals and categorize them into different grades. My father was working at the same mine and his work usually involved fixing and maintaining the electronics equipment, transformers, and things like that, which were used in the mineshafts. Actually, both my mother and my father lived in Japan before they came to North Korea, they were what's called *book-song-kyo-po* (북송교포), so naturally, they had a great deal of interest in Japan. I actually learned some basic Japanese from my grandmother, and even some classic Japanese pop songs and folk songs.

Generally speaking, I think kids in North Korea spent their weekends pretty much the same way they do here in South Korea when I was growing up. I mean, there may be a one- or two-hour difference in the exact schedule, but Saturday mornings were spent at school, with free time starting in the afternoon. The way kids played, though, was a little different. In South Korea, you see a fair amount of kids playing on their own, but in North Korea, the idea of playing alone, or even spending time alone, is pretty alien. We always had at least ten kids gathered together, usually more; I can't remember ever playing with just one other kid. It's as if the tenets of communal living were pounded into our very bones.

When I was younger, we were all taught that the Western world, especially America, needed to be regarded as the enemy. In North Korea, we're taught that during the Korean War (1950–53) the Americans carried out some kind of slaughter in Sincheon County (신천). That's the kind of thing they display at the museum there. When you're constantly taught these types of things, you really feel like Americans, or "Imperialist America" as we used to say in North Korea, was truly the enemy. I later discovered there's a big difference between the War Museum (전쟁기념관) in Seoul and that in Sincheon, where I grew up. Here, they show you the exhibit and let you judge things for yourself. In North Korea, though, they show you things at the museum and then they reinforce the message that they're trying to make. They tell you every terrible thing that happened and make you feel like you have to fight back, to resist. In South Korea you feel whatever you want to feel after you see the exhibit, and that's that. But in the North, we were always taught to express our thoughts about the United States and to reach the conclusion that we must annihilate America, our enemy. We were taught that we had to destroy the

United States and unify our country in an attempt to spread communism and our socialist ideology. After seeing these exhibits in the North we would then be rounded up to attend rallies where everyone would shout out certain slogans and generally strengthen the feeling of enmity against America and the West. It was almost like some sort of cult. One interesting thing I should point out is that when I arrived in South Korea I discovered that America is written with the Chinese character for beauty, *mi* (미 - 美), but in the North it's written with the character for rice, *mi* (미 - 米).

You have to understand that when I was younger I thought of Kim Il-sung as a deity. Kim Il-sung died when I was in the fourth grade, and when it happened I just couldn't believe it. Honestly, because I was so young, I had no sense of what death actually was, even though I had already lost my father and my grandfather by that time. To me, the idea of Kim Il-sung dying was, in a word, impossible. I thought of him as a god. Basically, all of North Korea belonged to Kim Il-sung and, now, to Kim Jung-il (김정일)—everything is for them. You could actually go to any location, any spot, in North Korea when I was living there, and there would be a portrait hanging of one of them. Any place where you might say to yourself, "Wow, what a view! Wouldn't it be great to just take my shoes off and cool my feet in this stream and indulge in a little romance," there would always be a portrait of them. It was like some kind of advertising, for example, with a picture of Kim Il-sung hugging a bunch of children.

To give you a better idea of how crazy it was, if your house catches on fire, the first thing you have to rescue is the portrait of the Dear Leader. There's a portrait hanging in every single house, and if there's a fire, you have to go get it first. If the portrait happens to burn with the rest of the house, then you might be put on trial at one of the weekly general assemblies. Every school has an office whose task it is to research the ideological history of Kim Il-sung and Kim Jung-il. These offices are sacred places and have perfectly ironed white carpeting, and you can only go in after you've put on bright white slippers. Once you're in the office, you have to maintain perfect posture, and wear neat, tidy clothes. Then you open up your book to read about the ideas and thoughts that a person puts forth and then discuss it with the other kids. Basically, there's no real difference between the way people in South Korea feel psychologically about God and the way people in the North think of Kim Il-sung and Kim Jung-il.

In terms of the way I thought about the South, all I had was what I was taught. In North Korea no one actually has any animosity towards the South. They just teach us that the South has become a puppet and that it's completely under America's thumb. South Korea was a lot poorer than the North a while back, in the seventies, for example. Yet the North hasn't changed its attitude at all since then. We're still taught about that situation, so we're told how students can't go to school in the South because they can't afford the monthly tuition; how kids shine shoes and work for American GIs to try and make enough money to pay the tuition; how people in the South just barely scrape by; how the South is so much off than us; how we have to unify our country and embrace the South into the arms of Kim Il-Sung and Kim Jung-il so that they can study and live happily like we do. That was the education I received and that was what I understood and what I thought I had to do, until I left North Korea, that is. I didn't know for myself whether capitalism was good or bad. Essentially, I was like the frog in the well[1] that just eats whatever it's being fed, so I didn't know anything else.

The thing is, in North Korea you're taken away and put in a prison camp if you say just one wrong thing; an entire family could be rounded up just in one night, actually. The people who were living there so happily just yesterday are gone the next morning and the house is absolutely wrecked. That's what happens in North Korea if you say the wrong thing. The punishments are really so severe. In North Korea, the media and communications system aren't very advanced, so it's not like South Korea where you can hear about stuff that's happened on TV or on the radio. The fastest, most current news you get in the North is by word of mouth. No matter where you go, conversation is the medium through which you hear examples of what's going on in the world.

One of the worst things I remember hearing through word of mouth was about all the North Korean women being sold off to China for money. Basically, it's the same thing as being sold into slavery, since they're paid for with money. They're bought by Chinese people like any other purchase, and then worked like slaves in China. It's said that in China men are very possessive with women, and that if you go really deep into the countryside there are families where none of the brothers have been able to find wives—seven, eight brothers, sometimes, and not one of them married, but that when they are married, it's because they've gone down south, to someplace like Sacheonseong (사천성), and brought home some fat, ugly woman that nobody else wanted. It's not like they're unmarried because they can't make a good living, and it's not that women don't want them, it's just that there just aren't any women around in China. Importing women from North Korea is almost the only way for them. And since there's a shortage of women, I've heard that sometimes a family of brothers will even share one woman. They'll actually break her legs so she can't run away and sit her down and basically just feed her and rape her over and over.

That bleak picture being painted, I had never ever really considered escaping from North Korea. But according to my mother, who was a teacher and had always been very clear on how children ought to be educated, since she lived in Japan until she was nine years old where she experienced life in a capitalist society, she knew that something was wrong with North Korean society from a very young age. She never spoke to us about it, but she knew, and I think for a long time she thought that there was simply no way to leave.

It was in 1996 that our lives reached a new low, though. Just scraping by became more difficult than ever before, and so my mother decided that we would have to go to my relatives abroad for help; we just wouldn't be able to make it in North Korea, she concluded. My mother then arranged to go to the Duman River[2] (두만강)—a river that flows east from Mount Baekdu (백두산), and forms part of the border between China and North Korea—and get help from relatives in China. She only got all the way to the Duman River because she managed to secure a transit pass. In North Korea if you want to travel through any region, you need a transit pass. It's used when people travel on things like trains, for example. And so my mother got a transit pass to the Duman River to go to the riverside and contact our relatives in China. While all this was all going on, however, she contracted a very serious fever. This was in 1996, when a near-epidemic paratyphoid infection was raging across the country. When she caught this fever, she was confined to a sickbed for around forty days. Fortunately, she managed to survive the infection, even though she was given no medicine.

When my mother came home from the trip I just couldn't believe how she looked. Her face was nothing more than a skull covered with a thin layer of skin. Her eyes were sunk deep into their sockets and she was nothing but bones. While she was sick, I think it really struck her that the North was so wretched that you couldn't even buy medicine to treat yourself when you were sick. A number of different factors like that all came together at the same time and I think it was then that she decided for good that we had to escape.

In retrospect, my mother's illness actually turned into a stroke of luck. There were some *kyo-min* (교민)—people of Korean descent living in China—who were going back and forth between North Korea and China who saw my mother and felt so sorry for her. I think one of them in particular saw that she was practically at death's door, and so I guess they thought that if she was left in North Korea she really would die. Since my mother was trying to find her relatives, anyway, they were willing to help her find them and kind of take us on as companions. One of these *kyo-min* ended up managing the whole thing, actually. It was August at the time, monsoon season, and they got my mother on one of those stretchers that are used to transport injured soldiers, and my eldest brother and everyone else helped to carry the stretcher across the Duman River border. At the time, my second-eldest brother and I were alone in our hometown. My mother and eldest brother went first to get help from some relatives, after which my mother got sick and came home, and we all took off together.

When we crossed the border into China, it was a little difficult getting around. There were four of us, so no matter where we went, people would notice us. Even if we did something like take a train, we were noticed by people, so we couldn't make a living in a big city. So, with the help of our relatives, we made our way to the Chinese countryside. We were just looking for some place safe, some place with no Koreans, and eventually settled in a rural area called Cheonjin, near Beijing. We were essentially in hiding, keeping an eye out for an opportunity to get into South Korea, yet we needed money. Plus, if we were really going to make it all the way to the South, we needed to figure out a route. Above all, though, we needed money. While we were hiding out in the countryside, my two older brothers and my mother worked to save money while I went to school. I actually attended Chinese school for about six months.

Actually, there's a fairly small group of people who help North Koreans in China. It's not like just anyone will lend a hand in a burst of compassion, however. Often it's churchgoing people who help the most, which is how I became a Christian myself eventually. There's a lot of pressure put on people by the Chinese government not to help North Koreans who have fled the North. Today I think that there are something like 300,000 North Koreans in China, but that may not be an exact figure; no one's really sure, in fact. The thing is, anyone who tries to help North Koreans cross into China and is caught is seriously penalized. If you're caught, you're fined between two and three thousand yuan, which amounts to about a year's wages for an average laborer. Hence it's really dangerous, and people don't take to helping us very lightly. Still, the people that actually end up helping us truly believe that they are doing God's work. They have faith and think of their work as an appointed task. They really are amazing people.

During this time that we were in China, when people asked me where I was from, I would simply say I was Korean.[3] I had a cousin in China while I was there, so when people asked me my name, I could use my cousin's name. I had to improvise like that.

It was the church, in the end, that finally gave us the opportunity to come to South Korea. Actually, most of the Korean missionaries in China are there to help North Koreans, and in my case, Korean priests did a lot to help me and my family out because it was really hard for us there in China. When we decided to come to South Korea, it was a priest we asked for help, for example.

I flew to South Korea in July 1999 with a fake passport, claiming I was Chinese by citizenship. That was first time I had ever taken an airplane, so I was really taken aback. The first thing I noticed was how green everything was. That was the first time I had ever seen land from the sky, and so it was so exhilarating. I can't say I was really nervous about landing in Seoul at the time. It was more that I was completely dazed and out of it, so much so, in fact, that I couldn't even hear the beating of my heart. I had no idea what to think coming into Seoul, and so came in with kind of a hazy fog surrounding my thoughts.

When I finally got off the airplane I was really surprised at how many cars there were on the asphalt roads. It felt a lot different from being in China, for example, and it was so much cleaner in Seoul, too. Coming from an underdeveloped country as I did, all we had were red and white lines on our black asphalt roads, and cars that barely moved. In retrospect, I think the thing that really blew me away, more than anything else, were the cars and the roads in the South.

Anyway, the priest I was with was only interested in running a program that helped North Koreans settle successfully in South Korea, and so initially, I ended up just being educated under that priest. The reason he had helped bring me to the South in the first place was because he wanted me to follow in his steps and become a priest just like him. His goal had been to use me as a missionary in an effort to spread the gospel to other North Koreans at the time of reunification. I came to the South with that priest because I agreed to this condition. The priest didn't know anything about the official government program for North Koreans, and so I stayed in a country church for one month, living, essentially, in total ignorance of everything. This all took place in Geumsan (금산), a small city that is famous for ginseng, in South Chungcheong Province (충청남도).

Actually, to be completely honest, I came to South Korea under false pretenses; I arrived here under someone else's name on a Chinese tourist visa. When Chinese people turn 19, the government issues them with a certificate of residence that is similar to a copy of one's family registry in Korea. In China, however, there isn't a picture attached to it, so I could forge a certificate quite easily. All I had to do was have the father call me "son" and the whole thing was done without much trouble. I put my picture on that person's certificate and borrowed his name. That's part of the reason that younger people can come to the South so easily with a Chinese tourist visa, and that was also why I had to leave after only being in Geumsan for one month—I had to renew my visa.

The priest wanted me to switch my visa so that I would be an exchange student under his tutelage, but he found out he couldn't do that, because it turned out that Korea was having major problems with illegal Chinese migrant workers at the time. The South Korean government started threatening the priest I was with, saying that, if I wasn't sent back to China, he himself would be denied entry to China in the future and possibly denied entry into other countries as well. The priest got confused and didn't know what to do, so he called the National Intelligence Service (NIS) and told them that he had a North Korean with him, not a Chinese boy. Someone at the NIS told the priest to report this to the nearest police station. After a brief investigation, I was sent to Hanawon (하나원), the government-operated center to assist North Koreans in their readjustment to Korean society.

At Hanawon, I was part of the third group to go through there, only one year after its establishment. These days Hanawon is on something like its thirtieth or fortieth group. Anyway, when I was there, they didn't really know what to do with us because the program was so new. As a result, they brought instructors from outside who taught us in a wide range of fields. They'd say, "Politics is like this, South Korean society is like this, the economy is like this... " To tell you the truth, everything sort of just passed over me; it was all in one ear and out the other. Also, I was only a teenager at the time, so it was pretty lonely being there by myself. Even though I was young, I had to live and study amongst adults most of the time, which also made it hard because I was unable to relate to most people.

The education at Hanawon opened my eyes up to a lot of things. I think they were testing us a lot to gauge our reaction to certain things, like a kind of "human nature" program meant to open our minds up. We were also taught a lot about economic markets. Hanawon is located in Anseong (안성), Gyeonggi Province (경기도), and so we went to a lot of markets in Anseong to learn firsthand how things worked. For the most part, though, we studied South Korea's economy. In the morning, the first thing I would do was read a newspaper. We would read the newspaper one by one in our first class and the instructor would explain the difficult words to us. I think that newspaper education class was the best class there. Then, after that, there was something like a Korean economics class or Korean culture class.

I ended up staying at Hanawon for exactly three months, after which I returned to Geumsan to see the priest once again. It was in Geumsan that I went back to a regular school for the first time in years. I was a first-year middle school student at the time, three grades lower than what I should have been in based on my age. My mother said that, because I had gone such a long time without studying formally since leaving the North, I should reacquaint myself with the learning process step by step and at my own pace. I wanted to learn everything about Korean society, so agreed that starting in the first year of middle school was the right thing to do.

At the time, I was learning mostly from my priest. He was of the belief that Korean society had taken a wrong turn somewhere along the road and that Koreans were no longer in tune with the ways of the Bible. As a result, I spent all of my time with the priest and was unable to get out of the countryside. Even in Geumsan itself I wasn't able to see a lot and so felt like I wasn't able to learn how the culture was different in the South very well. The priest just told me that I had to pray alongside the Holy Spirit every morning before going to school because he was worried that I would become too taken with capitalism and its destructive culture. So, I prayed alongside the Holy Spirit everyday at dawn and every evening upon returning home from school. I didn't even go to an arcade, an Internet café or a singing room one single time during that period in Geumsan. My routine consisted of coming and going to school, my home, the church, and the library everyday. I was eventually allowed a cell phone as a means of the priest checking up on me and knowing where I was at all times. There was a forcefulness at the church that to this day, I believe, is like an obsession for them.

Since arriving in the South, I think the opportunity to learn is the best part about living here. I was only allowed to learn what the government deemed appropriate in the North, but in the South I can learn about anything I want all on my own. People have a lot of money here in the South and so people can study at their whim, almost like it's a luxury. In the North, people live to eat and nothing more. I just think that people nowadays are becoming really cold and distant as a result. When I was in Geumsan, for example, I did things like write letters to friends in school by hand; I gave friends gifts on their birthdays; I wrote love letters to girls. Kids my age don't do those kinds of things anymore, though. I don't know if this makes me some kind of traditionalist or anti-technological, but it's how I feel.

The worst thing about living in South Korea, well, it was absolutely shocking to learn that a parent dropped their kids from the fourteenth floor of an apartment building and then jumped to their death right after. That was really horrifying. Even though life is much, much harder in the North, parents would never think about killing their own children. Parents there think that, even if they have to die, the children should be left to live. That's why there are so many kids in the North that have to beg to find food; their parents don't have enough money and food to raise their children. These kids even have their own name in the North, in fact, *ggot-jae-bee* (꽃제비). Why would parents kill themselves and their children at the same time? I can't understand that, not for the life of me. I mean, here in the South, nothing is lacking: food, clothing, shelter. The priests at my church would say that South Korea has become too materialistic, saying that the answer lies in a return to the Bible, in response to this.

These days I'm a student. I'm in my graduating year of high school. My mother always says that life is over for people of her age. She asks me how she can start life anew after living more than half her life in the North. She asks me how she's supposed to find happiness this late in life after all she's been through. That's when she tells me that she's just glad she has enough food everyday to go about her life as she pleases. She tells me that because I got to the South when I was young, I have a whole future ahead of me with so many possibilities to choose from. She wants my brothers and me to be really successful in life and not to waste our lives by being ambitionless and lacking in goals. A lot of students are studying hard in the South these days, but many of them are not doing it the right way and that saddens me. It just makes me want to ask others who have come from the North, "Hey, we had a really brutal time getting here and all you want to do is live out your life having fun?" Koreans say that people should return to nature to find happiness, but in cases like mine it's different; I still have to live like my mother did in the 1960s in order to carve out a future.

A lot of people don't realize it, but society is becoming harder to live in. If reunification is to come about, we from the North have to play a larger role in bringing it to fruition, in being a bonding agent between the South and North. I don't think the South can do it on its own because Koreans in the South don't understand the mentality of those in the North. Going it alone will only cause South Koreans to fail in realms like business as well. Nowadays a lot of businesses are moving up North, so they need people like us to help them. However, if we from the North just waste our time having fun and not taking anything seriously, what would people say? Doing that will only make it impossible to save our homes in the North.

My mother is working really hard for my two brothers and me, practically bending over backwards for us. She travels all over Korea—Seoul, Busan (부산), Jeju Island (제주도)—to lecture on what it's really like for North Koreans right now and to educate those in the South who still have no idea of what it's like for those of us here. Because my mother is working at such a superhuman pace, my brothers and I can't go wrong in life. My two brothers and I are most grateful for that and will always put our mother ahead of ourselves in life. It's funny, but these days if people ask me where I'm from, I speak with great pride about my hometown. I don't think I've ever felt the need to be ashamed about where I'm from. After all, there are now thousands of people from the North in South Korea.

There is no doubt that reunification needs to happen, but I think it will be up to the South to absorb the North, at least economically they'll have to, because our survival depends on it. If it were the other way around, everyone on the Korean peninsula would die; we can never go that way. That's partly why I think there has to be another war on the Korean peninsula, with everything changing in the aftermath. It has to be something like what happened with the Americans going into Iraq. If not, it's going to take the death of Kim Jung-il or an act of God from high up above. I think radical changes are needed in North Korea, because it's not going to happen on its own. In the case of the former Soviet Union, Gorbachev initiated reforms that led to the collapse of the regime, even though the people were against the reforms. With China, too, Deng Xiaoping initiated reforms that led to great change. Something like a change of leadership has to happen in the North because it will be impossible to change anything as long as Kim Jung-il is still alive. I do believe, though, that once the North adopts a more open-door policy people will begin to live much better than they are right now.

"Although the swearing-in ceremony was really not traumatic, what was traumatic for me was going into the American Embassy and renouncing my American citizenship."

Gary Rector 유게리 (59)
Korea (America)
Translator and Editor
35½ Years

Gary is well known and respected by many in the foreign community in Korea for the articles he has contributed to English-language dailies over the years. A citizen of Korea since 1994, he arrived in 1967, a 24-year-old looking for experience in the Peace Corps. More than three decades later, he is still here—and loving it. Columnist, editor, translator, advertising writer, traditional percussion aficionado, linguist, Gary is indeed a rare breed of "foreigner" living in Korea.

I CAME TO KOREA as a Peace Corps volunteer. I had been finished with college for about two years and working at the time. I didn't have the money to go to graduate school, so I thought an experience with the Peace Corps might be good. Since I was interested in languages and was hoping to go on to the University of Indiana's Graduate School of Linguistics, I thought that it would be nice to go and live in a country where they speak a non–Indo-

European language. I didn't particularly care which one, although I listed Turkey, Iran, and Ethiopia, actually. Anyway, I got a letter from the Peace Corps about this public health care program in Korea, so I started reading up on Korea. I read Bishop Richard Rutt's *Korean Works and Days*. It's a very appealing portrayal of Korea, about the old days. At that time I thought it sounded nice and I wanted to go to Korea with the Peace Corps.

The training site for Korea was in New Mexico, where we were trained for fourteen weeks in public health, cross-cultural issues, and Korean language. The language teachers were from Yonsei University (연세대학교). I thought that even if Korea was a backward country, at least economically at that time, it's still clearly a very civilized country with a history. My whole time as a volunteer I was in the Gyeongsang Province area (경상도). We had a month of in-country training in Seoul and after that we went into the countryside. At first I was in Cheongdo-gun, Geumcheon-myun (청도군 금천면), which is north of Miryang (밀양). I was there for six months working in a township office. For three months after that I was involved with a special project where some other volunteers and I set up a small health center in the main village of Chilgong-myun (칠곡면), just north of Daegu (대구). It was a small place where mothers could bring their children for their shots, a maternal and child health-care clinic kind of thing.

Everyone was very friendly to us. In the countryside, everybody knows everybody else's business, and as soon as I moved into my first boarding house, the whole village knew I was there. I would get strange visitors coming to check me out. Market day was once every five days back then. People would come around and drag me off to the market and get me drunk. I spent the first month in a semi-intoxicated state. I decided that, if at all possible, I would try to eat or drink everything that was given to me, not only to be culturally sensitive, but also for the experience.

When I first arrived, many more people dressed in traditional clothing, both in the countryside and in Seoul. I got off the plane at Gimpo (김포) Airport and there were still Quonset huts. We took a bus into the city and there were sections of the road into Seoul that weren't paved yet. Seoul still had electric trolleys for public transit in those days. We saw little thatched-roof huts along the way and some old men sitting on raised wooden floors, drinking or something, even though it was a cold December day. I remember seeing an ox cart coming down the hill where the Hilton Hotel is today, and I thought to myself, "Hmm, this is the biggest city in this country and here I am watching an ox relieving himself!"

I remember back then that there was only one bridge in Seoul that connected the north and south sides of the Han River, aptly called the Han River Bridge. When they first started building other bridges, they simply numbered them First Han River Bridge and then Second Han River Bridge, and so on. It became apparent rather quickly that people weren't going to be able to remember where which bridge was! What's more is that the bridges were numbered chronologically rather than where they were located, so soon after that they started renaming them for the parts of town they connected.

Anyway, after that first experience in Chilgong-myun, I was reassigned to the Dalseong-gun (달성군) Health Center. I spent most of my time there doing tests in the lab to see if patients had active TB, or going around to schools to give immunizations, because those were things you could do without a superb command of Korean. After two years of doing that, I did one more year at the Family Planning Association in Daegu, helping teach the local government workers how to work audio-visual equipment, because that's pretty much show and tell.

I finished in early 1971, whereupon the Peace Corps office in Seoul asked me if I would like to work on training programs for incoming volunteers. So, I went to Hawaii for four months and helped train a new group. I returned with them to Korea and continued working for the Peace Corps for about a year and a half. By that time I had become very interested in Korean music and wanted to stay on a little longer. I was also becoming more confident with my ability to speak Korean.

One of the major factors that made me fall in love with this place was Korean music, especially percussion. When I was working with the Peace Corps staff I started studying a couple of instruments. When another former Peace Corps friend of mine, Jan McQuain, was playing with a farmer's band that was traveling around the country, they came up to Seoul and performed once. It was then that I went completely crazy for the *jang-gu* (장구)—the hourglass drum. I was determined to learn that instrument. For the following fourteen years I really only worked part-time, just enough to support myself, so I could play the drum. That was a major thing that kept me here for a decade and a half. Although I used to dance in farmers' bands quite often, I don't really do that anymore. Even after fourteen years and my teacher's death, I continued to play with his other students. That was one of the major things that kept me going here and by that time, the late eighties, I really felt like I had taken root here. I would say the music was a very important part of my life until about 1990.

It was sometime around then that I first contemplated changing my citizenship to Korean—probably as early as the mid-eighties-wondering what it would be like, but my father was still alive and healthy and I thought I might have to go back to the U.S. and help him at some stage, so never followed through on any of those thoughts. In 1987, however, my father died of a heart attack. After that, I couldn't think of any reason why I'd have to go back to the States, so in 1990 I decided to apply for Korean citizenship.

I didn't think I wanted to move back to the States because one of the biggest selling points for me, as far as work was concerned, was the fact that I knew Korean well. Also, I'd been involved in editing and writing from back in my high school days, but I thought that going back to the States and trying to break into a writing or editing job at 45 years of age probably wouldn't be a good idea. If I had Korean citizenship I could own property and I could own a business without hassle, instead of having to worry about somebody sponsoring my visa and having to go through the routine over and over every year.

To attain Korean citizenship, I had to get some documentation from the United States. Long before this, I had lost my Social Security card in a fire and asked my mother to send me the numbers. Unfortunately, she got two of the numbers reversed, of which I was unaware when I sent away for the documentation. I got a letter from the IRS telling me they couldn't give me the documents because the Social Security number was wrong. After a series of letters back and forth, the dust finally settled—four years later—and I was finally able to file my application for citizenship. Initially, the immigration officials do some interviews to help them confirm your motivations for wanting to become a citizen of Korea. Also, they do a financial background check. They want to double-check all of the information you've submitted.

In my case, I was already somewhat known in the community; I'd been writing for a newspaper for four years and I'd been on television. I wasn't famous by any means, but I think the people in the government trusted me. One of the interviews you have is with the police, and I got called in to my local police station in Seongbuk-gu (성북구). The officer asked me if I'd ever been in trouble with the law in Korea. I confessed to him that I'd violated curfew back in the days when everyone had to be indoors by midnight every night, to which he replied: "Bah, that doesn't count! I've violated curfew, too!"

Anyhow, after you've passed the background check and the police interview, you're scheduled to take your written exam. There were more than twenty of us at the time of the test, of which only two were of non-Asian descent. Six were Japanese, four were Vietnamese, and the others were Chinese. The proctor addressed the room by mentioning that those of us who were of Asian descent probably wouldn't have any problem with the exam. He then turned to me and said, "But this might be difficult for you Americans." So, it was extra special that I got a perfect score. I don't think he knew who I was or the level of Korean I could speak, because he hadn't done any of the interviews.

After the written examination, there's a final oral interview with either the Minister or Vice–Minister of Justice. In my case it was the Vice–Minister, which was funny because he was from the first place I was assigned to with the Peace Corps, so we had more to talk about. The minister will usually talk with an applicant for ten minutes, but we had that connection, so we talked for about twenty minutes. In total, it took about five and a half months to attain Korean citizenship. I was sworn in on November 9, 1994, in a ceremony in which I and 23 others I received our certificates of citizenship. Everyone also gets a few gifts, like a Korean flag.

I felt relieved to know I could get on with other things after all that. Although the swearing-in ceremony was really not traumatic, what was traumatic for me was going into the American Embassy and renouncing my American citizenship. I didn't want to renounce my American citizenship, but the United States and Korea both insist that you do so within six months; otherwise you'll lose the citizenship you applied for. I went in to the American Embassy and I had to explain to them why I was doing it and they pointed out that I was relinquishing this and that, etc. Then you get a document officially stating the renouncement of your citizenship. I don't like the term "renounce," but that's what they use; I prefer to call it "giving it up."

Almost immediately afterwards, I had to get my Korean passport so that I could go to Saipan with a group from the publishing company I was working with at the time. When I put my passport in with the whole group, it turned out the American Embassy didn't want to give me a tourist visa without interviewing me first. They saw my passport—Caucasian face with a Korean name—and had to interview me. They even brought in a guy that could interpret in case I couldn't speak English. I talked with one of the consuls there. They didn't think I was going to become an illegal alien if I entered the States, so they gave me an American visa that is easily renewable as long as my passport is valid, so that was nice. That made me feel a little better, knowing that even though I'd renounced my American citizenship I was still allowed to visit whenever I wanted to.

It might look funny to other people, but I don't feel strange about using my Korean passport at airports throughout the world. When I've gone overseas I've sometimes had trouble going into other countries, but when I come back to Korea, there's no problem at all. When I went to Saipan that time, for example, they pulled me out of the line and questioned me at the airport. Another time when I went to Hawaii, a policeman followed me and kept on asking me all these questions like, "You're not really Korean, are you?" What a headache! The biggest problem I had was going into Indonesia, though. I was taken out of the customs line and into this airport police station where there were all these mafia-looking thugs, the immigration people kept badgering me, trying to get me to confess to having a different passport. They didn't believe that I was a Korean citizen, even when I told them to call the Korean Embassy so they could see and hear me speak Korean to an official there. They refused to do that and kept me detained for 45 minutes. That was the worst experience I've had at an airport. It turns out it's a bigger problem going somewhere else than it is coming back into Korea!

Now, however, I feel free to do what I want to do. I don't worry if someone is going to issue me a visa or not anymore. I'll never forget the day I took my foreigners registration card out to Mokdong (목동) and said, "I've just come to say goodbye. I will never have to see you people again, thank God!" They just laughed. I showed them my citizenship card and they thought that was really funny.

Koreans still refer to me as a foreigner, but it doesn't bother me, because I know they're referring to my ethnicity, not my nationality. When I tell Koreans that I'm from America but I'm a naturalized Korean citizen, they think that's great and will introduce me to other people and say, "Gary's a Korean!" Koreans still regard my ethnicity as being some fundamental part of me. And that's true; it is. No matter how much Korean I learn or how Koreanized I become, there will always be that underlying background that I have, and I acknowledge that that's there. When

Koreans go to the U.S. and become American citizens they still regard themselves as Koreans in the sense that they have that connection with their Korean background, even though they're Americans. I don't think there's anything wrong with that, necessarily.

For people who want to gain Korean citizenship today, I think it might be harder now, as more and more people are becoming naturalized citizens. At the time I did it, around a hundred people were doing it a year. Today, it's up to several hundred a year, I believe. I didn't find it a problem at all personally, so I don't know if I have any advice to give. They were very kind and polite to me when I did it, unlike the people at the immigration office in Mokdong, for instance. If you can't cross that threshold, though, then you shouldn't do it. You have to be absolutely certain. I asked myself if I was willing to stay here the rest of my life and make this my home. Will the time ever come when I want to move back to the States or make my home somewhere else? I was able to answer myself truthfully and the answer is no. I want to stay here. This is where I have my friends and my livelihood. I wanted to cast my lot with these people. If you're not certain that you want to give up your nationality in order to become naturalized in Korea, then you shouldn't do it.

"In terms of advice to foreign women who are marrying a Korean man, you have to talk with your husband or boyfriend before coming to Korea. Lay down the rules and tell him what is possible, what you can give, what you can do. Make sure everything is clear."

Rowena de la Rosa Yoon (36)
Korea (Philippines)
President of ISKA,
Public Relations Expert,
Journalist, and Editor
8 Years

As president of the International Spouses of Koreans Association (ISKA), Rowena is responsible for providing a great deal of support and assistance to foreign wives of Korean men. On top of founding and running the support group, she has also been adamant about working full-time since arriving in Korea, something her husband's family initially was not happy about.

MY HUSBAND and I got married in Manila. A month after the wedding, we came to Korea. That was eight years ago. When we first met in Manila my husband was working at a travel agency. I had a friend who happened to be his friend, and I think they came across the topic of girlfriends one time and this friend of mine found out that this Korean man was looking for a Filipina girlfriend. My girlfriend then set up the meeting between my husband and I. It wasn't that I was looking for a foreign guy or anything, though. I was just busy working, and one day I came to meet this guy introduced to me by my friend. It was not a serious meeting, however. But after the meeting he started to call me up and invite me out to lunch or dinner or to watch a movie or to go to the opera—those sorts of things. That's how we became friends. And after that, the friendship became deeper and deeper, and so we started building a relationship that was more than friendship.

Before 1997, when a Korean man married a foreign woman his wife automatically became a Korean citizen. The woman had to decide within six months whether she was going to keep her Korean citizenship or not. So what I did was—because I was so adamant—I said, "I cannot understand everything here: I don't know the language, I don't know the culture, I don't understand anybody who says I should change my nationality! Why should I change my nationality? It's my identity; I'm a Filipina." I ended up keeping my Filipino citizenship for about six years. Those six years were really hard for me, though, because every time I wanted to leave Korea I had to go to Immigration and get a re-entry permit and pay a lot of money. It was really bureaucratic.

Aside from the re-entry permit, the visa given to foreign spouses also needs to be renewed every year. And when you renew your visa, it's the same bureaucratic procedure. You have to go to the district office to get the family records and then take the family records to the Immigration Office, proving to them that you're really married to a Korean and that you live with a Korean family. They don't have marriage certificates in Korea like other countries, for example. The only thing you have to prove you're a legal spouse is the family registry.

One more problem I had during this time was when my family and I traveled outside the country. I had to go to the foreigners' line at customs with my Filipino passport, yet my husband and son had Korean passports and so went to the Korean line. Sometimes they would look at the passport of my son and ask, "Where's your mother?" and so they would call out my name and I would have to go there. After six years of this, my husband was fed up and told me to change my nationality and so that's what I did. I'm now a naturalized Korean citizen and the three of us all have the same passports.

Another challenge over the years here has been my husband's parents. Actually, before my husband and I got married in the Philippines, I had been to Korea one time to meet his family. I had a basic fear of Korean culture and that was that it's a very patriarchal society. Contrary to what some people think about Korean parents-in-law mistreating all foreign sons- and daughters-in-law, though, his parents treated me very well. However, when I told the parents that I wanted to work, I was told that a woman should stay at home.

In Korea when you marry you have to marry the whole family, not like in my culture where when you marry it's a union of the two; just the two of you become one. In Korea you have to marry the whole clan, so when I first moved to Korea it was like a bombshell hitting me. "I'm educated and I'm a professional," I said to my husband. "Why should I stay at home? What am I going to do at home?" I was supposed to be a decoration or something, which was absolutely shocking. The thing was, I had a job when I was in the Philippines and my background is in journalism and public relations. When I married my husband, I knew I had to leave my job in Manila, but I told him that I had to work as soon as

I set foot on Korean soil.

When we finally did arrive in Korea, though, I went to Korean school instead of getting a job. Since I couldn't speak the language, I knew I had to learn it before I went to work, and so I took some Korean language courses. But because I had been working for so long in the Philippines, eight years in fact, I was not comfortable with the idea of my husband giving me an allowance. I hated it! I didn't want that kind of life because I had been so independent my whole life. When I became a Korean language student and I was getting an allowance, I said to my husband that I didn't want to study anymore; I wanted to get a job. When my in-laws learned of my decision to get a job, however, they all protested: the mother-in-law, the sisters-in-law—I have three older sisters-in-law who are all housewives—even the younger brother-in-law told me that a wife should stay at home! But the thing was, it was a real struggle for me going to that school everyday and having to take an allowance from my husband, so I told him I was going to work whether he liked it or not. "I'm going to find a job and I'm going to work," I said.

Still, the family continued to protest, one against all; me against the whole family. As a result, I felt isolated and told my husband that if this was the way things were going to be, I was going to leave. "I'm going to pack my things and leave," I told him. My mother-in-law found out about this and told me that the woman should always submit to the husband, to which I then said, "Well, I'm going to show you how a Filipino woman acts!"

When I packed up my things they thought it was all for show. I actually bought a plane ticket and I left Korea and went back to the Philippines, though. My husband tried to find me by phoning my parents and friends, but I didn't talk to him until I phoned him three weeks after arriving in Manila. He wanted me to come back to Korea and said that he had fought with his family over this—he even had a fistfight with his brother. "Come back to Korea," he told me, "and we'll build our own territory. Nobody will bother you. You can do anything you want here." I told him he was a liar and that I had laid down my cards on the table before our marriage. There were two questions going through my mind then: one was if he really loved me, and the second was if he just felt ashamed that a foreigner had left him, because he's the first son in his family.

We were still husband and wife, though, so I believed in his sincerity. I tried to understand him and realized he was distraught, and so ended up coming back to Korea. Yet this time when I came back, I started work immediately. I began work at the *Korea Herald* as an editor and I was so happy—nobody in my husband's family could say anything, and by that point we were living on our own, as we'd moved out from my parents-in-law's house. From time to time I also worked at what then was called *Korea News Review*, a weekly news magazine put out by the *Korea Herald*, but is now known as *Korea Now*. Apart from that, I also proofread the bi-monthly scholarly magazine of the Korea Foundation, called *Korea Focus*. I did all this for about one year, until I got pregnant. When I got pregnant in 1997, I had to take time off work because I had to give birth to the baby. This was also at the same time that the Korean economy was on the brink of collapse because of the Asian financial crisis.

After I gave birth to the baby I was planning on going back to work. Initially, however, I couldn't go back to work because there was no babysitter to look after my baby. It's really hard to find a babysitter in Korea, so I became a housewife and a mother that first year of my baby's life. After about a year, I started taking some part-time editing work, leaving my baby with an *a-joom-ma* (아줌마)—middle-aged woman—when I had to leave the house. I was also writing articles at this time for newsletters and for newspapers like the *Korea Herald* and some other publications. About two or three years into this line of work my baby was old enough to leave at daycare, so I could return to the workforce and get a full-time job.

I had to apply at a lot of places before I found a job at the Korea Information Service, where I work right now, because it's not so easy for a married woman to get a job in Korea—a foreign, married woman at that. It's really outrageous, actually. It was also difficult for me because all the ads said "Native Speaker Needed." "Native speaker? But I'm from the Philippines!" I said in my introductory letter. When speaking to one particular company, I wrote, "I'm sure by 'native English speaker' you mean either someone who is British or American, but for your information English is the official language in my country. As such, an extensive and intensive English curriculum is an integral part of our curriculum and it's the language of the government, schools, and business in the Philippines, so I'm applying for this job based on my qualifications." They noticed this from my application and called me for an interview the next day. When they called me, they said, "Is this the house of Rowena de la Rosa Yoon?"

"Yes, this is she."

"This is the company you recently applied to. May we talk to your husband?"

"My husband? What does my husband have to do with this?"

"Well, because you applied for a job here we'd like to talk with him."

"Why would you want to talk with him? I'm a professional. I'm the one applying for the job. Anyway, he's not here right now. He's at work and I can't bother him at work right now."

I got the Korean man who phoned me very angry, so at last he just said, "Okay. Come for an interview tomorrow." When I told my husband later that night, he felt very ashamed and couldn't believe what happened.

The following day I went in for the interview and I was the only person who was a woman and the only person who was not a native English speaker. The man who greeted me said they were very impressed with my introductory letter, which is why they had asked me for an interview. So anyway, this really conservative looking Korean man conducted the interview and this was his first question: "If you come here and work in this office, who's going to cook for your husband and who will take care of your son?" I was boiling inside and I told him that I had come for the interview as a professional and had set aside domestic matters before coming to the interview. I hadn't gone there because I was a housewife; I had gone there because I was applying for a job I was qualified for.

When I eventually applied for a job at the Korea Information Center, I was relaxed. I went to see them and they were very nice, very professional, and after I went home I was not expecting that they would phone me back. However, they ended up calling me and offering me a job. I've been here ever since then, about three years.

In terms of my other work, my role in the International Spouses of Koreans Association (ISKA) has a longer history. When I came to Korea eight years ago, I didn't know the language. I didn't even know what I was supposed to do and what I was not supposed to do. In short, I didn't know anything. Everyday my husband went to work and I had to go to school or I had to stay at home alone. Early on, I went to McDonald's or KFC or some other fast food restaurant because that was the only food I knew. Whenever my husband got home at night, I wasn't able to make anything for him, so he was hungry all the time. I didn't know how to cook and couldn't find a cooking school that taught in English. These were some of the early problems I faced.

In my first Korean language class, I met a lot of women like me. On top of that, there were also other women that shocked me with their stories. There was one foreign woman I studied with, for example, who always said she was hungry. I'd ask her why she was always so hungry and she'd tell me that she couldn't eat much at home. The reason she wasn't eating much was because her husband and father-in-law always ate first and she and the mother-in-law could only eat the leftovers from the men's plates. I told her that was inhuman, but she just said that her mother-in-law had taught her that. Even on days when we didn't have class, this woman would lie to her mother-in-law and say that she had class just so she could get out of the house and not have to be with her. After hearing about this, I told her there should be a support group here in Korea for spouses of Korean men. For four years I was looking for a group that offered support and assistance to spouses of Koreans, but I didn't find one. As a wife, the only support I had was the church, and that was the reality of being a foreign wife of a Korean man.

I used to contribute articles for the United Nations Educational, Scientific and Cultural Organization (UNESCO), and one time they were organizing forums on various issues in Korea. In November 1997 somebody from Korea UNESCO Cultural Exchange Services called me up and told me that they were going to have a forum on the lives of foreign women with Korean husbands. There were ten foreign wives at that forum and I was the moderator. I asked the women what issues were important for them. For six months after that forum, I was trying to convince other women that we needed a group. I eventually posted an ad with the *Korea Herald,* and on March 25, 2000 we launched ISA, the Inter-cultural Spouses Association, which was the title ten of us women decided upon. There were about forty women from 15 countries in total who joined the club at the time. We soon changed this name to the ISKA—International Spouses of Koreans Association—just before the website was launched, because the original title was somewhat misleading.

Before the website was launched, we would meet once a month at an informal gathering, such as over dinner or on a picnic, where we could talk about our problems or anything in general. It was hard to get consistent turn outs, though. If a wife didn't have a child, then it was very easy for her to come to the meetings. Yet once she had a child she didn't come to the regular meetings. Right now, if we have more than ten women, then we can gather. We try and adopt a policy that no matter how far you are, no matter how busy you are, you can always get in touch by taking advantage of the Internet services we have. So, if a couple leaves Korea they can always keep in touch with us through the website. We also try and help women who have been battered, for example. We have contacts with shelters for runaway wives. We also have connections with specialists like lawyers and other people who provide legal assistance. We now have more than 200 women on our list from more than thirty countries all over the world. Nowadays, when a woman marries a Korean man, they can be sure that there's a support group here. They will never experience what

I experienced eight years ago by not having a support unit there for me. The revolution started at my home but it's moved out from there. They will not be lonely; they will not feel isolated.

In terms of advice to foreign women who are marrying a Korean man, you have to talk with your husband or boyfriend before coming to Korea. Lay down the rules and tell him what is possible, what you can give, what you can do. Make sure everything is clear. Keep in mind that not all Korean marriages are scary. If you have a traditional husband it's going to be a little bit hard. Tell the man that there is nothing permanent in this world except change, and that Korean husbands cannot cling to traditions forever. Even though not all change is always for the good, I think a lot of people are scared of change in Korea because they have been in that mode for centuries. If a woman meets an open-minded man, I'm sure they will not have any problems.

"My friends in Taiwan go so far as to ask me, 'If you're from Korea and you've lived in Korea your whole life, aren't you Korean?' In Korea, people will then ask *hwa-gyo* like me, 'You may have lived in Korea for a really long time, but how are you not Chinese?' There are times when I feel that I don't belong anywhere and that to be *hwa-gyo* is simply to be *hwa-gyo*."

Dr. So Seung-gul 소승걸 (25)
Taiwan
Dentist
25 Years

One of hundreds of thousands of Chinese-born foreigners living in Korea, or hwa-gyo *(화교), Dr. So is an eloquent speaker and a very patient man. Though he experienced some degree of racism and prejudice while growing up, he has always managed to maintain a very positive outlook about living in his "second" home.*

I WAS BORN in Seoul, though my parents are both Chinese. They are legally Taiwanese, but they're originally from the Shandong Peninsula, on mainland China. Years ago, sometime during my grandfather's generation, my mother and father immigrated to Korea from China. I am the third generation of *hwa-gyo* (화교)—Chinese emigrants. Actually, all the Chinese living in foreign countries are called *hwa-gyo*, and so I am the third generation from my family to be *hwa-gyo* in Korea. However, neither my parents nor I have ever changed our nationality even though we've lived in Korea our whole lives. For my parents, they've just never considered changing their nationality; I haven't either. People from my parents' generation have traditionally always had a stronger tendency to keep Taiwanese nationality. As that generation gets older, however, such loyalty to the Taiwanese citizenship weakens a little. We think, "Why should we change our nationality? We're Chinese." It's the older people who think that way the most, yet I do, too. If I change my nationality and become Korean, I'd be giving up my country, and that is the last thing I could ever do. At the end of the day, I'm still Chinese and will always be Chinese. Even when I was growing up, I always considered myself Chinese. Basically, the question is like asking Koreans if they're North Korean or South Korean. Koreans would never say, "I'm South Korean." The same rings true for me—I'm Chinese. China is one nation; it is only the ideologies that divide the two countries of mainland China and Taiwan. These days, I just say I'm Chinese when asked where I'm from. When asked specifically about my nationality, I then say that I'm Taiwanese.

Anyhow, while growing up in Seoul I went to Chinese schools. Actually, I went to *hwa-gyo* schools all through my childhood and adolescence: kindergarten, elementary school, middle and high schools. They were all Chinese schools in Korea. I was receiving my education in Chinese at the time. We learned Taiwanese history along with world history, and learned Chinese history separately. We learned Korean history in world history class as well as in Korean language class. I studied in Seoul, but I had many more Chinese friends than Korean friends. I talked with friends in Korean, but we took separate Korean classes at school.

We *hwa-gyo* learned Korean as a second language, and so my friends in Korea, who were almost all Chinese, would talk in Chinese to me.

When I was younger, I always felt there was discrimination in one form or another. As a child, I hung out mostly with Chinese kids, having few Korean friends at the time; I only had a few Korean friends in the neighborhood then. When we went out, the thing I hated most was when Korean kids made fun of us. Fortunately, with children discrimination would never usually go past that point. I did, however, hate it very much when kids would say, "*sswal-la sswal-la*" (쏼라쏼라) and "*jjang-ggae*" (짱깨) to me. I got into a lot of fights with other kids whenever they would say those things because it sounded like they were making fun of the Chinese language. Another thing I hated was when kids corrupted the Korean word for "China," *joong-gook* (중국), and said "*jjoong-gook, jjoong-gook*" (쭝국, 쯍국) instead. I've always disliked Koreans' strong pronunciation of that word since I can remember.

Nowadays I try and just deal with such racial encounters in stride, with a grain of salt, because I've changed a lot as a person. For example, today when somebody says "*jjang-ggae*" in front of me, I respond somewhat facetiously by saying, "What's all this about 'jjang-gae'? Do you want to eat at a Chinese restaurant or something? And by the way, do you even know what that word means?" In fact, these days I'd say I experience a lot more outright discrimination from the Korean government than I do from Koreans themselves. For example, the government won't issue resident cards to *hwa-gyo*. We are simply ignored for the most part and treated differently. In Korea foreigners are limited in buying real estate and there's a regulation that we can't employ more than a certain number of people if we own our own business. I'm not sure of every law exactly, but there are a lot of restrictions like that for us as foreigners. As a result, some foreigners decide to switch nationalities—to become naturalized Korean citizens—in order to open their own factories here.

Anyhow, while I was attending university, I was able to calm down about this very thing a lot. I began to understand that Koreans never had any bad intentions when they were saying things like *"jjoong-gook"*; they were just ignorant of what they were doing. I've shared this revelation with my friends over the years, believing that such awareness can spread effectively to many others. I've noticed my friends don't use such words around me anymore, and can only conclude that by changing people one person at a time we can bring about a greater amount of change, little by little.

Actually, it was during those six years that I attended Kyung Hee University's (경희대학교) Dental College that I made a lot of good friends, and was fortunate to receive a great deal of assistance from. I was only able to graduate from university thanks to my friends. To tell you the truth, I went through a lot of difficulties in university because I was taught entirely in Chinese until high school. At first, I found it really hard to keep up with the other Korean students. I was confused and felt like I was left behind much of the time in class, so my aim at university became to make as many friends as possible, deciding not to show people as soon as we met that I was Chinese or a foreigner. I figured doing that would only isolate myself from everyone else. I think it worked because my friends would often forget that I was Chinese. Whenever I said, "You know, I'm a foreigner," they would only realize it then and say back, "Oh, right. You're not Korean." It was because of the way I socialized that I was able to meet friends more naturally. While talking with my friends sometimes, I would occasionally say something that indicated I was a foreigner, though. For instance, I'd say something like, "Korea is..." instead of "our nation is..." or "our country is..." The two last phrases are what Koreans would say more naturally than what I said. It's just that I think of myself as Chinese, as a foreigner, so in truth, although it may cause me some annoyance from time to time, for the most part I just let the issue blow over and not think too much about it. That's partly why, when Koreans call me a foreigner and tell me that my Korean is really good, I don't say a thing; there's nothing I can say. I've lived in Korea for so long that all I can really respond with is, "Well, I'd hope my Korean is this good after so long in the country! By the way, why do you ask?"

When I return to Taiwan for visits, things are a little bit different, however. I don't feel like it's my "home" per se. I liken it more to thinking, "I'm here in my country, and my country is Taiwan." That's not exactly the heartfelt emotion that most people feel when going back home, though, is it? To be perfectly honest, it's really hard being *hwa-gyo* because in a sense, *hwa-gyo* belong neither to Korea nor to Taiwan. It's as if we're a people who don't belong anywhere, and so we can be discriminated against, even in Taiwan. When in Taiwan, I feel there's something a little off and the reason is that I speak Chinese differently. My friends in Taiwan go so far as to ask me, "If you're from Korea and you've lived in Korea your whole life, aren't you Korean?" In Korea, people will then ask *hwa-gyo* like me, "You may have lived in Korea for a really long time, but how are you not Chinese?" There are times when I feel that I don't belong anywhere and that to be *hwa-gyo* is simply to be *hwa-gyo*. By the same token, I've never felt like the proverbial *wang-dda* (왕따)—ostracized person—however;

I've always had friends around me, and so never felt like I was *wang-dda*.

Anyway, for me the best part about living in Korea is that this country has four distinct seasons. I don't particularly like the weather in Taiwan, as it's always hot and humid. I always feel that Korea is blessed with four separate seasons, with different fruits available in each season. Though I have to admit that another good part to living in Korea is its nightclubs!

On the other hand, one bad thing about life in Korea is that everyone is leading a really hectic life, with no time spared for themselves. It seems as if everybody is under constant pressure and always moving. Even though I wish life here moved at a slower pace, it's impossible. In other countries, Canada for instance, people live a lot more relaxed. They enjoy life and lead happy lives. In Korea, however, you have to be very rich or else it's really hard to live such a lifestyle. To give you a specific example, patients at my dental clinic often say, "My gums hurt," and I then ask them, "Are you stressed out? Are you tired?" Because this actually influences their teeth and their mouths, when you're stressed out or tired your gums hurt a lot more and can get easily inflamed. In that way, this kind of hectic lifestyle is the worst part of Korean life.

I'm really happy at work these days, all things considered, though. The head of the clinic is a really nice man and I enjoy my work as a dentist, taking care of patients. There are times, though, that I feel a little lonely. When I was in university and high school, I was always with my friends. Now that I'm out of school, everybody is all over the place and so it's hard to spend time with close friends. Occasionally, when I have a hard day, I like to go and have a drink somewhere with a friend, but I can't find anyone to do that with anymore. Everyone is so busy with their own lives and lives far away—even my girlfriend is in Canada—that I sometimes go home a little lonely, only to drink a couple of beers by myself and then go to bed.

Still, I'll most probably continue living here in Korea. We usually have to decide where to live when we enter university, and in Korea, according to which university we go to, our lives are determined as such. So, as long as I work as a dentist, I think I have to live in Korea. Yet I have no plans to become a naturalized citizen. As I've already mentioned, I'm Chinese first and foremost. Of course there would be many benefits if I were to become a naturalized citizen, but if I were to do so, I would be the first So (소)—my family name—of my family lineage here in Korea. Maybe I'm still young, but I think of being Chinese as a little more important than all the benefits that come with being a naturalized Korean citizen. I don't know what it will be like when I get older, but for now I feel that strongly about retaining my Taiwanese citizenship. In the future, I'd like to tell my own children that they are Chinese.

As a sidebar, many of us *hwa-gyo* believe that we should marry another *hwa-gyo*. Actually, it used to be a family rule, up until the generation of my parents, that *hwa-gyo* were not allowed to marry Koreans. They were much stricter about things like that back then. Years ago, in fact, I thought that I should marry a Chinese person, too. However, as I grew older and met more women, I began to think differently. Today I don't think the nationality of a prospective partner is so important. Of course I don't ever want to forget my roots, but at the same time I don't want to be *wang-dda* by being alone in the country where I live now. In addition, I think it's okay wherever I go, whatever I do and whomever I marry, as long as I act on my convictions and know who I am at heart. I actually have a Korean girlfriend right now and am thinking about marrying her. Whatever I do, I'm going to act on my principles and hope that I get along with people in this country as long as I'm here. If I don't socialize with Koreans, and instead just stay to myself, I'll never be successful; simply having lots of money doesn't necessarily spell success.

"I have very good Korean friends. I can frankly tell you that I prefer them more than Iranian friends. They are very good at friendship. When I need help they help me; when I am happy they are happy with me; when I am sad they are sad with me."

Shapour Nasrollahi (34)
Korea (Iran)
Restaurant Owner
14 Years

Born in Iran in 1968, Mr. Nasrollahi Shapour or Dr. Shapour, as his friends call him, grew up in Iran before moving to Canada. After spending some years in Toronto with his family, he found himself on the eastern edge of Asia, almost mistakenly, and the rest is history. A little under a decade after arriving in Korea, Dr. Shapour became a naturalized Korean citizen, and is now the proud owner of one of the finest curry restaurants in Seoul, The Persian Palace.

THE FIRST TIME I came to Korea, I was on the way to Canada. I was supposed to land in Japan, but by accident I came to Korea and stayed here for two or three days. On the airplane here, there was a Korean man behind me and we got to talking. He ended up inviting me to his house. He was a professor at Seoul National University (서울대학교), and so the next day he invited me to his school, just to go and see it. When I went there, I saw some foreigners. One foreigner in particular, he was from Jordan and studying the Korean language, explained many things about Korea and Korean to me.

Anyway, after those few days in Seoul, I went on to Japan. After I had been in Japan for one or two months, I decided to come and learn some Korean. At first, I only planned on staying in Korea for two months, but then two months became four years, four years became eight, and eight years became fourteen.

Upon returning to Korea all those years ago, I visited one Iranian businessman who was living here. We were from the same hometown, and so he was a big source of support for me in the beginning. He rented a small room for me, but later on I found a place for myself, a place specifically for foreigners, in Daehangno (대학로), called International House. I stayed there for one or two months. I found that Korea was a beautiful country and I decided to continue with my language course for one year. For that year, I was also working part-time, from 9:00 to 11:00 a.m., after which time the Iranian businessman I had befriended taught me business. For two years, I learned business from him. That's when I started to do some import and export for myself, but for very small amounts of money, "400 or "500. I did that for around four years.

I eventually went to study the Korean language again, going on to Hanyang University (한양대학교) to study medicine. In Iran I also studied medicine, so I continued my medical studies at Hanyang University until 1997, four years in total. In 1998 I was admitted to Seoul National University's psychiatric program, where I studied psychology until 2002. It was then that I started the business I still have to this day, The Persian Palace, a small restaurant that I'm very satisfied with today. I've always had a dream to have a small restaurant because my hobby is cooking. In fact, after I graduated from high school, I had always dreamed of cooking, but not as a chef. I had always invited my friends to my house and cooked for them. Some days I cooked for my family, but my family was always against the idea of me as a chef. They believed that a chef was not a good or suitable job, so they pushed me to study medicine. Now, however, I have self-satisfaction; I'm very satisfied with my work.

I've now lived in this country for a long time. I believe I can see the changes that have taken place here much more clearly than a Korean can. I'll give you an example: the city structure. You can be in an area and then return two or three months later and it has completely changed, with new buildings. Everything here changes continuously, especially the structure of the city. Another thing I've noticed is that people here have become more fashionable and that Korean men have become nicer to Korean women. When I first came here, I always wondered why Korean men treated women the way they did; they were not nice to them. Years ago, when I would pass people in the street, I never witnessed a Korean man carrying a purse or a bag for a woman, but these days I see this type of thing very often. Another thing is that middle-aged couples never used to walk together; the man would walk ahead and the woman would follow. That's changed, too.

Another change has to do with foreigners. When I first arrived here there were not a lot of foreigners. It was mostly just American soldiers and missionaries then; there were no illegal workers here back then. So, when I used to walk the streets, everyone looked at me very curiously. People were very nice and showed a lot of respect to foreigners, but after a lot of foreigners came here as illegal workers I noticed a change. For example, by 1995–1996 everyone with black hair and dark skin was suspected of being an illegal worker, especially if your clothes were not very clean. They were treated very differently from white people or Americans, for example.

As for me, I never had an experience like that because I'm an educated person and I never had a money problem in this country. I've always been working and I take care of my appearance. Some foreigners that I studied with at Seoul National University have had experiences similar to what I just mentioned, but truthfully, Koreans treat Americans, or people with white skin, differently than other races. Koreans may think that these people come from a more advanced country than Iran, for example, so they are better than us. Sometimes I can sense that.

Nevertheless, 99 percent of my friends are Korean. I have a lot of Korean friends and I know a lot of Koreans—more than 1,000 people; more than 1,000 people know me and consider me their friend. I've never had a bad experience in this country and I'm very happy with my job; I'm very happy with the studies I did; I'm very happy with my life and friends. I have very good Korean friends. I can frankly tell you that I prefer them more than Iranian friends. They are very good at friendship. When I need help they help me; when I am happy they are happy with me; when I am sad they are sad with me. So, I can trust my friends.

Another thing I like about Korea is that this is a peaceful country, a very safe country. If you were to go out at night at 2:00 a.m., nothing would happen to you. If you were to compare Korea to the U.S., or other countries, when you go out at night you don't feel as safe. People here are friendly with foreigners, at least with me, and I have good friends, a good life and I'm happy here, which is why, in 1998, I decided to change my citizenship.

It was not difficult for me to get Korean citizenship, compared to some other foreigners. When a country grants you citizenship, for example the United States or Canada, the government is mostly concerned with how useful a particular applicant will be for that country. In Canada, the government attaches points to certain things about an applicant, such as completing one's doctorate and having money, and after you get 60 or 70 points, they award you with citizenship. In Korea, the procedure is similar. Firstly, I completed my studies here. Secondly, I have money. These are two important factors. Also, I can read and write the Korean language. Of course I had to take a test, but it was not difficult for me. The government considered that I was educated here, I have money, and they believe that I am useful to Korea. But if, however, I had only a high school diploma and no money, the government could not trust me. Now I'm not married, and in Korea when applying for Korean citizenship as a single, foreign man, it's not an easy task. I think the two points that helped me were my education background and my savings, which the government has on file. They have copies of your bank accounts and your diploma, for example.

Originally, when I told my friends and family back home of my decision to become a naturalized Korean citizen, of course they were not very happy. My mother cried for two or three days, actually. My brother was very upset with me, too. But I tried to explain to them that I live in Korea, I am happy, and if I want to live in Korea for a long time I need Korean citizenship because there are a lot of benefits for me, especially if I'm running my own business. Even when you have money in this country, there's problems with your visa, contentious issues, like going to the immigration office—that's just too much of a headache. Now, though, with Korean citizenship, I can do business as a Korean would do business.

I face different challenges now that I have Korean citizenship. I remember last year when I went to England, and in Heathrow Airport I showed my Korean passport and the officer said, "Oh, you don't look Korean!!" The immigration officer was Indian, so I asked him, "Do you look British?" after which he then said, "Okay, you're alright." Later I went to France and they said, "You don't look Korean!" I said that my mother is Korean and they said, "Oh, okay," and they gave me the visa.

Regardless of my citizenship, however, I still believe Iran is my home as much as Korea is my home too, my second home. Even if I live here for twenty or thirty years, my heart remains Iranian and my soul is Korean. I am a combination. Half of my body belongs to Korea and half to Iran. Fourteen years is not a short time. Almost half of my life I've lived in Korea, and I expect that eventually it will be more than that. Still, I cannot say I am Korean because Koreans think I'm playing with them. I tell them I'm Iranian, but I have Korean citizenship. That's it.

The truth is, to change one's nationality is not a big deal. The important point is why you want to change it. Do you want to change it because you'd like another nationality? Because you need it? Or because you're happy and you want to stay here? In my case, I am happy and I want to stay here. I believe that the place where you are happy and satisfied with your life is your home. It is not important where I am from originally. I have my Korean citizenship and I'm very happy with that. So, if someone wants to change their citizenship to Korean, I advise it. If you are happy in this country and if you want to live in this country, change your citizenship. Why not? Koreans are nice people.

"In the end, be prepared to bend over backwards. When you're thinking to yourself that you can't yield any further, it's important to realize that the person you're dealing with is most likely bending over backwards as well. If you're not prepared to do this, be prepared to run into a lot of walls."

Suzanna Samstag Oh (44)
America
Editor, Translator, and SamulNori Expert
23 Years

In a land where few Western women make Korea their home for life, Suzanna should be a role model for what it takes to make it in Korea. Fluent in Korean, she is the proud mother of two, as well as arguably the most knowledgeable foreigner on SamulNori (사물놀이), one of the best known Korean music groups in the modern era.

I n 1980, when I arrived in Korea at the age of 21 with the Peace Crops, I immediately began my Korean language and culture training in Chuncheon (춘천), which lasted for two months. I was trained to be a tuberculosis control worker. My group was responsible for making sure Koreans took their tuberculosis medicine. Also, we taught basic health education, such as family planning, nutrition, cleanliness, and what to do to avoid having tuberculosis in your home. I remember Korea as being very hot when I arrived. I got sick once, some kind of intestinal flu, but it didn't dampen my enthusiasm. I think at that time I was still so dizzy from the whole experience that I didn't have a lot of time to look around. I didn't have much time to network with previous volunteers either, but we did have some people with us who were our culture teachers, and helped out with our training, who had been here for many years.

One of the most fun things that we did as volunteers at the health center was *ka-jok-bang-moon* (가족방문)—family visitations. We would get on a little bus and then drive on the country roads for a couple of hours. We'd visit patients to make sure that they were taking their medicine properly and check-up on their general health. Those excursions were wonderful and we were fed incredibly. People were very glad to see us and we were the hit of the countryside. We were taken very good care of. Seeing the countryside and participating in rice planting and harvesting was an awful lot of fun, too. I was mainly being dragged around, though. It was basically me going in to work in the morning and finding out the day's itinerary on the spot. I didn't have enough Korean in those days, and I looked at my tour of duty as a two-year commitment. I didn't have any lofty expectations about how I was going to change the world; I thought my tour would be a couple of years to mellow out after an intense four-year college experience.

I did have a couple of very interesting experiences at the time, however. One time I had gone to Daegu (대구) for my language training and when I came back to where I was staying, which was a beautiful, traditional Korean house, my room was lit up in bright lights. All these people were in the courtyard and some kind of exorcism was being performed on someone in the family. At first I thought they were exorcising me! I guess the family had some kind of problem that required the services of a shaman, *moo-dang* (무당). They had thought I'd be gone another day, so they were using my room and they had the shaman there.

Anyway, in January '81 we received a phone call from the main Peace Corps office in Seoul, ordering all the volunteers to come for a big meeting. At the meeting we were told that the Peace Corps budget had been slashed by Congress. Even though our tour of duty was supposed to last into the middle of 1982, we were told that our program was to be cancelled immediately, so the Peace Corps gave us several options: we could be sent back to the United States with no prejudice; we could be sent to another Peace Corps country—I was offered Tonga, which I flatly refused, or we were offered a deal with the Korean Immigration Department whereby we could stay in Korea for another year on a Peace Corps visa. I elected to stay in Korea.

What I did immediately was go to Seoul National University (SNU 서울대학교) because I had seen an article about their American Studies Institute in the *Korea Herald*. I met with the director and asked if he needed any assistance. He was a very nice man and offered me a job as an office assistant. I told him of my desire to pursue a graduate degree after which some calls were made to the Ministry of Education and I was awarded a scholarship. The scholarship provided me with an apartment, which I shared with two other foreign students, and a full scholarship to study at SNU, along with a living allowance. I was very fortunate.

The first thing I did there was study the Korean language through a year-long language program they had. It was very funny because there were so few foreign students that there were times when I was the only student in the class. What's more is that my

Korean teacher believed my score would reflect her teaching ability, so when I would take her tests, all by myself sometimes, she would come over and ensure my perfect score! I didn't care particularly whether I made mistakes or not, however it was of paramount concern to her!

After that I did an M.A. in English literature. I couldn't study Korean literature, but I did take classes in Korean literature as soon as I was able to. I found that very interesting, and my professors pushed me to pursue more inter-disciplinary studies, even though there were no American or Korean Studies programs available in Korea at that time.

What's interesting is that I was going to school in Korea during a time when there were the fewest classes ever offered in history, due to the high amount of demonstrations. We'd start off the semester and get two classes or so in, and then all hell would break loose because of the student demonstrations and the tear gas. I used to go through a pair of contact lenses a month because of that. It was a year of extremely violent demonstrations on campus. I remember walking up the main steps of Seoul National one time and there being this particular odor to the air. It smelled like a barbecue with burning hair. All these people had gathered around a student who had set himself on fire and then jumped off a building. In another instance I witnessed a self-immolator almost immediately after he'd set himself on fire. That type of thing was pretty regular; once a month a student was either shot or jumped from a building. It became a joke to say you were attending a university at that time because no professor was able to hold class under those circumstances, nor did they particularly want to. You'd get two classes or so in at the start of the semester, and then when the professor realized toward the end of the semester that they were running out of ways to salvage the academic year, they'd ask you to write a paper. That was your education. College education during that time was virtually non-existent.

At that time there was some anti-Americanism, but not as prevalent as you see today. The issue at hand was the Korean government itself. The Kwangju (광주) Uprising had taken place in 1980, right before I came to Korea, and with the country being run by a military dictator, people were disappearing without a trace. It was incredible for me to watch all of that because, being an American Studies major, I'd read about the birth of democracy in the States, but there I was watching it happen right in front of me in Korea. In that sense, I don't think I missed out educationally, even though I couldn't attend class in the formal sense.

Along with my academic pursuits, I was learning about traditional Korean performing arts at the training center in Gangnam (강남). I first started mask dance in about 1982 or so. I had seen a little ad on this poster outside some building which said "Looking for students for mask dance." I thought it sounded interesting, and I love dance, so I went to see their weekly Saturday performance, and they were just so incredible. I had studied dance before and I really appreciated the physicality of their movements.

It was at that point that my Korean language learning really took off because the teachers only spoke Korean and the students were required to actually do what the teacher was telling you to with their bodies. It wasn't like reading a book and memorizing vocabulary; if they told you to do something, you had to do it. The wonderful thing about dance, which I recommend to Koreans who want to learn English, is when learning how to do something in a foreign language, there is so much repetition. Learning mask dance isn't only about learning the dance—you have to memorize the script. It's very complex, but beautiful. You have to memorize the songs and learn how to play the instruments.

It was about that time I became involved with SamulNori. They weren't very well known then, and when my Korean language teacher had found out about them, she thought it would be good for a cultural experience. When I saw them my whole life changed.

To give you some background on this, "Samul" (사물) refers to "four things," in this case, four instruments: two drums and two gongs. *Buk* (북) is the barrel drum, *jang-go* (장고) is the hourglass drum, *jing* (징) is the large gong, and then *ggwaeng-gwa-ree* (꽹과리) is the small gong. The term "Nori" (놀이) means "to play," but it also refers to "artistic accomplishment." Directly translated, SamulNori means "the playing of four things," yet properly understood, it implies "the mastery of four percussion instruments."

SamulNori is such an interesting phenomenon because it's not traditional. Some people are of the belief that SamulNori is a thousand-year tradition, but it's not. It's actually just a band! Four guys with backgrounds in traditional music formed a band in 1978. It's a modern manifestation of traditional elements, deliberately conceived for performance on a stage, whereas one of the traditions it comes from, *nong-ak* (농악), is actually not the traditional term for that—it's a term that the Japanese used. Many people know it as *nong-ak*, or "Farmers band music," which suggests something as simple as farmers who would just all of a sudden stop planting and pick up an instrument to play. When these four guys got together, they realized that this "farmer's music"—I'll just use that term for convenience's sake—needs a lot of members, like 40 people, it's played outdoors, and you can't really present it on the stage. So they took some of the rhythms from *nong-ak*, the idea of presentation as a seated performance—because you can perform much more complex rhythms when you're seated than you can while you're dancing, this part of the tradition coming from *moo-sok* (무속)—ceremonial music—and they combined all of these elements into a group. They put together a show that was under two hours, performed on a Western stage, and faced the audience. These kinds of things were all calculated to make it presentable to audiences, which historically is not the case in traditional music. They then coined the name SamulNori, the group I ended up managing.

When they performed at the Asia Society, which was about the time that I got to know them—again it was the old story of having to leave Korea in order to become famous—a *New York Times* critic raved about their performance. When they came back to Korea, their momentum started to gather and people here thought, "Well, if the *New York Times* thinks they're pretty good, then maybe we should check them out!"

When I saw them perform, I wanted to go and learn how to play this instrument, even though previously I had never had an interest to play any musical instrument. I found out where their studio was and gathered up the courage to go there. These four guys had no interest in teaching anybody, however, especially not a foreigner who could hardly speak Korean, so they gave me the blow-off. I was determined not to give up, though. I came by all the time and attended all of their performances. I was the ultimate groupie! Finally, they conceded and let their driver teach me, and so I said okay because I just wanted to learn.

I arrived at the studio everyday at 6:00 a.m., which turned into 7:00 usually, as the driver wouldn't show up for the first hour, forcing me to sit on the steps outside their rehearsal space until the guy showed up. The driver knew some of the music, but he wasn't trained and he didn't know how to teach. I tried as best I could for months and months, though, until finally I said, "You know, why don't you give me a key and I'll come in and practice by myself until you get there, so you don't feel like you have to come down here so early because you're too tired or hungover." They then gave me the key to the place and I'd go in there and clean up everything first thing in the morning.

Since they'd gone and performed that one time in New York, they began receiving lots of letters from people wanting them to perform at other festivals. Now, the four members of the band didn't really read English, so they would open these letters and simply drop them wherever. I'd then come into a studio with a pile of letters strewn everywhere and stuff piled into drawers. One day when they were out performing somewhere in the country and I didn't go, though, I thought I'd take the opportunity to organize things. I took out everything—letters, papers, pamphlets, records—and laid it all out in the rehearsal room, which covered the entire area! When they came back to the studio they found all of their stuff neatly organized into two file cabinets. I was a little scared of their reaction because I had rifled through all of their stuff, but they just said, "Oh, thanks." I made them aware of the letters in English asking them to come and perform, then asked them if they wanted me to reply, to which they said, "If you want to."

All of a sudden, everyone I replied to received this letter in fluent English and I guess the band members realized that they had a manager. We began building up our contacts near the end of '83 and by the beginning of the following year we traveled extensively. I tried to balance going to school and then going with them on tour as the explainer/interpreter/translator. After they'd play in one place, they'd usually go back for a lecture and I'd be responsible for explaining while they played.

It was after this that we became a part of two wonderful things. In 1986, Korea hosted the Asian Games, and then in 1988, Seoul hosted the Summer Olympics. We did an incredible amount of touring in support of those two events, and everything was memorable because we met and collaborated with so many fabulous musicians. We were caught up in the growing interest in world music, so we'd go to studios and work with people like Peter Gabriel, for example. In 1988, we were even asked to accompany the Olympic Torch from Greece to Seoul! I was the tour manager while the band traveled around and followed the torch and played. These were all things I know I never imagined, and I doubt the rest of the band did either. For me it's fascinating to look back because it was so hard to get into their inner circle, originally. The only reason I stopped doing it in the end was because I had no personal life for ten years. I was their roadie from 1983–1994.

For those ten years, I was working with and managing four men who were nothing short of musical geniuses, and the reaction to their stage performances while they were in their prime was magical. The founder of SamulNori, and my boss, Kim Duk-soo (김덕수), however, was a very, very difficult person to work with. Many people cannot manage artists. They think that everyone has to be treated equally, and that just wasn't true in this case. We were unequal. There were many tears shed because if everything wasn't perfect with the performance, whether it was my fault or not, I usually got dumped on. It was a real emotional strain.

By 1994, I had come to the realization that I wanted, and

needed, a life outside of the band. I had to ask myself if I had the energy to continue, if trying to keep up with life on the road was what I wanted my life's work to be about. I ended up going through a withdrawal period when I left, but being their manager was so high pressure and I'd felt that I'd done enough. By then, anyway, the original group had broken up. Kim Duk-soo had managed to irritate just about everybody by that point! Choi Jong-shil (최종실) had wanted to go back to school and finish his college degree and Kim Duk-soo told him that he had to decide to stay with the group or quit to go to school—he couldn't do both—so Choi Jong-shil left. Lee Gwang-soo (이광수) also left.

Fortunately, before I left SamulNori I had been scouted by *Newsweek*. They were going to start the Korean edition of the magazine and they needed people who could speak Korean well in order to check the translations. While I was still managing SamulNori I flatly refused, but later acquiesced and did some work part-time on weekends. When I left the band I went to work for them full-time. These days, however, I've changed careers again and am involved in early childhood education, working to provide kids with learning experiences that are really fun and interesting. I make my job choices based on my ability to properly accommodate my children. I'm not a high-powered career type and I have no serious ambitions. Money is not my sole purpose for waking up in the morning. The thing that's made me happiest lately has been working on the LATT Children's Theater in the past year which, interestingly enough, causes me to draw on my ten years with SamulNori. The thing with working in publishing now, and especially with developing material for children's English learning, is that I've spent so many years learning how to speak Korean that I find I have a lot of knowledge when it comes to language acquisition.

If I were to offer any advice to people who are thinking about living in Korea, I would first say that you have to have a sense of humor. Never take yourself too seriously. The best thing is to be able to sit down and laugh at whatever happens to you during the day, because a lot it is bound to be hysterical if you sit back and think about it. Another virtue to have is patience. It takes a really long time, but once you're in, you're in—whether you want to be or not. Give yourself a lot of time to do things and don't expect things to happen immediately. In the end, be prepared to bend over backwards. When you're thinking to yourself that you can't yield any further, it's important to realize that the person you're dealing with is most likely bending over backwards as well. If you're not prepared to do this, be prepared to run into a lot of walls.

Personally, I've led a charmed life. I've met people here in Korea that I could have never met in the United States, like Katherine Graham, as well as being involved in the diplomatic community here and being invited to numerous embassies. If I had simply lived out my life in the States, what are the chances of these experiences happening there for me? Zero. Thinking about it in that context, I've had a very amazing life. And it just gets more interesting as it goes along. The future will take care of itself.

"... Koreans under the Japanese and during the Chosun Dynasty were more or less a downtrodden people. On occasion, qualities of creativity and imagination were shown but basically they were downtrodden. With liberation from Japanese rule came a sudden burst of over self-confidence."

Dr. Horace Underwood III 원일한
(86; 1917–2004)
America
Professor Emeritus and President of the Board of Directors of Yonsei University
71 Years

Born into a young, post-dynastic Korea, Dr. Underwood lived through the Japanese occupation of the Korean peninsula. He was interned in Seoul after the bombing of Pearl Harbor, only to go on to serve in World War II and the Korean War. Soldier, educator, translator, Dr. Underwood was a fountain of information on one of the most important eras in modern Korean history. He passed away at the age of 86, in 2004, shortly after giving this interview.

M Y GRANDFATHER arrived in Korea in 1885 and is considered the pioneer Protestant missionary in Korea. My grandmother came a few years later and they were married here. My grandfather was primarily a minister, but he was also the founder of Yonsei University (연세대학교), along with a host of other interests. They had one child, my father, who returned to Korea later as an educational missionary, not a minister, strictly a layperson.

My father was the president of Yonsei University for a time during the Japanese occupation. I was born here in 1917, the oldest of five children, and lived in Korea until 1923, at which time my father went back to the States for three years to follow up on some graduate work. I returned to Korea at the age of nine and remained until I was 16, when again we left for the States. I was a junior in high school at the time and I remained in America until I graduated from college. I returned to Korea again in 1939 and stayed until 1942 whereupon I was repatriated to America to fight in World War II. I joined the U.S. Navy and spent the war years in the Pacific. I came to Korea once again in 1946 to work with the military government and at Yonsei. I've pretty much spent all my time in Korea ever since the Korean War broke out. It's funny because in my own mind, all of my youth was spent in Korea. However, if you add up the years it doesn't appear so. Anyway, after I retired, I remained on the Yonsei Board of Directors. I'm also on the board of a number of church organizations in Korea. Ours is a missionary family. We're all missionaries with the Presbyterian Church USA. I have three sons, the oldest son came and taught here at Yonsei for a number of years and is now director of the Fulbright Program in Korea.

When I was born in 1917, the Japanese had already been in Korea for quite some time. From all I've read, the first ten years of the occupation were especially rough, culminating in the March

First Movement of 1919 (*sam-eel-jul* 삼일절). Although the Japanese never admitted it, it was partly because of that independence movement and partly a change of mood in Japan that in the 1920s there was a relatively mild government here. At the time the local policeman was king and very authoritarian, but they were not so terribly harsh in their treatment. Now of course, March First was very harsh—many people were tortured. In fact, there was this male student I remember seeing at Yonsei with no nose because it had been cut off by the Japanese during the March First Movement.

I would say, though, especially as foreigners, we were not bothered very much by the Japanese. For the most part, we had to notify the police if ever we were to go somewhere and we'd have to register with them when we arrived; there was always a regulation of one sort or another; always some sort of bureaucratic hassle. For Koreans, however, life was much harsher, especially in the business world. Oftentimes when a Korean would request a permit for his business, the authorities would delay and delay until finally they'd apologize that the permit had already been granted to someone else, like a Japanese person. I was not aware of this as a young boy, though.

As the 1930s rolled around things in Korea began to get rougher. I can't give you exact dates, but it was in the thirties that the Japanese started insisting that Korean children start being taught in Japanese. There was a Korean school right across the street from our Seoul Foreign School, and I still remember how Korean children would be speaking Korean together before they entered the gates to their school and then switch into Japanese as soon as they crossed the threshold. In a couple of years, these kids weren't allowed to speak Korean at all. As the Japanese campaign in Manchuria began to heat up and Japan began to really assert its influence in the Orient, things in Korea got worse for Koreans. Effectively, the Japanese were trying to turn Koreans here into Japanese—they wanted to stamp out Korean culture.

Every year there would be a smallpox, cholera, or some other sort of epidemic and the Japanese set up these checkpoints along the roads to give injections, sometimes forcibly. I was told that the Japanese decreed the Korean *han-bok* (한복)—traditional dress—as wasteful because it was white and got dirty easily, and so Koreans were issued darker clothes. Japanese policemen would stand at the entrance to villages and smear tar or black paint on the clothing of Koreans who hadn't adhered to the decree. There was also "thought control" and oppression during this time. A number of Yonsei's university faculty, for instance, were arrested and placed into either prison or these "thought schools" where they could look forward to being "cleansed" of all thoughts not Japanese. In turn, they were taught "proper" Japanese thoughts through various methods.

With greater oppression on the Korean nationals came greater restrictions on the foreign community in Korea, as well. The whole shrine issue, for example, became a very bitter issue for the Christian community, both foreign and Korean. The Japanese insisted that the Shinto shrines weren't simply religious, but national. On certain occasions, representatives had to visit the shrines to indicate their loyalty to Japan, and they tried to compare it to saluting the flag. Most in the Christian community felt that this was idolatry, that they were being forced to go and worship at Shinto shrines. Persecution ensued and people refusing to go found themselves in prison. The first person to blow the whistle was actually a missionary. Later on, the shrine issue was taken up in church circles and became a very bitter source of contention, both at the time and after the war, among those who had adhered and those who had not. Some Japanese even insisted on placing Kamidana, literally "God shelf," but better known as "baby Shinto shrines," in many Korean homes. My family had no particular trouble, though when we went traveling, especially in 1941 and after, we had to have a police escort travel with us.

Actually, after 1941 we were all forced to leave: all foreigners were deported in June of 1942 by the Japanese. After Pearl Harbor, everything shut down. My family was either under internment or house arrest. My father and I were interned and my wife, brother, mother, and sister were under house arrest until we were repatriated in 1942. There was an exchange. With my father and I, though, internment "camp" is a grand word. There were only 13 of us, actually, in the Methodist seminary building. We were all in one room together and had another room that we could sort of use as a kitchenette with electric heaters when our food was sent to us by my mother under house arrest. Anyway, we were all interned until May 31, 1942. We were then shipped to Japan and were interned there for two weeks before we got on board the *Gripsholm* and were repatriated at Lorenzo Marcus, in what was then Portuguese East Africa, and which is now called Mozambique.

When we returned to the U.S., I knew I'd be subject to the draft, so I volunteered to serve in the Navy. I heard about the language program and I figured with my experience in Korean and knowledge of some Japanese I could be helpful. I was a non-warrior in the Pacific Campaign, however. I joined the language school in January '43 and finished in March. I was assigned to

Pearl Harbor to interrogate prisoners of war as part of the intelligence team. We were later in the Philippines for about a month, searching for possible collaborators. Mostly I was a desk warrior in Pearl Harbor, though. After the Japanese surrendered, I was assigned to mine sweepers in the western Pacific and operations in Japan for about five or six months.

Although I wanted to get back earlier, I was only assigned to Korea in May of 1946 to work in the education section of the military government. At the time, Korea was bubbling and there were lots of problems and quarrels—it was just boiling. Various things like the Yeosu (여수) rebellion were a part of this boiling. To what extent these incidents were actually fostered by North Korea would depend on which end of the political spectrum you're looking from, I suppose. Some acknowledge that there was genuine unrest and genuine reason for it, but stimulated by agents from the North. From the American side of things, the functioning military government was not excellent in the carrying out of all its functions.

Anyway, I did this until the summer of '47 when I was finally discharged. I returned to Yonsei as a missionary and was teaching there until the Korean War broke out. The day the Korean War broke out, June 25, 1950, our mission was having its annual meeting down country in Daecheon (대천), so 50–60 of us were not in Seoul. Our whole group took off to the south that day and when we got to Daegu (대구) I decided not to leave. I sent my wife and only son at the time to Japan and tried to get myself back up to Seoul yet couldn't. I heard the South Korean government had moved to Daejeon (대전), so I went there. I knew quite a number of people in the Korean government, people who were my father's friends, so asked them if I could be of any assistance. They then asked me to join the American Army observer team that was working with the government, and so that's what I did. I worked with the 24th Division from July 1 to August 5 or 6. It didn't seem right to work with the Army as a missionary, so I enlisted in the Navy and was sent to Japan in early August, joining the Naval Headquarters there who were planning the Incheon (인천) landings. The Incheon landings took place on September 15, 1950.

I was assigned to the 5th Marines when they came up from around the north side of the Han River as far as Yonsei campus, until one of my good friends, Bill Shaw, another Korean kid, was killed. I was still in Seoul when General Macarthur, in grandiose fashion, declared Seoul "secured." Seoul was far from secured, but if Macarthur says so, then it must be, right? At the time, Seoul was very badly destroyed. Seventy to eighty percent of the city was decimated—rubble. When the North Koreans attacked, the South Korean forces evacuated the city. After the Incheon landings the North Koreans fought for the city block-by-block. The streets of Seoul were littered, among other things, with barricades every couple hundred yards. Fighting back into Seoul, the city got rather badly shot up. At one point I was on a hill overlooking Seoul Station and looking down at the rather awesome sight of Severance Hospital going up in flames. Driving through the city, the big buildings were still standing but heavily pockmarked with shell holes. Almost everything that could burn did.

Those of us involved in the Incheon landing were in our combat uniforms with our helmets on when all these fat cats from Tokyo in traditional dress arrived in Seoul. We were in the center of the Capitol Building, and the glass from the dome was trickling down. Anyhow, that's when they told me I wasn't supposed to be up near the front lines. The company took me back to division headquarters and I then returned to Japan near the end of September. I was then put on assignment up Korea's east coast to report the status of North Korean naval materials. We eventually met up with a Korean capital division and I became an unofficial interpreter/advisor to the capital division for about ten days or so, until the Chinese swarmed in and we had to bug out, when I was withdrawn to Japan. I was then assigned to a naval advisory group in Busan (부산), and I was there until the armistice talks started, at which point I became the senior interpreter from July of '51 until the end.

At the armistice talks, we had five delegates on either side and everything had to be said in Korean, Chinese, and English. When the Korean side spoke, their interpreters would translate almost immediately into Chinese and English. When our side spoke it would be translated into Korean and then Chinese. My role was to do the translation from English into Korean. Although this process was tedious, it was also so vital, as each interpreter tried to leave no room for misinterpretation. I believe there's an Italian saying that captures this well: "To translate is to betray," or something similar to that, that no two languages can be translated perfectly into one another.

In the first month of the talks I was getting into a real sweat because we were dealing with concepts that were foreign to me; I'd never learned them. Anyway, my brother and I made a handy vocabulary list which we used for about a month or so. My favorite example is this: what's the distinction between "armistice," "truce," and "cease-fire" in Korean? In any case, I believe there are only two words in Korean, *jung-jun* (정전) and *hyu-jun* (휴전).

The armistice talks ended up being very bitter on both sides. I think that originally our people had thought in terms everybody going back, but before we made any decisions we demanded to see the prisoner of war exchange list. In December of '52, the North Koreans came up with a list of around 13,000 soldiers, which caused our people to blow their stack. The Communists had boasted how they'd amassed many thousands of prisoners of war, and even been quoted through Geneva, yet the number of American prisoners of war they had from the early days of the war that weren't on that list caused our people to get madder than hell as a result.

By January we'd arrived at essential agreement on everything save the repatriating of prisoners. By March or so, the Communists hinted that they might be able to accept something if the request weren't too great, and so I went down to interrogate the POWs. I'd have to look it up in my book to be sure of the figure, but I think it was somewhere between 65–70 percent of the Chinese who didn't want to be repatriated, while 70–80 percent of the Koreans were of the same mind. In the case of the Chinese, they genuinely didn't want to go back where they came from. In the case of the Koreans, it was more a case of mistaken identity because there were a lot of Koreans who should never have been in the POW camps in the first place. The prevailing tendency of the U.S. troops at the time was to round up all young men who were not in uniform under the assumption that they were infiltrators or spies. The North Koreans drafted a lot of young people to march them north for training, yet they were South Koreans who were in the North Korean army and they were treated as prisoners of war, as such. In any case, the Communists, as it turns out, blew their stack over that fact. And so, from May of '52 until April of '53 the talks were in virtual suspension. We'd meet every two to three weeks and after learning nothing had changed, the meeting would adjourn and we'd wait another month or so.

In April of '53 it was suggested that we exchange the sick and wounded because there'd be no question towards their repatriation. This opened the door. In the meantime, from modern intelligence sources we've learned that the Russians advised the North to adhere and get out of it. So, the volunteer repatriation was to be screened by the Indians and it was agreed to by both sides. President Rhee was very much opposed to this because he thought the Indians were all Commies and would do everything in favor of the North, but that didn't happen. The North were more bitter in the sense that they were shocked, I think. When we asked them where were the thousands of soldiers unaccounted for, they replied that they'd released them at the front. We took this to mean they'd been drafted in the North Korean Army. Quite a number of North Korean POWs were South Koreans that had been captured and then recaptured.

Looking back after all this time, Koreans under the Japanese and during the Chosun Dynasty (조선시대) were more or less a downtrodden people. On occasion, qualities of creativity and imagination were shown but basically they were downtrodden. With liberation from Japanese rule came a sudden burst of over self-confidence. Isabel Bishop wrote nearing the end of the Chosun Dynasty, before the Japanese came, that "Korean people have been suffering oppression at the hands of aristocrats. Someday, when they are liberated from this oppressive regime, they will do remarkable things." That's very perceptive and exactly what I think.

We had a cholera epidemic in 1948 where some 10,000 people died. Another cholera outbreak happened in the eighties, in which only ten cases broke out. That's the difference of forty years. When I was a kid growing up in Korea, we had to take worm medicine at least once a year because Koreans were infested with tapeworms. That's no longer an issue. Also, although Korean women are still discriminated against tremendously, their position now in comparison to what it was is incredible! For good or for ill, the eldest son no longer sacrifices his education so that his brothers and sisters can go to school. Family ties these days are certainly still strong, but not as strong as they once were and in one way this is regrettable, but in another it's a plus. Levels of loss are unavoidable whenever there's change in social structure. The elderly may not be as respected as they once were fifty years ago—no offspring would have dreamt of taking their elderly father or mother and abandoning them in Jeju Island (제주도)—but this doesn't happen with a high level of frequency today. Look at the Korean change in diet for crying out loud! Before World War II, a Korean meal would consist of a big bowl of rice—four people eating barley and rice mixed together—a bowl of soup, and one or two pieces of *pan-chan* (반찬)—side dishes—and none of their food would be fresh or even green.

    Also, in America, the West, we tend to put top value on various abstract concepts such as honesty, integrity, the company, or the nation. We may not like to admit it, but we sacrifice relationships through this value system. In Korea, the top value is placed on the inter-personal: people related to you, people from your hometown, people from your school, people with whom you work—whatever the interpersonal connection may be. Although in the West we do get mad at whistle blowers from time to time, and we do have the West Point protective association and other such things where loyalty has priority over honesty, nevertheless, as a society

Westerners value honesty first. In Korean society, it's the other way around, so I think it's this polar opposite value system that Westerners not only have a hard time grasping, but a hard time accepting.

Appendix & Endnotes

Appendix

Visas Issued by the Republic of Korea

A–1 Diplomats This applies to foreigners: diplomatic missions of the countries recognized by the Korean Government, consular officers assigned to represent their countries in Korea, foreigners granted privileges and/or immunities equal to diplomatic mission in accordance with treaties or international customary practices, and their immediate family members. (During mission)

A–2 Official Duty This applies to foreigners who carry out official service of the countries or international organizations recognized by the Republic of Korea, and their immediate family members. (Term of duty)

A–3 Agreement This was created to apply to foreigners who are exempted from alien registration or deemed necessary to be exempted from it according to the agreements with the Republic of Korea, and their immediate family members. (During term of agreement or length of agreement)

B–1 Visa Waiver This was created to allow nationals of the countries which have made visa waiver agreements with the Republic of

Korea to do activities under the agreements. However, income-generating business, or paid activities in Korea are excluded. (During period of sojourn stipulated by agreement)

B-2 Tourist/Transit This applies to foreigners who desire to visit Korea without a visa for pleasure or transit. (During period designated by Minister of Justice)

C-1 Temporary News Coverage This applies to foreigners who want to engage in temporary news coverage or report activities. (90 days)

C-2 Short-term Business This category is available to foreigners who are going to engage in marketing research, business liaison, on-the-job training, counseling, contract, pilot operation of export-import machines as well as installment, repairs and inspection on them during the short period of time. (90 days)

C-3 Short-term Visitors This category applies to foreigners who visit Korea for pleasure, transfer, medical treatment, relative-visiting, goodwill match, events, conference, cultural art, training, religious ceremony, academic data-gathering, and for other purposes similar to the above during the short period of time. However, profit-making activities are excluded. (90 days)

C-4 Short-term Employment This visa applies to foreigners who wish to employ themselves on temporary entertainment, model for advertisement and fashion, lecture, research, technique-instruction and so on during a short term. (90 days)

D-1 Culture/Art This visa is available to foreigners who wish to be occupied in academic or art activities which are not for the

	purpose of profits-making. This category includes foreigners who long for professional research or being instructed Korean traditional culture or art. (2 years)
D-2 Students	This visa category is designed for students who wish to pursue academic courses of study or research at junior colleges or higher educational institutions or educational/scientific research organizations. (2 years)
D-3 Industrial Trainees	This visa is available to individuals who are going to participate within industrial companies in the Republic of Korea, in a formal training program which must be related to the following companies: (a) Industrial firms which directly invest money into foreign countries or have joint venture relations with foreign companies (b) Industrial firms which offer techniques to foreign countries (c) Industrial firms which export plants to foreign countries. (2 years)
D-4 General Trainees	This visa category is reserved for foreigners who are coming to Korea to be trained or educated by educational institutions or organizations other than organizations under the D-3 status described above. The D-4 visa does not involve individuals who receive money from training organizations or have the D-3 visa. (2 years)
D-5 Residence Reporters	Foreigners who are visiting Korea to work on behalf of foreign information media such as foreign newspaper, television, magazine, and other reporting organizations while stationed in Korea. (2 years)

D–6 Religious Workers	The D–6 visa must meet the following qualifications: (a) individuals who wish to be engaged in religious activities for Korean branches or pertinent religious organizations as the members of religious or social welfare organizations in foreign countries. (b) individuals who are invited by religious or social welfare organizations in Korea in order to do activities on social welfare or religion. (2 years)
D–7 Intra-Company Transferees	The D–7 visa is granted to professional personnel who are transferred to branch offices, affiliated companies or resident offices in Korea from foreign companies abroad, with over one year of service in head offices, branch offices or other business offices of foreign ones. (2 years)
D–8 Treaty Investors	This category is available to foreigners who, as professionals of foreign joint venture companies, wish to engage in the field of manufacture and technology as well as its management. The D–8 visa include those who are dispatched to the company as managers or technical experts, except for foreigners who are hired in the Republic of Korea. (2 years)
D–9 Treaty Traders	D–9 visa is available to foreign professionals who desire to carry on an enterprise or participate in trade and other commercial enterprises after founding their companies in the Republic of Korea. This category includes foreign citizens who wish to work for private or public organizations in Korea in order to install/repair of import machinery and so on, or supervise building ships and industrial plants, except for individuals hired in Korea and treaty investors under the D–8 status. (2 years)

E–1 Professors	This category applies to foreigners who, as qualified individuals specified by the Educational Law, wish to instruct special fields of study or engage in the guidance of research at junior colleges or higher educational institutions, or the institutions corresponding to such levels. (2 years)
E–2 Teaching Foreign Languages	The E–2 visa is available to individuals who have the the qualifications specified by the Minister of justice and desire to instruct foreign languages at foreign language institutions, educational institutions of elementary school and higher levels or their annex language research institutions, or language training institutions attached to public/private companies or broadcasting stations, or other institutions/organizations corresponding to such institutions as described above. (1 year)
E–3 Research	E–3 visas are granted to foreigners who, as individuals who are invited by public or private institutions of the Republic of Korea, want to be occupied with study or research in the area of natural science or research and development of sophisticated technology in industry. This category does not contain individuals who apply to E–1 status. (2 years)
E–4 Special Tech. Instruction	This visa category applies to foreigners who wish to work at the invitation of public or private institutions in the Republic of Korea with a view to offering technical knowledge in the area of natural science or special technology involved in specialized fields in industry. (2 years)
E–5 Specialty Occupations	"Foreigners in specialty occupations" who have qualifications for a lawyer, certified public accountant, medical doctor or other individuals who are qualified for specialty occupations, and wish to be involved in such

	specialty occupations as laws, accounting, medical services and so on may be eligible for E–5 classification. Please note that individuals who fall under E–1 status are excluded from this category. (2 years)
E–6 Arts and Entertainment	This E–6 visa is available to foreigners who, for the good of profit-making, wish to be engaged in art activities such as music, art, literature and so on, and such activities as entertainment, performance, play, sports, advertisement, fashion modeling, and other occupations corresponding to those above. (6 months)
E–7 Other Particular Jobs	This visa category applies to foreigners who desire to desire to work for public or private organizations as a cook, teacher of schools for foreigners only, etc., other than those in E–1 status through E–6 status. (2 years)
E–8 Indutrial Trainees Employment	This visa is available only to those who meet the qualifications that are stipulated in the presidential decree, among the industrial trainees who has successfully completed their two-year period training with no serious mistake. (1 year)
F–1 Visiting and Joining Families	F-1 visa is granted to foreigners who wish to stay in Korea to visit their relatives, join their families, be supported by families, help household affairs or with other purposes corresponding to those above. This visa category involves the following individuals: (a) who wish to help household affairs of diplomats stationed at their embassy or consulate; (b) who wish to temporarily stay with their families or relatives having A–1, A–2, A–3 status or having alien registration completed: (c) who wish to stay for a long period of time without

	participating in employment activities; and
	(d) who have not been granted the F–2 status as a wife/child of a person having F–2 status.
	(e) a wife/child of a Korean. (2 Years)
F–2 Residence	This visa category is available to individuals (including spouse and children) who have continuously lived with their permanent address in the Republic of Korea. This visa also includes the following category: (a) Children underage of a person who has F–2 status; (b) A woman who, as a wife of a Korean national, has never acquired a Korean nationality before; (c) A woman who, as a wife of a person having F–2 status, has continuously stayed in Korea; and (d) Individuals who have especially contributed to the Republic of Korea or who have valid reasons to continuously stay there. (5 years)
F–3 Dependent Families	F-3 status may be granted to individuals who meet the following requirements: (a) A spouse of a person who applies to one of D–1 status through E–7 status; (b) Children underage and unmarried of the person described in the above (c) However, individuals who are involved in D–3 status are excluded from this visa. (Same as attendant's period of stay)
F–4 Overseas Korean Residents	This visa category is reserved for the Overseas Korean residents whom the Minister of Justice permits to stay in Korea for special reasons among them. (2 years)
G–1 Other	This visa is available to foreigners who are not eligible for A–1 status through F–3 and H–1 status. (1 year)

H–1 Working Holiday	A national of countries which made agreements or memoranda on "Working Holiday" with the Republic of Korea is entitled to apply for this visa. The young foreigners may be engaged in short-term working activities while in Korea only to meet their expenses for sightseeing, unless they are engaged in the work fields contrary to the purport of the agreement/memoranda or the fields stipulated by domestic laws. (During period of sojourn, as stipulated by government)
M–1 Military	(Length of tour of duty)

Migration Offices

Seoul	82-2-2650-6239	319-2, Sinjeong 6 (yuk)-dong, Yangcheon-gu, Seoul Subway: At Omokgyo (Mok-dong Stadium) Station exit 7. Go straight for about 10 minutes.
Incheon	82-32-889-9903/10	1-17, Hangdong 7 (chil)-ga, Jung-gu, Incheon Bus: Take Incheon City Bus #3, #12 or #24 to Jungbu Police Station. 10 minutes on foot
Incheon Int'l Airport	82-32-740-7013	Incheon International Airport Immigration Office mainly handles procedures pertaining to entry and departure of Korea.
Busan	82-51-461-3030	17-26, 4-ga, Juang-dong, Jung-gu, Busan Subway: Juang-dong Station (Busan Subway Line No.1) 10 minutes on foot.

Gimhae Airport	82-51-972-1610/	Gimhae Airport Immigration Office mainly handles procedures pertaining to entry and departure of Korea.
Jeju	82-64-722-3494	673-8, Geonip-dong, Jeju-si, Jeju Directions: Take any city bus to Jeju Girls' Commercial High School.

Alien Registration

Korea Customs Service: http://www.customs.go.kr/hp/homepage/eng/index.htm

Visa Extension

Extensions for tourist visas are possible in special cases such as accidents, health problems, flight cancellation, etc. Applications for visa extensions can be made at local immigration office at least one day before the day of expiration.

Re-entry Visas

Immigration Bureau: www.moj.go.kr/immi/08english/indexe.html

A Korean embassy or consulate can issue two types of visa: a short-term visa for the visitor who wants to stay up to 90 days and a special long-term visa for periods longer than 90 days. A visitor with a special long-term visa is required to apply for alien registration at a local immigration office within 90 days of arrival.

Tourist, Business, and Work Visas

See the Ministry of Foreign Affairs and Trade for more information: http://www.mofat.go.kr/mission/missionsmapen.mof

Quarantine

For more information, refer to the following Internet sites:
1) National Veterinary Research & Quarantine Service: www.nvrqs.go.kr/extra/english/index.asp

2) National Plant Quarantine Service: www.npqs.go.kr
This is a document issued by the chief of a district or branch office in Korea for the simplicity of processing and shortening the time of visa issuance. As well, in certain cases, this document is required before applying for a visa to Korean consulate abroad. The objects of this certificate are as follows:

Disposition by Notification, Accusation, Negligence Fine

A disposition by notification is an administrative and simple disposition rather than a formal trial to ease an offender's burden and simplify the process of administration. When the chief of a district office, branch office or immigration processing center has obtained conclusive evidence of the offence as a result of an investigation, he may give the offender written notification to pay a fine.
When the offender of this Law has paid the fine in compliance with notification,

he/she shall not be subject to any further criminal punishment concerning the case in issue. However, when the offender of this law does not pay the fine within the designated period, the chief of a district or branch office shall file an accusation thereof.

In the case of minor offences such as negligence of various obligations of reports, the negligence fine shall be imposed and collected by the chief of a district or branch office.

The person who has accepted the disposition of a negligence fine may raise the objection against the chief of a district or branch office within thirty days from the informed date. When an objection is raised, the chief of a district or branch office shall notify the competent court without delay, and the competent court notified thereof shall judge the negligence fine pursuant to the Non-Contentious Cases Procedure Act.

1. Investigation, Examination and Decision

An Immigration officer may investigate a person who is suspected of immigration offences. In case there is considerable reason to suspect an immigration offender and he/she flees or might flee, the immigration officer may detain the foreigner. The chief of a district or branch office will examine and decide when the immigration officer has finished the investigation on the suspect. The chief of a district or branch office may give the offender a written notification to pay an amount equivalent to the fine. This disposition may be burdened on the offender with a departure order.

When the offender does not pay the fine within the designated period and in the case of serious offence, the chief of a district or branch office shall file an accusation. When the suspect desires to file an objection against the deportation order, he/she shall file it with the Minister of Justice by way of the chief of a district office, branch office or immigration detention center within seven days from the date on which he/she received the deportation order.

2. Detention

A. Detention of a foreigner under suspicion

- In case there is considerable reason to suspect that a foreigner falls under any of the terms in the sub-paragraphs of Article 46, and he/she flees or might flee, the immigration officer may detain the foreigner after obtaining a detention order issued by the chief of a district office, branch office, or immigration processing center.
- The period of detention shall be less than ten days. However, under unavoidable circumstances, this period can be extended only once within the period not exceeding ten days with the approval of the chief of a district office, branch office or immigration detention center.
- When the suspect is detained, the immigration officer shall notify his legal proxy, spouse, lineal relatives, brothers and sisters, family, counsel (hereinafter referred to as "legal proxy", or a person designated by the suspect, of the time, place and the reason for detention in writing within three days.
- The person detained by the detention order, or his legal proxy, may file an objection against the detention with the Minister of Justice, by way of the chief of the office, branch office, or immigration processing center.
- The Minister of Justice, upon receipt of the objection, shall review the relevant documents without delay, and he shall, if the request is deemed groundless, reject the objection by a decision and he shall, if well-grounded, order by decision to release the suspect from detention.

B. Detention of Deportee

In case a foreigner to be deported cannot be repatriated immediately, the immigration officer may detain him/her until the deportation is available. Other processes such as notification of detention or objection against detention are the same as the above.
Temporary Detention of Foreigners
The immigration officer may temporarily detain a foreigner falling under any of the following sub-paragraphs in an immigration processing center. In this case,

the detention period shall not exceed forty-eight hours:

- A person who has not been permitted to enter the country because of not fulfilling entry requirements
- A person who has been admitted on a conditional entry visa and who flees or has a considerable reason to deem that he/she might flee.
- A person who has been ordered to leave the Republic of Korea and who flees or has a considerable reason to deem that he/she might flee.
- When the immigration officer is unable to repatriate a foreigner temporarily detained within the scope of 48 hours because of the unsecured transportation for departure, disease, or other unavoidable reasons, the officer may extend the period of detention within this scope which does not exceed 48 hours by getting an approval from the chief of a district or branch office.

3. Disposition by Notification, Accusation, Negligence Fine

A disposition by notification is an administrative and simple disposition rather than a formal trial to ease an offender's burden and simplify the process of administration. When the chief of a district office, branch office or immigration processing center has obtained conclusive evidence of the offence as a result of an investigation, he may give the offender written notification to pay a fine.

- When the offender of this Law has paid the fine in compliance with notification, he/she shall not be subject to any further criminal punishment concerning the case in issue. However, when the offender of this law does not pay the fine within the designated period, the chief of a district or branch office shall file an accusation thereof.
- In the case of minor offences such as negligence of various obligations of reports, the negligence fine shall be imposed and collected by the chief of a district or branch office.
- The person who has accepted the disposition of a negligence fine may raise the objection against the chief of a district or branch office within thirty days from the informed date. When an objection is raised, the chief of a district or branch

office shall notify the competent court without delay, and the competent court notified thereof shall judge the negligence fine pursuant to the Non-Contentious Cases Procedure Act.
− When the chief of a district office, branch office or immigration processing center deems, as a result of his investigation, that the case would entail punishment not less than confinement, he/she shall immediately file an accusation thereof

4. Deportation, Departure Order and Recommendation of Departure

A deportation means that the offender of Korean Immigration Laws and, falling under any parts of article 46, shall be deported from Korea against his/her will by the chief of a district or branch office.

− When the chief of a district office, branch office, as a result of his examination, concludes that the suspect falls under any of the sub-paragraphs of Article 46, he may issue a deportation order to the suspect. The deportation order shall be executed by the immigration officer.

When it is impossible for the chief of a district office, branch office or immigration processing center to repatriate the person ordered to be deported immediately, he may detain him/her at the immigration processing center, or other places designated by the Minister of Justice until repatriation of the said person can be effected.

A departure order means that the offender of Korean Immigration Laws shall be ordered to leave the country by the chief of a district or branch office. The differences from a deportation come from the seriousness of the offence or the process of disposition and there is a difference in a follow-up action.

− For example, if a foreigner who has overstayed and has been illegally worked for a long time wants to leave Korea voluntarily with his/her own expenses, he/she shall get a departure order instead of a deportation.
− In a follow-up action, an offender of deportation shall be put on the list of entry

prohibition for a long time, on the other hand, an offender with a departure order shall be restricted from issuing a visa for a certain period.

A recommendation of departure means that the minor offender of Korean Immigration Laws shall receive a recommendation of departure by the chief of a district or branch office.

Endnotes

Introduction

1 See Yahoo.com's Korean-English dictionary at http://kr.kordic.yahoo.com/search/kordic
2 The pure Korean of this term is *wae-gook sa-ram* (외국사람). Due to the fact that pure Korean ostensibly has no "roots," I only examine the meaning behind the term *wae-gook-een* (외국인), which has Chinese roots. Also of note is the fact that *een* means the same thing as *sa-ram*, that is, "person."
3 See James C. Whitlock Jr.'s *Chinese Characters in Korean*.

Section I: Working in Korea

1 These statistics are all taken from the Republic of Korea's Ministry of Justice Report on Foreigners (2002).
2 According to the Labor Ministry. See the *Korea Herald*, "Work-permit scheme aims to improve rights of foreign workers," August 1, 2003; Kim Sung-mi.
3 See the University of California (Davis) for more information on this at http://migration.ucdavis.edu/mn/ArchiveMN/jun2002-15mn.html.

4 See the Korean Federation of Small and Medium Size Business's (KFSB) website at www.kfsb.or.kr

5 See the Korean Investment Service Center's website at http://www.kisc.org/

6 Ibid.

7 Ibid.

8 Ibid.

9 See the Korea National Tourism Organization's website at www.knto.or.kr

10 Names that appear with an asterisk (∗) beside them indicate that the person did not wish to use his or her real name. Every interviewee in this book with an asterisk beside his or her name has opted to use a pseudonym instead.

11 Throughout the course of this book, I use the government-sponsored romanization system adopted by the South Korean government in 2000 for all place names. However, for those that can read Korean, I always provide the place name in Korean as well.

12 With all other Korean words (i.e. non-place names), I have chosen to transliterate them into English phonetically, electing not to use the government's official romanization system, except in the case of kimchi, soju and hagwon, for which I have chosen to use the most common spelling of those three words. I know this may seem confusing for someone not familiar with the Korean language—one system of transliteration for Korean place names and another for Korean vocabulary—but I can assure you that I am doing it with these exact readers in mind. The uniformity that is the government's new romanization system is definitely its strength, but because it does not distinguish between syllables, on top of not acknowledging certain sounds (like the H sound), I have chosen to phonetically transliterate all Korean words into English for this book.

Section II: Social Relations with Koreans

1 See Haejin Elizabeth Koh's "Confucianism's Influence On Marriage In The Chosun Dynasty Of Korea" at http://www2.soc.hawaii.edu/css/dept/owr/Haejin.html for more information.

2 The Ministry of Justice plans on abolishing the family registrar system in 2006. The

ministry will instead introduce a system that creates separate records of birth, death, marriage and adoption for each individual family member. See the *Korea Herald*, "Patriarchal family register to be abolished in 2006" August 23, 2003; Choe Yong-shik.

3   This was as of April 2003. See the Republic of Korea's National Statistic Office's website at www.nso.go.kr for more information.

4   People interested in contacting this organization may do so at www.iska.co.kr

5   See "Homosexuality in the Korean Historical Record" on Utopia-Asia's Website at http://www.utopia-asia.com/korlife2.htm for more information.

6   Ibid.

7   Ibid.

8   Ibid.

Section III: People of Korean Descent

1   See The Korean American Resource and Cultural Center's website at http://www.krccweb.org/html/hisifq.html for more information.

2   Ibid.

3   See the *Korea Herald*, "Russia's Koreans look for roots," October 9, 2003; O Youn-hee.

4   See the *Korea Herald*, "Ethnic Koreans find roots, job," April 26, 2003; Lee Sun-young and Kim So-young. These facts were compiled in December 2002.

5   See Haejin Elizabeth Koh's "Confucianism's Influence On Marriage In The Chosun Dynasty Of Korea" at http://www2.soc.hawaii.edu/css/dept/owr/Haejin.html for more information.

6   This was taken from Molly Holt's, "A Personal Viewpoint - 43 Years of overseas Adoption," presented at the Global Overseas Adoptees Link (G.O.A.'L) Conference in August, 1999. See http://www.goal.or.kr/english/adoptionissues/molly1999.htm for more information.

7   Ibid.

8   Ibid.

9   See the *Korea Herald*, "Patriarchal family register to be abolished in 2006" August 23,

2003; Choe Yong-shik.
10 See the Republic of Korea's Ministry of Health and Welfare's Website at http://english.mohw.go.kr/index.jsp
11 Ibid.

Section IV: Teaching in Korea

1 See the Republic of Korea's Ministry of Justice's website at www.moj.go.kr.

Section V: Learning in Korea

1 See the Ministry of Justice's website at www.moj.go.kr.
2 See the *Korea Herald*, "Colleges to pick 6,002 foreign-educated students," July 10, 2003; Choe Yong-shik.
3 Ibid.
4 See the Republic of Korea's Ministry of Justice's website at www.moj.go.kr.

Section VI: At Home in Korea

1 This is in reference to a traditional Korean tale called "The Frog in the Well," *oo-mool-an gae-goo-ree* (우물 안 개구리). The story is well known among Koreans for highlighting the misunderstanding that can come about when someone is sheltered and ignorant of certain facts that many others know.
2 The Duman River is commonly referred to in English by its romanized name from Chinese, the Tumen River.
3 In point of fact, it's impossible to perfectly translate what the interviewee says here because of the linguistic and cultural divides. He actually uses the term *cho-sun-jok* (조선

족) here, which, if translated literally, means "someone of Chosun lineage." The reason this word becomes complicated is because of it's reference to both the dynasty that last ruled over Korea, the Chosun Dynasty (조선시대), and the name that North Koreans generally refer to their country as, *buk-cho-sun* (북조선). That's why I've translated it as I have, "Korean," in order to eliminate any potential confusion. Koreans themselves are quick to point out that *cho-sun-jok* are not "Korean," even though they are of Korean descent, which is yet another complication surrounding the word.